The Female
Stress
Syndrome

Second Edition

THE FEMALE STRESS SYNDROME

How to Become Stress-Wise in the '90s

Second Edition

GEORGIA WITKIN, Ph.D.

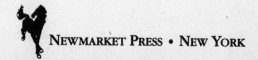

NEWMARKET PRESS • NEW YORK

Second Edition
                10 9 8 7 6

Library of Congress Cataloging-in-Publication Data

Witkin, Georgia.
    The female stress syndrome : how to become stress-wise in the
'90s / Georgia Witkin. —Second ed.
        p.   cm.
    Includes bibliographical references and index.
    ISBN 1-55704-099-0 (hc). — ISBN 1-55704-098-2 (pb)
    1. Women—Psychology. 2. Stress (Psychology) 3. Women—
Mental health.   I. Title.
HQ1206.W77   1991
155.6'33—dc20   90-27062
                                                            CIP

Quantity Purchases

Companies, professional groups, clubs, and other organizations may
qualify for special terms when ordering quantities of this title. For
information, write Special Sales, Newmarket Press, 18 East 48th Street,
New York, N.Y. 10017, or call (212) 832-3575.

Manufactured in the United States of America.

This is more than an acknowledgment. This is a dedication to the following special people in my life who have reduced *my* stress through their support.

To Esther Margolis, for her commitment to my work as my publisher, mentor, and friend.

To Keith Hollaman, my editor, for his midnight oil, his patience, and his impatience.

To Susan Rosalsky, my assistant editor, for her care and keen eye.

To Nancy Stedman, for her impressive research, recommendations, and revisions.

To Joan Lippert Indig, for her tireless data collection, kind words, and constant curiosity.

To all my colleagues and associates at Mt. Sinai School of Medicine in New York City, who so generously shared their research, ideas, time, and experiences with me and, ultimately, with you: Dr. Richard Berkowitz, Chairperson, Department of Obstetrics, Gynecology, and Reproductive Sciences; Dr. Kenneth Davis, Chairperson, Department of Psychiatry; Dr. Gertrude Berkowitz; Dr. Raul Schiavi; Dr. Patricia Schreiner-Engel; Dr. Daniel Navot; Dr. Philip Luloff; Dr. Michael Quadland; Dr. Marjorie Luckey; Dr. Alexis Karstaedt; Dr. Adele El-Kauch; Mary Anne Williams; and Jacqueline Torres.

To my dear friends and family:

Dr. Jorge Coco Radovic, Dr. Robert Benjamin, Dr. Roy Witkin, Milton Fisher, Clifford Hertz, Dr. Constance Freeman, Larry Abrams, Dr. Birgitte Mednick, Dr. Gordon Ball, Anne Johnson, Bob Berkowitz, Roberta Gallagher, Richard Gold, Susan Sprecher-Gold, Barry Mills, Esther Newberg, Bob Levinson, Dr. Robert Reiner, and Dr. Barry Weintraub.

To my loving mother and mentor,
Dr. Mildred Hope Witkin-Radovic,
for teaching me the secrets of life,

and

To my fabulous daughter Kimberly Hope,
for writing the teen stress syndrome chapter
and for teaching me the facts of life,

All my love, always.

Contents

Preface

IT HAS BEEN A DECADE SINCE I STARTED RESEARCHING THE FIRST EDITION OF *The Female Stress Syndrome.* It was the first book about those stresses and stress symptoms that are frequently or uniquely ours, and I had hoped it would be the last book about female stress we would ever need. But here we are in the '90s, and more than ever our lives are spinning out of control. In the '80s we wanted to do it all. Now we find that we have to do it all. In the '80s we fought for choices. Now new roles are added to old roles, and the sense of choice is gone again. In the '80s we had to learn to take control of our lives. Now we have to learn how and when to give up some control. Less stress this decade? Not a chance!

This edition of *The Female Stress Syndrome* covers female stresses, old and new: fertilization facts, mommy tracks, daily crime, biological clock time, PMS, posttraumatic stress. The middle-aged male executive is no longer the sole profile of stress. Homemakers and children have joined the ranks of the overstressed, along with widows, teenage girls, and female executives of every age. Young women in the "twenty-something" generation are facing economic confusion, dating in the age of AIDS, and marriage decisions in the age of divorce. Women in their thirties are dealing with their fertility and infertility, putting their time into their careers, and taking time out. Women in their forties must decide what to do when they hit the "glass ceiling" in their office. Women in their fifties are "sandwiched" between their not quite independent children and their dependent, aging parents. Women of all ages are facing unprecedented social and personal changes. More than ever, we need this book. Read it and use it.

INTRODUCTION

Complete freedom from stress is death.
HANS SELYE

IT'S NOT THAT WE AREN'T WARNED ABOUT STRESS. WE ARE. We are warned every day about the potential dangers of stress. We are told that stress can be held responsible for high blood pressure and low blood pressure; for overeating and loss of appetite; for fatigue and for hyperactivity; for talkativeness and for withdrawal; for hot flashes and for cold chills. We are advised that under stress we are more susceptible to infection, depression, accidents, viruses, colds, heart attacks, and even cancer. We worry about the aging effects of stress and then worry about the effects of worrying! We are stress-conscious and stress-concerned. But we still are not, however, sufficiently educated about female stress.

Our stress education is inadequate because it's still mainly focused on men and their life-work patterns. Executive pressures, corporate games, professional expectations, Type A behaviors, and competitive behaviors have been described by the experts mainly with men in mind. For years newspapers, books, magazines, television specials, and lecturers have discussed the serious effects of stress on men—high blood pressure and heart problems, in particular. But did you know that high blood pressure and heart problems are the number one killers of women also?

Women, after all, live in the same world as men. We, too, get cut off in traffic, hassled at work, and disappointed in love. We, too, worry about our families, become frightened by the future, and are surprised by the present.

Women become depressed, unable to sleep, withdrawn, irritable, childish, frightened, anxious, listless, and distracted under stress, just like men. Under stress, women can lose interest in food, sex, or friends, just like men. Our blood pressure may climb, our heart rate may double, our breathing may become fast and irregular, our hands and feet may become cold and clammy, our mouth may become dry, and our digestion may seem to stop altogether—just like men.

In addition, women experience some stresses all their own. Men do not menstruate, become pregnant, or go through menopause. Men do not typically have to justify their marital status to an employer or their sexual behavior to their family. Women must deal continually with society's mixed messages: We are most often expected to be sexy, but not sexual; to have a child, but remain childlike; to be assertive, but not aggressive; to hold a job, but not neglect our home. Et cetera.

These special, all-female stresses—both physiological and psychological—result in many symptoms of tension that are unique to women, and many others that are found more frequently in women than in men—symptoms ranging from loss of menstruation to crippling panic attacks; from transient headaches to life-threatening anorexia. And yet when women complain of these symptoms of tension and stress, we tend not to be taken as seriously as men are. Whereas men are given serious tests and treatment for their ailments, many physicians still prescribe tranquilizers for women, or tell them, "Go home and try to relax. Your problem is just stress."

"Just stress." I am still amazed when I hear that phrase. "Just stress" can trigger or contribute to diabetes, hypertension, and heart attacks. "Just stress" can trigger or contribute to depression, anxiety, insomnia, accidents, alcoholism, and drug abuse. "Just stress" can mimic senility, mental retardation, hyperactivity, and motor coordination problems. "Just stress" mediates all psychosomatic disorders, including ulcers, asthma, and allergies. And "just stress" can bring on the cluster of psychological and physiological symptoms women suffer that I call the Female Stress Syndrome.

My awareness of the Female Stress Syndrome did not, as you might imagine, come from a recognition of my own stresses and stress symptoms. I was as much a victim of female stress una-wareness as were my female psychotherapy patients. I was a full-time college professor, full-time psychotherapist, full-time mother, full-time author of textbooks, part-time clinical super-visor, part-time consultant, semi-efficient homemaker, and in-efficient bookkeeper.

I was full-time stressed and part-time guilt-ridden. Like most working mothers, I was haunted by a long list of *shoulds.* I *should* be more active in the PTA. I *should* be baking or building with my daughter on snowy afternoons. I *should* be editing or billing *instead* of baking with my daughter on a snowy afternoon! Like most women, I was concerned with the shape of my body and wardrobe—or the lack thereof. Like most homeowners, I was plagued with put-off repairs and immediate emergencies. Like most people in their middle years, I was worrying about time running faster than I could.

Symptoms? Of course I had symptoms. Headaches, backaches, erratic premenstrual tension, unusual allergies, a touch of colitis, and a bit of cardiac arrhythmia. "Just stress," my doctor said. "Just stress," I reassured myself, and continued on my harried way.

Ironically, my Female Stress Syndrome awareness was first raised by a man, who was telling me about his daughter. She had a new marriage, new house, new baby, and a full-blown stress syndrome. She was very unhappy, and feeling very guilty about being unhappy. "I'd be overwhelmed by all that change and responsibility," he said, "but *she* thinks that she should be able to do everything and bake bread, too. Please tell her as a psychologist, woman-to-woman, that it's OK for her to feel stressed. That she can sympathize with herself and help herself without feeling guilty or inadequate. No one else is telling her that!" "Of course I'll speak to her," I replied; and I began to think about the many stresses that fall primarily on women.

My second consciousness-raising experience followed the next week. I was leading a stress-management workshop. Because it was sponsored by a hospital rather than a police department or corporation, the audience had more women than usual. I was fascinated. I gradually realized that the questions and concerns expressed by the women were different from those raised by the men. The women spoke of many more stresses that were long-term and largely beyond their control—the two factors that make stress dangerous to psychological and physical health! They spoke of unequal pay and unequal say. They spoke of double duties: housework and work-work. They spoke of sabotage on the home front: sometimes intentional, but more often not. And they kept adding, "No one takes my stress seriously until I am sick in bed for a week!"

Interested in this issue of women and stress, I then went over a decade of therapy notes about female patients. What stresses could women claim as their own? I found many:

- The stresses associated with our *physiology*—breast development, menstruation, pregnancy, and menopause.

- The stresses that can be associated with our *life changes*—becoming a wife, becoming a mother, being either during the divorce boom and economic bust, being a babyboomer after forty in a youth-beauty culture, becoming a not-so-merry widow, or reorganizing after children have grown and returned home.

- The *psychological* stresses often felt by the single woman who feels alone, the homemaker who is pressured to get out of the home and develop herself, the career woman who is pressured to get back into her home lest she lose her family, and the working woman who can never seem to catch up with bills or sleep.

- The *hidden stresses* that distract, distress, and deplete— tokenism, chauvinism, subtle sexism practiced by both men and other women, infertility, commuting, crime, and talking to two-year-olds.

- And the stresses of *life crises*, which fall largely on female shoulders—caring for an ill or dying parent, parenting a handicapped child, and making sure that life goes on after your divorce, your parents' divorce, or your child's divorce.

Like the stresses mentioned by the women attending my workshop, these stresses are also long-term and beyond immediate control. Like the women at the workshop, my patients felt the symptoms of stress, but were not taken seriously. Their husbands, doctors, and even their mothers too often said, "Get a good night's sleep and you'll feel better in the morning." When they didn't feel better in the morning, they sought a therapist and came to me.

I realized, in time, that the way I was able to help them most was to reassure them that their stresses were not "all in their minds," but rather in their daily lives; that their symptoms were usually not in their imaginations, but rather in their bodies. This is what I am still doing in my private practice, my regular columns, lectures and television appearances, and in this new edition of *The Female Stress Syndrome*. In effect, I give the "permission" we all need to take our stress seriously.

When I first wrote this book it was to help even more women educate themselves about female stress and the unique ways in which it affects our lives differently from men's, because of biology and conditioning. The first edition was a handbook of women's stress; think of this 1990s edition as a women's handbook of stress: our stress, our children's stress, our partner's stress, and our parents' stress. It is meant to help us help ourselves and all those we love. I hope this book will also help educate the men who are professionally or personally concerned for the women in their lives.

Educating ourselves about Female Stress Syndrome symptoms, however, is only half the solution to a healthier life. Unfortunately, many of us become expert at identifying and describing our states of tension and symptoms of stress, but don't go beyond that. We find ourselves in the same stressful situations again and again. We recognize that we've been there before, but we cannot change our reactions, no matter how upsetting. We have yet to take the next step, that of stress *management*, which I also emphasize in this book and believe is as important as stress education. To reduce stress and achieve some control over it, we not only need to know and recognize our problems, we also need to gain an understanding of their causes and learn how to deal with them. I hope this book helps you help yourself live with female stress so that you can manage it rather than have it manage you. Knowledge is power, so read on.

1 GOOD STRESS, BAD STRESS, AND FEMALE STRESS

MEN AND WOMEN MAY BE CREATED EQUAL, BUT THEY ARE CERTAINLY NOT identical—particularly when it comes to stress. Research continues to uncover fascinating differences between most males and females, some of which are good news for women and their relationship to stress.

For example, females seem to survive birth stress better than males. Although 105 males are born for every 100 females, by the end of one year there is already a reversal in the male/female ratio. Not only is the early female mortality rate lower than the male rate, but females usually live longer as well.

Women also seem to grow older more gracefully. They tend to retain use of their legs and hands longer, show less gray hair, fewer sight and hearing deficits, and less memory loss, and maintain greater circulation of blood to the brain.

Since women typically have a greater fat-to-muscle ratio than men, women have better protection from the cold, better buoyancy in water, and a slower release of energy supply. This is a boon to women who are long-distance runners or long-distance swimmers. It also helps women cope with long-term stress, since stress tends to constrict the surface blood vessels that keep our hands and feet warm; stress tends to increase sweating, which chills us; and stress tends to suppress appetite, which makes it necessary to have an alternate source of energy.

From Eleanor Maccoby at Stanford University comes the information that females probably react to touch more easily than males. Might this mean that females get more pleasure from being stroked and caressed than males? Perhaps. Might this mean that females' stress can be soothed more easily by holding, hugging, and touching? Probably!

Some studies show that females are more sensitive to pain than males, other studies show no difference—but *no* studies show males to be more sensitive to pain. How is this good news? Although a low pain threshold may lead to an overconcern with body ailments, it can also provide an early warning system for stress symptoms that require early intervention. This sex difference may even contribute to longer life expectancies for women than for men.

Some research also shows a male-female difference in aggression control. After eighteen months of age, girls seem to gain better control over their tempers than boys (E. Maccoby and C. Jacklin*). This is another reason that females could be expected to evolve better verbal stress-coping strategies than less-controlled males. Females would assess information more efficiently and address problems more logically. An alternate hypothesis is that females may show less of a tendency to react to situations aggressively and, therefore, need less control. This, too, would enhance their coping capacity—they would think first, act later.

One area of female superiority certainly seems underutilized: the female's fine-muscle coordination. Although this would suit women for occupations such as brain surgery and fine art, in this society it still more often results in a woman doing needlepoint to reduce tension!

Now for the bad news concerning women in relation to stress. Because of our unique physiology and conditioning, women under long-term stress are in a position of double jeopardy: We are at risk for all the usual stress symptoms, from ulcers to hypertension to chronic fatigue, and we are also at risk for such

---

*For further information on the research and specific studies referred to throughout this book, see the Bibliography beginning on page 310.

additional stress-mediated disorders as infertility, premenstrual tension, and anxiety neurosis—symptoms that are either unique to women or are more frequently reported by women than men. Before detailing these specific female stress symptoms, though, let's first take a look at the general subject of stress and the ways in which the body reacts to it.

STRESS AND THE GENERAL ADAPTATION SYNDROME

Have you noticed how your heart seems to skip a beat or race after a near-accident on the highway? How about an unexpected encounter with a former lover? In each of these instances, your body is responding to signals from your sympathetic nervous system. It can, for example, increase your heart rate from about 70 beats per minute to 140 beats per minute when you are under stress.

Think about your most recent experience with stress. Since this can involve almost any demand or pressure that induced mental or physical tension, an incident will probably come to mind easily. You may remember being upset, frightened, excited, confused, insulted, elated, aroused, disappointed, annoyed, competitive, saddened, sickened, fatigued, exhausted, or surprised.

Stress can result from something happening around us, or from something happening within. It can result from a work problem, a family crisis, or a bout of self-doubt. It can be caused by factors as diverse as the aging of our bodies and the birth of a long-awaited child. It can be intermittent, rapid-fire, or chronic.

The primary effect of stress is to mobilize the body's "fight, flight, or fright" system. This means that stress stimulates the chemical, physical, and psychological changes that prepare us to cope with a threatening situation in these ways. This is all very well, of course, when the stressful situation calls for this type of action; we can easily speculate, for example, that the system evolved back when the "fight" impulse was directed toward defending one's territory or competing for a mate; when "flight" generally meant running for one's life from a wild animal; and when "fright" referred to confrontation with a natural disaster.

Suppose, though—as happens all too often in the '90s—that the stress you are confronted with does *not* require action. Suppose, for example, that you are late for an important appointment and are held up in bumper-to-bumper traffic. No movement, no escape, and no action. In this situation, relaxation would be of more use than the biochemical and psychological changes created by the fight, flight, or fright system.

As Hans Selye pointed out in the 1950s, our stress mobilization system is relatively nonspecific. That is, it mobilizes in a similar way to *any* strong demand, whether short-term or long-term; whether it requires action or restricts action; whether it brings good news or bad news. Winning a lottery, for example, stresses the body in much the same way as *losing* a lottery does! Both produce what Selye called the General Adaptation Syndrome— a bodily reaction to stressful situations that involves emergency activation of both the nervous system and the endocrine (hormonal) system.

Within the nervous system, stress messages travel along three pathways. They travel from the brain through motor nerves to arm, leg, and other skeletal muscles, preparing them for motion. They travel from the brain to the autonomic nervous system, which raises blood pressure, heart rate, and blood sugar level; releases reserve red blood cells needed for carrying oxygen to muscles; and slows intestinal movement (since digestion is not a priority in an emergency). And finally, they travel from the brain to the interior of the adrenal gland, which releases adrenaline into the bloodstream as a general stimulant.

The hypothalamus also receives stress messages transmitted from the brain along nervous system pathways, but from there a second system, the hormonal or endocrine system, is activated. This system works more slowly than the nervous system in reaction to stress, but it can maintain its effects on the body for longer periods of time.

Think of the hypothalamus as the emotion control center of the brain. From the hypothalamus, stress messages can be dispatched to many different glands. When signaled by the hypothalamus, the pituitary releases into the bloodstream hormones that activate the adrenal cortex. The adrenal cortex releases similar hormones, and together they raise the white blood cell count (affecting some immune and allergic reactions), alter the salt and water balance (gradually increasing blood pressure by changing excretion patterns), and stimulate the thyroid gland (increasing metabolism).

THE EFFECTS OF SHORT- AND LONG-TERM STRESS

Both the immediate action of the nervous system and the time-release action of the endocrine system function to prepare and maintain the body for life-saving action. If stress is short-term, there is usually no problem, since your body will have time to rest afterward. This occurs naturally when stress is part of a game, a sport, or even romance. The exhilarating feeling you get is "good stress," stemming from activities that are stimulating and can be terminated at will.

If, however, the stress is long-term and *beyond your control*, your body will not have a chance to rest, and the effects of this "bad stress" may begin to show. Your heart, after all, is a muscle, not a perpetual-motion machine. Soon you may feel missed beats, rapid beats (tachycardia), a sense of pounding, or even chest pains.

Breathing patterns also change under stress. Breathing becomes more rapid, often doubling its rate, and it also becomes more shallow, like panting. Under "good" stress these changes are adaptive. Under long-term or "bad" stress, they create problems. The nose and mouth begin to feel dry from rapid, shallow breathing, and, again, chest pains may develop from working the diaphragm muscles so hard.

Since signals to breathe come from a buildup of carbon dioxide in the bloodstream, rapid, shallow breathing can create another problem: Carbon dioxide is expelled *too* well and breathing messages seem to slow down. We feel out of breath and dizzy. This is called hyperventilation, a common symptom of prolonged stress. For quick relief of hyperventilation, you can breathe into and out of a paper bag. In this way, carbon dioxide that has been expelled is breathed into the lungs again, and the carbon dioxide level in the bloodstream is soon high enough to trigger the breathing reflex.

Some psychosomatic effects of "bad" stress are more difficult to manage than hyperventilation. Decreased rhythmic contractions of the digestive system and vasoconstriction of the gastric glands under stress can produce an upset stomach and constipation. (On a trip, we usually blame these symptoms on the water.) The output of certain hormones (glucocorticoids) under stress can gradually increase stomach acidity and, therefore, the risk of a peptic ulcer.

IMMUNITY PROBLEMS

According to research compiled by the Upjohn pharmaceutical company and others, hormones produced under stress suppress the number of certain blood cells which protect us against infections and cancers. This may help to explain why widows and widowers are at higher risk of illness for the first two months after the death of a spouse, why stress precedes sore throats and colds four times more frequently than it follows them, and why women under the chronic stress of caring for parents with Alzheimer's disease show reduced immune functioning. The evidence is piling up—we can't fight chronic stress and still fight illness efficiently.

Long-term stress can also produce a *progression* of side effects. The General Adaptation Syndrome, for example, shifts blood flow to large skeletal muscles and decreases flow to the gastrointestinal tract and to the skin. The first signs of such shifts might be cold hands and feet, then gradually a pale or sallow complexion, and finally migraine headaches or high blood pressure.

As another example, the endocrine glands under long-term stress cause the release of extra sugars for energy into the bloodstream, and extra insulin to break down these sugars for use. If too much insulin is produced, blood sugar levels will become too low (a condition called hypoglycemia). We feel tired and reach for a cigarette, coffee, cola, or sweets to give us a lift. Then even more insulin production is stimulated, and the low-blood-sugar cycle continues.

Sometimes long-term stress aggravates a preexisting condition or tendency. Think of this type of stress side effect as wear and tear on the body's weak spots. Researchers A. H. Schmale and H. P. Iker think that 80 percent of all diseases can be explained this way!

Look at the list of stress-related problems below. How many have you noticed in yourself? Your family? Your friends?

ulcerative colitis
peptic ulcer
irritable bowel
    syndrome
myocardial infarction
    (heart attack)
high blood pressure

cardiac arrhythmia
hyperventilation
asthma
rheumatoid arthritis
allergies
skin disorders

Sometimes the symptoms of stress are less serious than these but mimic serious diseases. This, of course, adds further worry to any stressful situation. I often hear patients in the midst of emotional traumas conclude that they have a brain tumor, coronary disease, or cancer, based on some of the following stress symptoms:

headaches

swallowing difficulties
   (esophageal spasms)

heartburn
   (hyperacidity)

nausea

stomach "knots" or
   "butterflies"

cold sweats

neck aches

chronic fatigue

dizziness

chest pains

backaches

urinary frequency

muscle spasms

memory impairment

panic attacks

constipation

diarrhea

insomnia

We know that the brain plays a crucial role in determining how the body reacts to stress. Here are the three important mind-body connections:

1. Remember those stress messages that travel from the brain through motor nerves to arm, leg, and other skeletal muscles? Their short-term effect is to prepare us for emergencies. Their long-term effect is to make those muscles fatigued.

2. Other stress messages travel from the brain through autonomic nerves to the heart, lungs, intestines, sweat glands, blood vessels, liver, kidneys, endocrine glands, and other organs. Their short-term effect is to gear up the fight, flight, or fright system. Their long-term effect is to exhaust these organs.

3. Finally, some stress messages travel from the hypothalamus in the brain to the pituitary and then to other glands that will release hormones. The short-term effect of these hormones is to raise energy production. The long-term effect is often to create imbalances—and nowhere is this more apparent than in the problems that develop in the woman's finely tuned reproductive system.

FEMALE STRESS

The stress symptoms I've been talking about can and do affect men and women equally; but, as I noted earlier, women are at risk not only for these ailments but *also* for less well-understood symptoms stemming from their particular physiology, life changes, and the social and psychological demands placed upon them. Most important, the majority of these stresses are long-term and beyond their control—the most dangerous type of stress one can experience. Stress-mediated symptoms that are unique to women include:

amenorrhea (loss of menstruation)	vaginismus (painful intercourse)
premenstrual tension/ headache complex	frigidity (inhibited sexual arousal)
postpartum depression	anorgasm
menopausal melancholia	infertility

Disorders that are not unique to women but that are reported more *frequently* by them include:

anorexia	anxiety attacks
bulimia	depression

These are the symptoms of the Female Stress Syndrome, and the sooner we make the connection between their appearance and the incidence of stress in our daily lives, the sooner we can help ourselves become healthier. Some women may already have recognized the importance of the mind-body connection by observing their own physical reactions when they are under chronic stress. Many have probably not recognized it, however, and will be relieved to be able to identify both female stresses and female stress symptoms. Remember, the stresses and symptoms of the Female Stress Syndrome do not replace, but rather coexist with, the general stresses and stress symptoms of everyday life. In the next two chapters we will examine the effects of this double dose of stress on the female body.

2 STRESS AND THE FEMALE BODY

WOMEN ARE ENDOWED BY NATURE WITH THREE COMPLEX PHYSIOLOGICAL processes that have no counterpart in men: menstruation, pregnancy, and menopause. These changes are all aspects of a very precious gift, of course—the ability to reproduce—but they can also be both the cause of and the arena for a unique set of stress-related problems. Again, we see how important the mind-body connection is in the development of the Female Stress Syndrome.

THE RISK OF PREMENSTRUAL TENSION/HEADACHE COMPLEX

Research has recently begun to document what women have always known: Premenstrual tension is real! During the seven to fourteen days preceding menstruation (and sometimes during or immediately after menstruation) nine of ten women of childbearing age experience some of these symptoms:

headaches
anxiety and nervousness
fatigue/lethargy
depression and/or
  crying jags
moodiness (alternating
  highs and lows)
backache and/or pelvic
  pain
fluid retention and
  bloating
food cravings (typically
  candy, cake, and
  chocolate)
sweating
swelling of the legs
changes in bowel
  rhythms

hot flashes
distended stomach with
  or without stomach
  upset
irritability
breast engorgement
  and tenderness
temperature changes
migraine
lowered sex drive
increase in accidents
  and errors
acne, blotching
flaring of allergic
  reactions
outbursts of aggression
thirst
loss of concentration

Between 10 and 20 percent of these women have symptoms severe enough for their families to call it "hell week." It is because these symptoms are so extensive that, until quite recently, many physicians dismissed premenstrual tension as an imaginary condition that gave women a good excuse for not coping with their daily lives. After all, how could such different kinds of symptoms (and fifty others not listed) be related?

But research over the past twenty years now shows that, indeed, more than half the surveyed female populations in three countries (the United States, Britain, and France) report psychological and/or physical menstrual changes. In fact, they are probably suffering from different subtypes of premenstrual tension. Katharina Dalton, the British physician who pioneered much research in this area, found correlations between the premenstrual phase and commission of violent crimes, death from accidents, death from suicide, and admissions to psychiatric hospitals among women. L. Rees reports a correlation between anxiety and the premenstrual phase. M. Abramson and J. R. Torghele found headaches to be the most frequently reported premenstrual symptom; and Gail Keith of the University of Illinois Medical Center finds that a sense of being out of control is the most frequent symptom.

Doris's case is not unique. She reports:

> I begin to become short-tempered and irritable as I get closer to my period—irritable in every way. I can't tolerate the noise, the heat, or my children's bickering. I can't even tolerate being touched or stroked. I find excuses to be angry at my family so I can self-righteously go off by myself for a while. Then there is my headache. It comes three days before my period and lasts for two! Aside from eating chocolate and sleeping, the world seems to be empty of pleasure.

Can Doris's problems be explained? Why do headaches develop premenstrually? Why do women become bloated? Tense? Depressed? Why do they become sugar-starved and feel like the Wicked Witch of the West?

Although psychological explanations sound good, they do not fit all of the data. For example, many women who do not suffer from premenstrual tension grew up with the same negative messages about menstruation as the women who do. Many women develop premenstrual symptoms only after the birth of their first child. Symptoms fluctuate with the menstrual cycle, increase as a woman reaches her 30s and 40s, and appear to be hereditary. Furthermore, *rarely* do women who do not ovulate have premenstrual stress symptoms.

The triggers, therefore, are probably within the body. The menstrual cycle is highly complex and powerful, involving the monthly gearing up of the entire reproductive system. Because it is an endocrine/hormone-activated system, its hormones travel in the bloodstream as do the stress hormones, thus reaching every tissue in the body. Also, like the stress hormones, the menstrual hormones set off various chemical reactions and metabolic changes in addition to reaching their target organs.

The cycle is governed by those two master glands, the hypothalamus and the pituitary. In the normal cycle, the hypothalamus signals the pituitary to release follicle-stimulating hormone (FSH), which causes several egg follicles in the ovaries to begin growing and secreting the first of the major female hormones, estrogen.

This powerful hormone begins changing the body to prepare for the fertilization of an egg. It causes the cells in the uterine lining to multiply and increases their blood supply. It works changes on the fallopian tubes and on the musculature of the uterus, the cervix, and the vagina.

In addition to these changes in the reproductive organs, estrogen affects the duct system in the breasts; the hormones from the thyroid and adrenal glands and the pancreas; the blood vessels; the chemistry of cholesterol and protein in the blood; and bone metabolism.

After nine or ten days, the high estrogen level in the blood triggers the hypothalamus to signal the pituitary to decrease its FSH output and release luteinizing hormone (LH). This induces ovulation from one egg follicle and a subsequent surge of the second female hormone, progesterone, from the follicle (now referred to as the corpus luteum).

Progesterone *opposes* estrogen—that is, it has an inhibiting or reversing effect on the changes estrogen has produced. Progesterone stops the growth of the uterine lining and further develops it to receive a fertilized egg. If the egg is fertilized and implants in the uterus, progesterone will continue to be secreted to support the egg's environment until the placenta takes over that function. Progesterone also begins reversing the changes in the uterus, cervix, and fallopian tubes.

Although the level of estrogen has gradually fallen as that of progesterone has risen, on about the twenty-first day of the cycle both are at high levels—and for many women, so is tension! Then if no pregnancy occurs, both hormones are abruptly shut off by the endocrine system's negative feedback mechanism: The high levels of progesterone signal the hypothalamus to stop the pituitary's secretion of LH, which in turn stops the ovaries from secreting progesterone and estrogen.

As the uterine lining breaks down and flows out (menstruation), both hormones are at their lowest ebb. But the lack of progesterone then induces the hypothalamus to signal the pituitary again to release FSH, starting a new cycle.

As you can see, if one part of this cycle is altered, the rest will also be affected. Thus, there are many possibilities for sources of premenstrual tension.

1. Rather than changes in actual hormone levels, changes in some women's sensitivity to hormones may explain premenstrual symptoms.

2. There may be withdrawal reactions to the hormones when they decrease before the menstrual flow.

3. Some research suggests that there is evidence that progesterone may be involved, since it is often deficient among women with premenstrual tension/headache complex.

4. Other research suggests that the estrogen-progesterone ratio may be a factor. When estrogen is too high or progesterone levels too low in relation to each other, symptoms seem to develop.

5. Fluctuations in chemicals involved in brain activity are being examined for sensitivity to estrogen and progesterone changes.

6. Since hormone imbalances and diet changes can affect water retention and electrolyte concentrations, this area is also being researched.

7. Changes in the way vitamin B_6 is utilized in the body premenstrually may lead to an increase in a hormone called progesterone in midluteal cycle. Progesterone can affect fluid retention, causing breast tenderness, swelling, and irritability.

8. Estrogen conjugation competitively inhibits B_6 activity. This may decrease levels of a brain chemical called serotonin, and this may encourage depression, food cravings, and mood swings. However, double-blind studies

have so far failed to show any improvement in alleviating PMS symptoms by taking B$_6$ as tracked against a placebo.

Can stress affect premenstrual syndrome (PMS) symptoms? Some say: Yes. According to gynecologist Sharon Diamond of Mount Sinai Medical College, stress influences the brain's hypothalamus, which in turn mediates the anterior pituitary and, therefore, the ovaries, which are the source of the progesterone and estrogen involved in PMS. This means that stress will aggravate most PMS symptoms, from acne to allergies. It can aggravate the premenstrual symptoms of temperature changes and sweating. It can alter tolerance for fatigue, aches, pains, and other people. But when Joseph F. Mortola, M.D., of Beth Israel Hospital in Boston asked twenty-five women to chart their PMS symptoms and their stress levels for three months, he found no correlation at all. In fact, eight of the women had their mildest PMS month during their most stressful month. It's more likely that PMS makes *stress* worse, says Dr. Schmidt of the National Institute of Mental Health. He gives an example: If someone hits you on the arm, you feel it. If someone hits you on a broken arm, you *really* feel it. In a study he and colleagues did in 1990, he found that when women were in the premenstrual phase, they felt stressed out by life events that didn't bother them at other times of the month. In other words, premenstrual symptoms will certainly feel worse, and may even be worse, when a woman is under stress. If she must deal with skepticism about PMS and lack of sympathy as well—more stress!

Fortunately, both medical science and home science have at least partial remedies for PMS. Let's start with science:

- Physicians have recently begun to prescribe antiprostaglandins to counteract premenstrual and menstrual cramping.

- Tranquilizers and antidepressants can be prescribed for mood changes, but in this case, awareness that mood changes are temporary and follow a premenstrual pattern may be just as effective—without the side effects of these medications.

- For breast tenderness, some doctors prescribe bromo-creptone (brand name, Parlodel), which inhibits the hormone prolactin. Prolactin was thought to produce PMS symptoms in certain patients by causing breast engorgement and decreasing the ability of the kidneys to excrete water. Although several investigators, through double-blind studies with bromocreptone, have shown that prolactin alone doesn't seem to cause PMS, it still seems to be effective in managing breast tenderness.

- Progesterone, which has been widely given for PMS because progesterone levels drop dramatically at ovulation, has now been shown to be no more effective than a placebo, according to Ellen W. Freeman, Ph.D., of the Hospital of the University of Pennsylvania in Philadelphia. So if you are taking progesterone for PMS, review this remedy with your physician and get a second opinion from a research hospital physician near you.

- Be aware that although in theory birth control pills should relieve PMS symptoms by suppressing many of the hormones that appear to contribute to PMS symptoms, no studies have proven their effectiveness so far.

- Be aware also that diuretics to reduce fluid retention should only be used under a physician's supervision. Dehydration creates electrolyte imbalances that can be lethal to heart functioning.

- Some women take low daily doses of vitamin B_6 beginning ten days before menstruation to manage PMS. If you want to try this, speak to your physician first and remain under his or her supervision while you are taking the vitamin because nerve damage can result if you overdose.

Now let's talk about home remedies. Home remedies include cutting back on salt intake to reduce water retention (don't overdo this in the summer); heating pads to reduce the discomfort of cramping in the pelvis and/or back; and aerobic exercise for thirty minutes a day, which fights depression and flushes extra fluid out of the body.

Many women find that minor changes in diet make a big difference; eliminating alcohol and caffeine, for example, can reduce outbursts and irritability. An increase in carbohydrates may help to increase brain serotonin, which in turn may reduce depression, tension, anger, confusion, sadness, and fatigue, and increase alertness and calmness. Perhaps this finally explains why some of us crave carbohydrates premenstrually; we may be self-medicating with potatoes, bread, pasta, cake, and candy to feel better! Try eating six small meals rather than three big ones to reduce hunger and prevent binging on the sweet carbohydrates you're probably craving.

Richard Schwab, M.D., director of emergency medicine at Holy Name Hospital in Teaneck, New Jersey, tells us to substitute complex carbohydrates such as grains, beans, legumes, and many fruits for simple carbohydrates such as sugar, candy, and sweet-tasting fruits. He calls the latter group the "short-change carbohydrates," since their nutritional value is low and they can actually aggravate PMS symptoms by stimulating too much sugar metabolizing after a brief high, leaving us lower in energy and in our mood.

Since PMS can contribute to the Female Stress Syndrome, all the self-help and stress-management techniques that are described in later chapters of this book may well make an important difference. Try them this month—if not for your sake, for the sake of those around you.

THE STRESS RISKS INVOLVED IN PREGNANCY

Pregnancy means change, and the stress of change often brings on female stress symptoms. If you are a mother, think of all that changed for you during pregnancy. Most obvious, of course, was the change in your body and perhaps your assessment of your attractiveness. Your health-care responsibilities broadened and alcohol, nicotine, and medication intake had to be monitored.

Your activity level probably changed as a result of morning sickness, which 70 percent of women experience as their estrogen level climbs. If your mate told you that your morning sickness was "in your head" and you knew that it was in your stomach, further stress was obviously added to an already unhappy situation. Your activity level may have slowed even more as your size and weight increased, but soon after delivery you came to suspect that you might never have a moment to sit still again.

Remember, too, how many financial changes were taking place: impending medical and hospital bills, perhaps the end of your wage-earning for a while, or the beginning of life insurance and savings deposits. And these expenses were just the beginning!

Women often find that their time frame changes during pregnancy. For many women, all plans become focused on the due date, and all experiences are remembered as being far from, or close to, delivery. It is even more important to an understanding of the Female Stress Syndrome to realize that many women do not have clear plans or expectations beyond that date.

Women may have studied reproduction in biology class, genetics and conception in anatomy and physiology courses, natural childbirth methods in Lamaze classes, gentle birth in LeBoyer's books, and neonatal care in maternity classes—but most have never studied mothering! Expectations of motherhood are often no closer to reality than a cartoon is to life; the demands and disappointments this can lead to contribute to the Female Stress Syndrome.

PREMOTHERHOOD

Premotherhood is a psychological period, not a time period. It may begin before conception, during pregnancy, or even after the onset of labor! Tension can build, drain energy from happy anticipation, and aggravate postpartum Female Stress Syndrome symptoms.

The cases of Sarah, Edna, and Sandy reflect some of the stresses that can be associated with conception.

> Sarah had been working as a production assistant in a Chicago advertising agency, dating Ray, and feeling good about her self-directed life-style. Although she stated that in principle birth control was the responsibility of both members of a couple, she preferred the sexual spontaneity that an intrauterine device gave her to the "clumsiness" of a condom. (They had both tested negatively for the AIDS virus.) Since she had, therefore, taken on the responsibility of contraception, she was particularly stressed when she accidentally conceived. Although she decided that she wanted the child, she found that she was upset about having lost control over this area of her life decisions, resentful of the changes that were coming, and guilty about her resentment.

Stress for Sarah, therefore, began during premotherhood, when she experienced a dip in the predictability of her life. Her pregnancy represented both a wish and a fear, and such ambivalent feelings are always associated with some degree of discomfort or stress.

> Although Edna's pregnancy was unplanned, it was a welcome surprise. Edna had worried that she and her husband were not ready for parenthood, that they had more "playing" to do before settling down to the responsibilities of a family. She also suspected, however, that they might never feel ready to make a conscious decision about having a baby, and might delay such a decision far too long. So she put her concerns aside, and prepared for delivery with great excitement. As the time for delivery loomed, however, the realities of parenthood began to frighten Edna and her husband. They became irritable with each other, and each began to see the other as responsible for their plight.

For Edna, stress had begun to build as she approached delivery. She felt that her course was set, that she no longer had a choice about parenting, and that she had betrayed herself by leaving the conception of her child to chance.

Sandy pondered the considerations of timing, finances, and emotional readiness before she and her husband tried to conceive a child. When the situation seemed right, Sandy was ready. Unfortunately, almost 15 percent of all pregnancies end in miscarriage or spontaneous abortion before the eighth week, and this was Sandy's experience. Following her miscarriage, Sandy's efforts to conceive again were unsuccessful for many months. By the time she did conceive, her anxiety level was high and her focus on motherhood was all-consuming. Even her relationship to her husband was overshadowed by the prospect of the mother-child relationship to come.

Fear and unrealistic expectations combined to produce a high level of stress for Sandy during her pregnancy. Again, motherhood stress began during premotherhood.

The cases of Sandy, Edna, and Sarah are by no means unusual—their stories are representative of many women's. Premotherhood concerns are a very real part of the Female Stress Syndrome. Some pregnancy fears are symptomatic of a generalized anxiety about the demands that are made on mothers, as in the case of Edna. Other fears, however, are probably literal—fear of miscarriage, of having a defective baby, of labor pain, or even of delivery procedures or cesarian section. Either way, motherhood becomes associated with fear.

For a woman who is fighting fertility problems, premotherhood can be nightmarish. She may spend years going to fertility specialists; trying laparoscopies, tubal surgeries, *in vitro* fertilization, G.I.F.T. procedures, L.I.F.T. procedures, hormone injections, and ovum donation. She invests time, money, and hopefulness. She alters her daily life, her sex life, and her life plans. She waits months for signs of conception, and then hopes for days that she won't miscarry. She wonders about the effects of the medications on her and on the potential baby. She wonders about the effects of infertility on her marriage and of basal temperature charts on her libido. She stops telling people about her problems because she becomes tired of their questions and afraid of them. She can't see a baby without crying or wondering how she might have brought this on herself. For the nonpregnant woman in the '90s premotherhood maybe her first brush with circumstances beyond her control.

POSTPARTUM DEPRESSION

Depending on the particular study you read, between 20 and 65 percent of childbearing women report maternity blues. Since postpartum (after-the-birth) depression rarely begins before the third day after delivery, it seems clear that hormonal and chemical changes are involved. But psychological stresses also play an important role.

Psychologically stressful changes begin with delivery. The woman is separated from her husband and family except during visiting hours. She is often separated from her baby except during feeding hours. Soon the new mother may feel isolated, vulnerable, and incapacitated. Her first days at home with the baby can make things worse. Mary remembers:

> I was totally prepared for natural childbirth, and totally unprepared for natural child-rearing. Despite my twenty years of formal education, I did not know how to sterilize a bottle without melting the rubber nipples. By the end of the week, every time my baby cried, I cried, too.

Teenage mothers struggle with further stresses after delivery. Becoming a mother may have solved an identity crisis, but it also may have created new ones: loss of freedom, of mobility, and of choice, and mixed feelings about parenting and its responsibilities.

Some women don't feel the baby blues until they have their second or third child. As Dora, who has four children, put it, "It is hard to see myself as pretty, witty, and wise, when I feel more like the old woman who lived in a shoe, and had so many children that she didn't know what to do!"

The postpartum depression should lift as the new mother rejoins her support system, sees that she can handle things, and finds that her body chemistry readjusts. Sometimes it does not.

As with some other Female Stress Syndrome symptoms, professional intervention may be necessary to break the mind-body chain of events producing, in this case, the depression.

THE STRESS RISKS INVOLVED IN MENOPAUSE

Even the most skeptical of physicians and mates usually view menopausal depression as "real." That is, they assume *physiological* changes within the woman can explain mood and behavior changes. She is more likely to receive sympathy and understanding at this time than when she is premenstrual or going through a postpartum depression.

Who can argue with the reality of the hot flashes that the majority of menopausal women experience? Who can argue with the reality of the permanent cessation of menstruation that results from the end of ovarian activity? These symptoms are neither imaginary nor psychosomatic in origin, all agree; therefore, menopause must be real.

The sympathy doesn't stop here. Physicians and husbands understand that menopause represents a landmark along the road to aging. Who can argue with the assumption that a woman will be depressed at the notion of aging? Who can argue with the idea that the loss of fertility makes a woman naturally defensive and irritable? Who can argue with the belief that when a woman feels older her sex drive decreases? Researchers can—*and do*.

It is ironic that much of this sympathy is unnecessary and may even be unhealthy: unnecessary because the most recent research points out that most women do *not* experience increased depression or any other type of mental illness during menopause; unhealthy because such sympathy may encourage women to feel defensive and devalued by assuming that they *should* feel that way during and after menopause.

The happy truth is that many women find the freedom from

fear of pregnancy liberating, both sexually and practically. With menopause comes a rite of passage into a period of personal choice and self-defined life-styles—free from premenstrual tension and postpartum blues, free from preparental anxiety, and filled with postparental relaxation.

> According to Lena, now sixty-two years old, the fun has just begun. At thirty-eight she started to plan for her retirement from mothering. She enrolled in a counseling program that had evening classes. By the time Lena reached menopause, she had completed her master's degree in social work, completed her full-time mothering responsibilities, and completed her ten-year plan to prepare for her second career. It has been five years since she began private practice, and she is pleased that she sorted her interests sequentially, rather than juggling them simultaneously.

Of course, this is not to say that menopause is always a time free from sadness and stress. Even in women who look forward to their life changes, there may be nostalgia for earlier times, a sense of loss of their ability to have children, frustration that their body is aging, and an anxiety associated with entering a later stage of life. Furthermore, menopause is a time of major physical change. Life change and physical change interact, once again. Female stress symptoms can reappear.

PHYSICAL CHANGES

Like the General Adaptation Syndrome itself, menopause affects nearly every organ in the body.

It begins gradually as the number of egg-containing follicles in the ovaries is reduced, so that the amount of estrogen produced when the pituitary sends out FSH falls below normal levels. Eventually the delicate hormonal feedback system is disrupted. The pituitary sends out more and more FSH and LH, because not enough estrogen and progesterone are coming from the ovaries to shut them off.

Because the remaining follicles develop more rapidly, the

cycle may be shortened by a couple of days. A follicle in a given cycle may not ovulate or form a corpus luteum, and without the proper amount of progesterone from this phase of the cycle, the uterine lining thickens without maturing properly. As a result, it may slough off in bits and pieces, causing spotting. When so little estrogen is produced that the uterine lining does not build up enough to flow at all, menstruation ceases.

Not surprisingly, the withdrawal of estrogen and progesterone from tissues that had been flooded with them monthly has its effects. Blood chemistry and blood vessels must adjust to the change. The adjustment of the hypothalamus, an area in the brain that controls body temperature, to the loss of estrogen is thought to cause the hot flashes that are experienced by two-thirds of menopausal women (it has been shown in research studies that the flashes cease if estrogen is replaced). The vaginal and urinary tract tissues tend to become dry and thin and thus more vulnerable to trauma or infections. Sometimes painful intercourse and urinary problems result.

Bone metabolism loses an important support with the withdrawal of estrogen and progesterone. Everyone, including men, loses bone mass with aging, but postmenopausal women lose it at a higher than normal rate. In fact, osteoporosis—bones made brittle by loss of minerals—will probably occur in about 40 percent of all women; many use estrogen replacement therapy to help prevent osteoporosis.

Finally, some women do experience anxiety and depression that seem to be related to the reduction of hormone levels—just as premenstrual and postpartum emotional effects can be.

INDIVIDUAL DIFFERENCES

As in all aspects of the Female Stress Syndrome, individual differences are important determinants of symptoms. L. Speroff, R. H. Glass, and N. G. Kase have summarized the influences on the average woman's menopausal pattern.

1. *Rate of hormonal changes.* Usually, menopausal changes begin a few years before menstruation actually

ceases, and the body has time to make a natural transition by approximately fifty or fifty-one, the national mean age for menopausal women. If this is the case, brief hot flashes and amenorrhea (cessation of menstruation) may be the only symptoms of menopause. Most women who experience hot flashes have them for about a year, although some women report ten or more years of these vascular changes. If, however, the hormone feedback to the hypothalamus is withdrawn suddenly, as with a total hysterectomy including removal of the ovaries, menopausal symptoms may be more severe and numerous. "Instant menopause" can produce instant symptoms: fatigue, insomnia, heart palpitations, back pain, and moodiness. In addition, any surgery can produce anxiety; surgical removal of reproductive organs can result in a profound sense of loss as well. Since messages of anxiety and loss can affect hormonal functioning through the complex hypothalamus connection, both "instant" and natural menopause symptoms will be aggravated by stress.

2. *Amount of hormone depletion.* Estrogen levels gradually drop as the ovaries become less active. Since the changes in the vaginal wall and the autonomic nervous system are related to estrogen depletion, symptoms of menopause such as dyspareunia (pain during intercourse), diminished vaginal lubrication, and hot flashes will be more severe among women who have greater estrogen depletion. Estrogen-progesterone-replacement therapy may relieve these symptoms as well as prevent osteoporosis and may even help prevent heart disease. Some women are not candidates for hormonal replacement therapy, such as women with a history of blood clots, active liver disease, or undiagnosed vaginal bleeding. The specific recommendation for women with a history of breast cancer and endometrial cancer has not been developed yet. These women may benefit from

the use of water-soluble jellies, which can relieve vaginal dryness with less risk; and a fan and a sense of humor, which may help make hot flashes bearable.

3. *Physical fitness.* Although menopause has genetic parameters, nurture also has an influence. Hormonal changes can lower resistance to infection by changing the acid/alkaline balance in the vagina and urethra; nutrition and exercise can help to restore resistance. Changes in calcium and fat metabolism are part of menopause; exercise and nutrition can help to compensate for some of the effects of these changes. In fact, as nutrition and vitamin awareness has improved over the years, the average age of menopause onset has been set back and menstruation onset has been set forward!

4. *The meaning of aging.* As with all mind-body syndromes, menopause has an autonomic nervous system component, a hormonal component, and a cerebral cortex (brain) component, with the hypothalamus as the information-processing and control center. If the thought of aging is distressful, this message will go from the brain to the hypothalamus to the autonomic and hormonal systems; and the General Adaptation Syndrome will gear up for a long-term stress situation. With menopausal changes also affecting these mechanisms, a woman may experience a *multiplication* of the symptoms of both stress and menopause. If, in addition, the symptoms themselves make her more anxious, we see a vicious cycle in which more autonomic changes lead to more hot flashes, and so on.

Many times of body change are times of stress, because we may feel our sense of control threatened. The changes associated with menopause, as with menstruation and pregnancy, are pre-programmed; we can make them better or worse, but we can't turn them off! This may increase anxiety and make many women feel helpless or victimized by their bodies.

Marilyn had always exercised, dieted, and maintained a youthful style of dress. She felt that her appearance and health were in her own hands and that her self-discipline was the secret of her "staying power." Although she thought that she had accepted the inevitability of menopause, she found that when menopausal changes began, her sense of control was threatened. She looked for, and of course found, every new wrinkle and age spot that appeared. She could no longer predict the rate of her body's changes, and her stress level rose. Feeling that she was fighting a losing battle, she lost her interest in dieting, exercise, and dressing attractively. She became increasingly depressed; soon Female Stress Syndrome symptoms, which she blamed on menopause, developed.

Does Marilyn's story sound familiar? Although the menopausal symptoms themselves may not be under full control, other areas of functioning are. Unlike Marilyn, women who maintain control of their weight, their exercise, and their time can help themselves reduce that feeling of being overwhelmed by inevitable physical changes. Take appropriate control over every area that you can while you are menopausal, and see Chapter 13 for more on the management of menopausal stress.

Depression and stress are not exclusive to changes in body state such as menstruation, pregnancy, and menopause. In fact, often these feelings coincide with body changes only because both come at the same time of life, not because one has been *caused* by the other. For example, a husband's retirement, a daughter's failing marriage, or the loss of one's own parent may trigger a depression mistakenly labeled "menopausal melancholia." The loss of one's office friends or autonomy may coincide with the postpartum period. To understand the Female Stress Syndrome fully, we must look in the next chapter at stresses not associated with preprogrammed body changes, and at the body changes that go along with these stresses.

3 FEMALE STRESS SYMPTOMS

SOME OF THESE SYMPTOMS OF STRESS ARE COMMON; SOME ARE LESS so. Some are unique to women; some are simply found more frequently in women than in men. Some involve a physical predisposition; others do not. They are all important aspects of the Female Stress Syndrome.

ANOREXIA NERVOSA

Donna cuts her food into many little pieces and moves them around her plate. She drinks her coffee and eats the lettuce in her salad, but will not swallow the meat she has put in her mouth. She coughs into her napkin to remove it. Donna is twenty years old, five feet, four inches tall, and weighs eighty-seven pounds. Although she has abundant energy for physical activities, within two weeks her malnutrition will endanger her life. Even then she will not seek help voluntarily. She feels fat and wants no interference with her dieting.

Donna's syndrome is called anorexia nervosa, and it is one of the many stress-related symptoms that are more frequently found among women than among men.

Under the stress of increasingly adult responsibilities, sexual anxiety, or self-conscious concern about their appearance, young women may begin to control their eating and thereby gain a sense of control over their other impulses as well. Soon their appetite is altered, but their body image is not. As young women like Donna become more and more emaciated, their self-image lags behind, and they continue to see themselves as needing to diet.

Why is this disorder so much more common among women then among men? The answer is not clear, but it probably involves female physiology. Appetite changes often accompany the menstrual cycle, for example. Premenstrual cravings for sugars, chocolate, and rich or spicy foods are common. The food preferences that accompany pregnancy are legendary. (Pickles and ice cream, anyone?)

Even if women were not more physiologically predisposed to anorexia nervosa, cultural messages probably encourage women to manage stress symbolically through anorexia.

Cindy was the oldest of many children and felt like a surrogate mother to her brothers and sisters. A little more was always expected of her, and she tried her best to live up to all expectations. Her grades were excellent, her friends were "nice," and her family was proud. By the time she was a high-school senior, Cindy was anorexic.

If Cindy is thought of as having "swallowed" others' demands all her life, the stage is set for her not "swallowing" anymore. By late adolescence, she was facing additional adult responsibilities. Not the openly defiant type to begin with, Cindy took control over herself in this passive way. Her rebellion was symbolic.

Theresa seemed to be using her anorexia to manage sexual anxieties. She actually delayed her own sexual development by keeping her body thin and childlike. Since her fat/muscle ratio was altered by dieting, even her menstruation was delayed. She dispelled her guilt over sexual impulses by denying her "appetites," and her fantasy fear of pregnancy was dispelled by a perpetually flat belly.

Although her mother thought Theresa would be tired from her constant dieting, she found instead that her daughter was over-active. Psychologists would suspect that Theresa's hyperactivity was yet one more attempt to manage unacceptable impulses, by keeping very busy.

There is no mystery as to how anorexia nervosa reflects an obsessional concern with appearance. Anorexics are often "approval junkies," trying to live on love and acceptance rather than food. If thin is in, they will want to be the thinnest. If fat means a lack of willpower, they will avoid being fat at all costs: by starvation, vomiting, enemas, and diuretics, to name a few.

At what point should family members worry about a dieting young woman? As soon as they see her dieting excessively without medical supervision, becoming obsessed with fasts, water diets, or fad-food diets. As soon as they suspect her body image is unrealistic. As soon as dieting interferes with her normal menstrual cycle. As soon as they find evidence of her using forced vomiting, enemas, or diuretics to control weight gain. Psychotherapy, family therapy, group therapy, and even hypnotherapy can all help if the problem is treated early enough. If allowed to become severe, anorexia is life-threatening. In fact, some reports say that up to 15 percent of severe anorexia patients die of malnutrition or related complications.

BULIMIA

How many women are thinking, despite these gloomy statistics, that they would gladly trade in their compulsive eating for a "mild case" of anorexia? Undoubtedly more women feed themselves than starve themselves when they are under stress. They chomp, chew, and sip, trying to sweeten up, spice up, to fill up their lives.

When gorging and binging become extreme and compulsive, the resulting stress symptom is called bulimia. Its source can vary, from too little satiety hormone (cholecystokinin, or CCK), to a complicated set of emotional factors, since food can have many different correspondences and meanings. Food can be tied to a memory of being mothered. It can provide a touch of home. It can be a reward, or it can be part of an attempt to gain strength and fortification. It can be a substitute for "taking in" sexual pleasure, praise, or love from others. It can be a safe outlet for anger: We can chew it, bite it, or cut it. It can be a safe outlet for dependency needs: we can hide it, stock it, and hoard it. The list may go on and on, but the symptom remains the same—uncontrolled eating.

> Gloria binged secretly. Publicly she complained that her sluggish metabolism was responsible for her weight. Privately, she used her obesity as an excuse for her lack of popularity. She periodically tried to diet, but felt too deprived to continue for long. When she was tense, she could imagine no other release, and told herself that her eating was a combination of a bad habit and good cooking.

Gloria was a food addict, and as with other dependencies, management of her symptom would be a lifelong problem. First she would have to recognize that she was no longer a helpless infant whose only active capacity for soothing herself was to put something in her mouth. She would have to understand that when she had finished her munching, the source of her stress had still not been dealt with! She would have to admit to bulimia. The stess triggers would have to be identified and alternative strategies for coping developed.

Bulimics run many of the same health risks as anorexics. Their diet becomes nutritionally unbalanced as they "just pick" at healthful foods to compensate for devouring desserts or junk food. Their biochemical electrolyte balance becomes threatened if they use forced vomiting, enemas, and/or diuretics to undo their loss of eating control. If they hide their bulimia by maintaining normal weight, the disorder is harder to identify and help is less likely to be offered. If they alternate between anorexia and bulimia, they are in double jeopardy.

DEPRESSION

Did you know that the rate of depression among women is twice as high as among men? Did you know that twice as many women are in psychotherapy as men? Did you know that the ratio of women to men in mental hospitals for depression is two to one?

Some say that these statistics only tell us that women admit to their depression more readily than men and talk more readily to therapists. But even the most carefully controlled studies confirm that about 8 percent of women, and only 4 percent of men, suffer from this type of stress overload!

Why do so many women respond to stress by becoming depressed? It may be that some women are socially programmed for depression. Boys are often taught to fight when something goes wrong; girls are taught to control their tempers instead. Boys are often taught to be achievement junkies; girls, to be approval junkies instead. Boys are often taught that failure is part of trying; girls are taught it is shameful. All this means that some women will be afraid to take control over the stresses in their lives. This is "learned helplessness," according to psychologist Martin Seligman, and it leads directly to depression.

But how about the new woman who takes charge, against all odds? Working outside of the house seems to be correlated with a lower risk of depression than full-time homemaking because there are more adults to talk to and laugh with at the office. But working women run into the same stresses as men—and then some. A woman who lands a job may find that she still gets less than her male counterpart. A woman who spends years building a career may find her aging is held against her. Her family may need the money but resent her absence. So when some major negative event befalls her, it is one event too many and, once again, depression may be the result.

Although some insist women are prone to respond to stress with depression because of their learning histories, others are suggesting that women may be somewhat biologically predisposed to depression. That is, stress may change the transmission of our nerve impulses, suppress the functioning of the pleasure center of the brain called the hypothalamus, use up energizing hormones called catecholamines (dopamine and norepineph-rine), or upset the production of serotonin and histamines which help to regulate brain functioning: and one major symptom of each of these changes is depression.

Whether depression is an attempt to preserve ourselves at minimal functioning level while we are under siege from stress, or whether depression is an unfortunate by-product of our bio-genetics, it is part of the Female Stress Syndrome. If you think you may be suffering from depression, you will probably say "yes" to most of the following items, according to Dr. Aron Beck, pioneer in depression therapy:

- When I think about the future, I feel discouraged.
- I don't enjoy things the way I used to.
- I am disappointed in myself.
- I cry more than I used to.
- It takes an extra effort to get started doing something.
- I don't sleep as well as I used to.
- I am less interested in sex than I used to be.
- I feel guilty a good part of the time.

Since depression includes thoughts of suicide, and suicide is among the top ten causes of death in this country, all depression should not be taken equally seriously. Most people who commit suicide are not psychotic at the time and not even at the lowest point of the depression. Most suicides occur during the three months after the depression begins to lift and some energy re-turns. It's best to assume depressions are cries for love and help.

Intervene by encouraging talk and then listening carefully. Listen for a sense of loss, guilt, or helplessness. A depressed woman will often overgeneralize the current stress into a picture of never-ending defeat, according to Dr. Beck. She will take the inconveniences of life as personal tortures and punishments, and probably filter out all positives and dwell instead on even the smallest negative in any situation. Instead of arguing with her about these distortions, help her understand that these feelings are symptoms of her stress-induced depression. And then help her get help. She may not have enough energy to organize a search for therapy by herself. Cognitive therapy, with medication in some cases, seems to be showing the fastest and longest results for mild to moderate depressions.

ALCOHOLISM

Statistics tell us that male alcoholics outnumber female alcoholics almost five to one in the United States, but, for several reasons, this probably does not accurately reflect the incidence of alcoholism among women. In fact, the ratio is changing. As greater numbers of women are working outside the home, their alcohol problems are becoming more obvious. As women deal with the stresses of what used to be a "man's world," their alcohol problems increase. Not surprisingly, so do those of homemakers who feel less and less support for their chosen role. More and more, women are seeking treatment for drinking problems. So, while alcoholism is not a distinctively female stress symptom, women must recognize it as an important potential response to stress.

Alcohol can act as both a sedative and a disinhibitor. Both functions can temporarily reduce a sense of stress. As a sedative, alcohol works like a liquid barbituate. At low levels it slows muscle response and induces a feeling of relaxation. As a disinhibitor, it affects the brain center for emotional behavior and allows the drinker to act out impulses with less guilt. The effect will vary depending upon which of the drinker's impulses are more guilt-associated. If, for example, it is your aggressive impulses that make you feel most guilty and stressed, a few cocktails may transform you into a woman who speaks her mind without hesitation. A few more and you may be speaking without consideration, forethought, or discretion as well. If, on the other hand, it is your sexual impulses that are ordinarily repressed, you might find yourself dancing on the piano after a few drinks. A stoic may become a crying drinker; an "earthmother" type may become a teenager reborn.

The problem with this elixir of relaxation and disinhibition is that moderation is difficult. Since the effects of alcohol are achieved by altering judgment, alcohol abuse is difficult to avoid. If one drink makes us feel good, we reason, two drinks will make us feel better. Right? Actually, as alcohol consumption increases, motor coordination is impaired, drowsiness progresses into drunkenness, and memory is diminished. We eventually sleep, but dreaming is suppressed and our intestines are affected. The day after is rarely worth the night before. Stresses have not been altered, and in addition our capacity to deal with them has been lowered.

At what point does alcohol use become alcohol abuse? The following brief summary is drawn from the definitions set forth by the World Health Organization, the *Comprehensive Textbook of Psychiatry*, 2nd ed., and Alcoholics Anonymous.

1. Frequent intoxication or drunkenness (four times per year or more).

2. Habitual use (drinks at dinner having an effect more than once a week).

3. Compulsive drinking (without real choice or control, or out of fear of not being armed with a drink).

4. Addiction (characterized by withdrawal symptoms, such as tremors, seizures, disorientation, or hallucinations).

5. Vocational, social, or physical impairment related to alcohol consumption.

When signs like these are present, the drinker is confronted with two problems: the original stresses and the alcohol abuse they have triggered. Both problems must be treated, and professional help is usually vital. Group therapy, family therapy, or individual therapy, with a trained psychiatrist, psychologist, social worker, nurse, or Alcoholics Anonymous leader all seem to work if the patient is motivated and the therapist is supportive and caring.

SMOKING

Woman's best friend—that is how some of us see our cigarettes. They keep us company during our morning coffee and solitary evening dinners. When we want to celebrate, a cigarette gives us a chance to savor our joy. When times are tough, we take time out for a smoke. (Ironically, nurses smoke more than any other group of career women—possibly because it is one of the few "legitimate" excuses they have for stepping off the floor.)

Smoking causes heart disease, lung cancer, and emphysema— some friend! It may surprise you to know that women, who are usually quite sensible about health matters, are not quitting smoking as quickly as men. Perhaps we are afraid that if we do, we will gain weight. Teenage girls, especially, are unwilling to give up the appearance of sophistication they think having a cigarette between their fingers brings. We choose not to see the disease that may lie a little farther down the road of our lives. We are held hostage by nicotine, an addictive drug.

Yesterday, Fran had surgery to remove a cancer in one lung. Today, Fran is struggling with her desire to have a cigarette. As she lies in her hospital bed, exhausted and breathless, she is amazed to find that nicotine has such an overwhelming hold on her. She asks a visitor if he has any cigarettes, and when he refuses to give her one—"Are you crazy?" he says—she feels ashamed.

Fortunately, society no longer endorses the cigarette as a sign of sophistication. Many people are disgusted by the smell of smoke, which interferes with good-tasting food and clean air. We are more aware of the yellowed teeth, the wrinkled skin, and the implications of poor health that smoking confers. These negative signals from society make it a little easier to quit or never start smoking.

But most smokers need more than society's disapproval to quit because nicotine is such a highly addictive drug. Help is abundantly available—from the American Cancer Society, the American Lung Association, from physicians and clinical psychologists, in video and book and seminar form. Some of this aid is free, and some costs quite a bit. Many people feel that if they pay a lot, they will be more likely to take the program seriously. If one of your reasons for smoking is weight control, you may want to look for a program that offers nutritional advice along with quit-smoking tips.

HEADACHES

If headache jokes were fact, it would seem that migraines occur exclusively among long-married women when they are approached sexually by their husbands. Although this is not true, migraines *are* more frequently a female then a male stress symptom. The question is, why?

It would seem that there is a predisposition to react to stress in this way built in to the female physiology. Glands, various blood vessels, and scalp muscles may, under the influence of some female hormones, be particularly susceptible to stress triggers. Blood vessels that constrict spasmodically in reaction to stress may eventually dilate painfully. The walls of the vessels are now irritated and the blood pulsing through feels like pounding pain. This type of headache is a true migraine. Prolonged contraction of the muscles of the face, neck, and scalp produces what is generally called a tension headache. And, finally, secretions from various glands to raise energy levels under stress can also change fluid retention and electrolyte balances, causing yet a third type of headache.

Although fast relief from headache pain is offered in myriad television commercials, relief from the stresses that cause migraine headaches is even better.

> Rosemary knew that her migraine attacks always followed situations in which she was enraged but felt that she couldn't express her anger. She claimed that she had had years of "nonassertiveness training," and feared that showing her anger would destroy her image as the patient wife and mother. She was, in fact, quite sure that her husband would stop loving her if he knew how often she felt irritable and annoyed at being taken for granted.

Imagine Rosemary's surprise when she began to request some appreciation from her family and got it! Her headaches gradually subsided, and she learned that her stress trigger had been an automatic fear of her own angry impulses. Other women have found that their dependency needs or sexual interests create similar conflicts and activate their headaches.

If the "unacceptable" impulse can't be identified or avoided, migraine may warrant a preventive medication (such as methysergide maleate) or ergotamine at its onset. Biofeedback techniques can be effective also, by helping women recognize autonomic nervous system changes *before* they reach headache proportions, and thus modulate fight, flight, or fright responses.

AMENORRHEA

If a girl has not started to menstruate by eighteen years of age, the diagnosis is "primary amenorrhea." If, however, there has been menstruation and it stops, the condition is called "secondary amenorrhea." Although both types of amenorrhea can be related to organic problems, stress is one of the most frequent causes of secondary amenorrhea.

The mind-body chain of events works like this: Stress is perceived and messages are sent through the nervous system to activate the fight, flight, or fright emergency systems. Since the reproductive system is not an emergency support system, its hormone levels are lowered and menstruation is not triggered.

Imagine this: A sexual encounter has caused Sally great anxiety, fear, and guilt. She is distraught at the notion that she may have become pregnant. She worries and worries and waits breathlessly for her period. Her period is delayed by her stress, and her anxiety increases. The scene is set for temporary amenorrhea.

Imagine this: Fran is about to leave home to attend boarding school. She realizes that she will be on her own in a real way for the first time in her life. She is fearful yet determined, nostalgic yet excited, reluctant yet committed. She is experiencing an approach-avoidance conflict. These strong mixed feelings have raised her stress level, and the scene is again set for amenorrhea. "Boarding school amenorrhea," in fact.

Imagine this: Carol has decided to transform herself into a facsimile of a *Vogue* model. She begins to diet drastically. She eliminates desserts. Then breads. Then fats. Then sweets. Her menus have been stripped down to celery and bouillon, and she has been stripped down to skin and bones. She has lost her stomach, her hips, her waist, and her period. Amenorrhea!

Imagine this: It is Lissa's last summer before college. This is her last chance to see if she wants an academic life or the life of a professional dancer. She joins a semiprofessional troupe and starts a round of classes at 6 A.M., rehearsals at 1 P.M., and performances at 7 P.M. She makes more and more demands on her body and is proud of its response. She gains a pirouette and loses a period—then another, and another. Again, amenorrhea.

Imagine the many other stressful situations that can also lead to amenorrhea. Depression, prolonged grief, and unrelieved anxiety can produce the same effects. Although mature women do not typically lose their periods, the menstrual cycles of young women are more vulnerable. In fact, young anorexics are frequently nonmenstruating.

A famous study of women college students shows how responsive the female reproduction system is to psychological and social factors. M. K. McClintock reported that although dormmates were menstruating at different times throughout the month when they first arrived at college, by the end of the school year their periods were synchronized far beyond chance or coincidence.

What can be done about amenorrhea? Relief from the stress is often enough, although sometimes a normal cycle returns even while the stress continues. Researchers tell us that some concentration-camp victims who developed amenorrhea when they were first imprisoned began to menstruate once again after a few months of confinement—even though their terrible circumstances had not been altered. Just as psyches can adjust to even the most stressful situations, so, too, can bodies often gradually adapt to stress and change.

Sometimes this does not happen, however. When stress-triggered amenorrhea continues and a normal cycle does not spontaneously reoccur, a physician should be consulted. Although the problem may not have started with an organic condition, chronic stress may lead to one. The physician may suggest therapy based on hormones or one of many new drugs.

The doctor may, however, suggest psychotherapy instead. Psychotherapy can help patients deal with the immediate stress causing the amenorrhea and helps to eliminate the risk of future stress symptoms by encouraging the development of more effective coping strategies for the future. Psychotherapy can also help women explore the cultural messages that make menstruation a high-risk target for the Female Stress Syndrome.

MENSTRUATION AND
SOCIETY'S MIXED MESSAGES

For many women, sexual stress reflects negative associations with female body functions. As we have discussed, it is women alone who menstruate, gestate, and lactate. They should feel unique, special, and proud. Instead, they often feel embarrassed, inconvenienced, and inferior. Why?

A look at some common taboos shows how women get the message that being female is a physically and psychologically unhealthy state of being.

> Don't swim during menstruation.
> Don't have intercourse during menstruation.
> Don't wash your hair during menstruation, because you will get sick.
> Don't handle flowers during menstruation, because they will wilt.
> Don't get a hair permanent during menstruation, because it will not take.

Menstruation is particularly singled out for negative attitudes. Just when a young woman is trying to cope with the stresses of adolescence, she begins to menstruate. In some cultures, this is a cause for celebration. In our culture, it must be kept a secret.

Jennifer's first menstruation started while she was at school. At first, she was frightened when she noticed red stains on her underpants when she was changing into her gym clothes. She was twelve and had no sex education at school. Her mother had never spoken to her about menstruation—or about anything else that personal, either. Jennifer had never allowed herself to think about "that part" of her body, nor look at her genitals with a mirror. She had only a vague notion of her sexual anatomy, and wasn't too sure exactly where her vagina was in relation to her urethra.

Jennifer had heard from the boys on her school bus that the

first "period" was the bloodiest. Her fear turned to worry. She didn't dare go to gym, leave the locker room, or even get up off the bench. She was trapped. She wondered when the cramps and headaches she had heard about would start. Maybe in a few minutes when the flow really began, she concluded. She was still sitting on the bench, frozen by her anxiety and confusion, when she was rescued by a teacher-in-training.

Advertisements for tampons and sanitary napkins emphasize the need to hide any signs of menstruation, avoid any possibility of an "accident," and forgo adjusting one's activities in any way. "No one but you will know," they seem to be saying.

Like Jennifer, many adolescents worry about hiding their secret month after month. They feel odd if they start menstruating early in puberty, they feel odd if they start late, and they feel odd *while* they are menstruating. It's certainly not hard to understand how females can develop negative feelings about a body function referred to as

> the curse
> being unwell
> on the rag
> sick time
> bleeding
> a visiting friend
> that time of the month

Once a woman starts associating her vagina with a "curse," it is but a short step to developing self-conscious sexual inhibitions.

INHIBITED SEXUAL AROUSAL

The term "frigid" is outdated, although it used to be quite commonly used. It conjured up images of unfeeling, uncaring, icy-cold women who were rigidly unresponsive to demonstrations of physical affection. In fact, the label was meant to describe a sexual dysfunction in which stress interfered with the swelling and lubrication of the female genitals in response to sexual stimulation—a problem that is now called inhibited sexual arousal.

Does this inhibited response mean the woman has no interest in sex or physical affection? Absolutely not! Often she enjoys the contact and is unaware on a conscious level of the source of her fight, flight, or fright reaction.

> Rhonda had looked forward to her honeymoon as a time of romance and privacy. She had lived at home until her marriage and had "saved herself" for her husband. When the time for lovemaking finally arrived, Rhonda found that "nothing happened." She liked being close with her husband, but couldn't share his sexual excitement. He, in turn, felt like a sexual failure, and soon the stress level climbed.

In sex therapy, Rhonda's stress was traced to her self-conscious fears of loss of control. She was concerned about what reactions were "normal." She was so busy worrying that she could not stop watching herself ("spectatoring") and abandon herself to the pleasure of the experience with her husband. Learning that flushing, spastic movements, nipple erections, rapid breathing, and utterances are all common relieved much of her stress.

VAGINISMUS

Another less common stress-related sexual problem is vaginismus. Women with vaginismus would like to be able to achieve normal sexual intercourse but find that involuntary contraction of the muscles surrounding the vagina make penetration painful or impossible.

> Flora told her doctor that she thought she had no vaginal opening. Although she had never examined herself with a mirror, she could not feel an orifice with her finger nor insert a tampon. Her doctor attempted a pelvic exam, but found that although

her vulva was normal, Flora's involuntary contractions of the pubococcygeus muscles were so strong that she could not be dilated for an internal examination or a Pap smear.

A number of stresses can be responsible for vaginismus, including fear of pain, fear of pregnancy, fear of intimacy, fear of punishment, fear of intrusion, fear of "contamination," fear of dependency, and fear of rape. Vaginismus is, in fact, very often the product of an early rape—by a stranger, date, husband, or even family member. The contractions that were meant to protect the victim from the stress of unwanted intercourse can remain and prevent desired intercourse.

In cases such as this, both the symptom and the stress need treatment. In her book *The New Sex Therapy*, Helen Kaplan recommends gradual dilation and accommodation of the vagina to the patient's own fingers in the privacy of her own home, as well as muscle awareness exercises where the woman identifies the muscles she uses to contract around her finger. She then recognizes these muscles and is able to relax them. If the inhibition seems unyielding, clinical psychologists and psychiatrists trained as sex therapists can help women deal with the underlying fear and stress.

ORGASM PROBLEMS

Perhaps the most common sexual stress symptom among women is orgasmic dysfunction. The statistics vary, but here are some approximations that give the general picture.

- Five to 15 percent of the female population surveyed reports never having achieved an orgasm. This is called primary orgasmic dysfunction. Most researchers, including William Masters and Virginia Johnson in *Human Sexual Inadequacy*, associate this condition with the stress created by guilt. Sexually repressive backgrounds seem common among those who suffer from it.

- Forty-five to 60 percent of the female population surveyed reports having difficulty achieving orgasm at certain times or with certain partners. This is called
situational or secondary orgasmic dysfunction, and is usually related to lack of sexual arousal due to the stress of
fights or fears. An orgasm requires an autonomic "letting
go" and giving up of control; fights and fears, on the other
hand, require "holding on" and a struggle *for* control.

There are many other stresses that can inhibit orgasm. Listen to
the women in a Westchester, New York, sex therapy group as
they discuss this problem.

"I realized, finally, that I was afraid of looking silly if I had an
orgasm with my boyfriend. I didn't know if I would make noise
or curl my toes the way I do when I come by masturbating. Then
I took a good look at him while he was coming. He became
spastic and noisy and I loved it. It made me feel great to be part
of that; so I let myself go also—and bingo!"

"You know, I never really *wanted* to let Eric give me an orgasm.
I didn't want him to have that kind of power over me—pleasure
power."

"Fred criticizes me about everything else, so I expected criticism
in bed, too. Now it doesn't matter to me anymore, because I
am not criticizing myself. Now I look at him as if he's crazy when
he starts in on me—and he stops! Since I began to feel that I'm
supposed to enjoy sex, he has picked up on that idea."

"Believe it or not, I was thirty years old before I tried to masturbate, and I was thirty-three before I had an orgasm. My secret
fear was that it would feel so good that I'd never want to do
anything else! Like women who can't stop eating or drinking, I
was afraid I'd have no control over this. The funny thing is that
now I feel the opposite way—since I can give myself an orgasm,
I am more relaxed about the whole thing."

Fear of punishment, fear of criticism, fear of abandonment, concern with appearing aggressive or selfish, reluctance to give a
partner the power of pleasure, anxiety about religious taboos,
misinformation, guilt, anger, and control issues can all raise female stress levels and inhibit the orgasmic response. After all,

the center for both stress and sexual stimulation is the mind.

Success rates for the treatment of both primary and secondary orgasmic dysfunctions are usually reported to be as high as 80 percent. These success rates reflect the achievement of an orgasm through *any* means: genital stimulation, clitoral stimulation, masturbation, and vibration—usually not through intercourse alone. For many women, orgasm through intercourse alone, without direct clitoral stimulation, is improbable. So why fight Mother Nature?

INFERTILITY

The Lerners were anxious to begin a family and tried without success for at least one year. Diagnosed as functionally infertile, Mrs. Lerner became more and more frustrated. She began to feel inadequate and helpless. She turned to the experts, but no organic problems could be found. Her concern with her infertility spread to a concern with abandonment. She felt pressed to take action, to take control.

An adoption seemed to be the next logical step. It restored her sense of decision. It provided her with a new focus of activity. It was a goal that she and her husband could share.

The Lerners did, in fact, adopt a girl and begin to parent together. Within the year, Mrs. Lerner became pregnant!

Most psychologists know couples like the Lerners. How do they explain a case in which the woman seems infertile, though no organic reason presents itself, until *after* she has adopted a child? The answer can lie in the Female Stress Syndrome. Fears and conflicts about mothering can produce stress, which in turn may mean women are more likely to use tranquilizers, drugs, alcohol, and cigarettes. But stress also interrupts and alters hormonal functioning, which in turn affects ovulation, which in turn provides a solution to the conflict—no pregnancy. Reproductive science researcher Adele El Kareh, M.D., Ph.D., tells us that the ovulatory mechanism can be disrupted at the hypothalmic-pituitary level by hypothalmic dysfunction secondary to stress, obesity, anorexia, systemic disease, or abnormalities in the ovaries or adrenal gland that affect circulating steroid levels. The incidence of infertility due to psychogenic, nutritional, and metabolic factors is 5 percent. Because more than one factor may contribute to a given couple's infertility, all possible causes must be addressed and investigated before attributing infertility to stress alone. These factors are:

1. male infertility factors, accounting for 30 percent
2. tubal or keritonal factors, accounting for 25 percent
3. ovulation factors, accounting for 15 percent
4. cervical and uterine factors, accounting for 10 percent
5. immunological incompatibility, accounting for 5 percent
6. unexplained, accounting for 15 percent

After hidden and unconscious fears are dispelled by parenting the adopted baby and stress is reduced, endocrine functioning may return to normal, and conception is more likely.

Great-grandmothers knew a lot about this Female Stress Syndrome symptom. They knew that tension could create temporary infertility. Their recommendation to a couple like the Lerners would have been, "Take a vacation together." It is still worth a try.

ANXIETY REACTIONS

Sylvia was waiting for a bus at the end of a hot summer day. The buses were full and a crowd of commuters swarmed around her. As bus after bus passed them by, Sylvia began to wonder if she would ever get home. She also began to wonder why her breathing was so very shallow and rapid. She felt as though she would have to monitor each breath or her breathing might stop altogether. Her palms, she noticed, were both cold and clammy, and although the air was muggy she was now shivering slightly.

More alarmed than bewildered, she started walking home rather than waiting a minute longer for a less-crowded bus. As she half-ran, half-walked, panic welled up. Her heart pounded and she feared that she would not make it home. Terror seemed to come in waves, each leaving her more exhausted than the last. She reached her door, but found that her hands were shaking so violently she could not use her keys. She stood by her door, desperate. Within minutes, however, the panic subsided, and she entered her apartment shaken and mystified.

Sylvia was suffering from a panic attack. Her fight, flight, or fright reaction seemed to come from nowhere. As in the case of Rosemary's headaches, the stress triggering Sylvia's reaction was also an internal conflict between a wish and a fear. Sylvia wished to break loose at the end of her work day but also feared that impulse. She had never tested the impulse, and had no idea where it would lead her. With professional help she came to accept her impulse and handle it realistically—and her panic attacks subsided.

The female-to-male ratio for anxiety disorders is a disturbing three to two. The reason for this is unclear, but part of it may lie in the way girls are raised in our society. According to J. H. Bloch's research, fathers in this culture emphasize achievement, self-assertion, aggressiveness, and self-aggrandizement in their sons, but expect their daughters to control these same qualities. Is it any wonder that women think of many of their impulses as "dangerous"? Is it any wonder that women see themselves as more fragile and vulnerable than men?

Anxiety attacks are best treated by professionals—psychiatrists, psychologists, and psychiatric social workers. Before, during, and after treatment, however, support systems are vital. So, too, is knowledge of crisis-intervention procedures, which can help until a professional is found. Read about these procedures in the last chapter of this book, and help others help themselves.

In addition to acute anxiety attacks, women seem to experience more general anxiety than men. Why? Perhaps it is because women are less likely to respond aggressively to stressful situations. Perhaps it is because women are presented with more anxiety-provoking situations and cultural messages that reduce their sense of control. Perhaps it is because women are more apt to notice and label fight, flight, and fright reactions as "anxiety." Perhaps it is because, until recently, girls and women have had fewer sports outlets for tension than boys and men have had. Perhaps it is because men may be less willing to admit that they are also anxious! Perhaps it is due to all the pressures that make up the Female Stress Syndrome.

Because the symptoms of panic attacks can mimic a mild heart attack, women often fear for their lives. This makes the adrenaline level go even higher, and women's symptoms become even worse. In fact, it is estimated that 25 to 30 percent of emergency room patients are confusing anxiety reactions with cardiac episodes. If all this sounds familiar, try these home remedies:

- Remind yourself that what you are feeling may be frightening, but it is not dangerous.

- Make your breathing slow, steady, and from the stomach, not the chest. After you exhale, rest a beat or two in order to mimic the kind of breathing we do when we sleep. Gordon Ball, Ph.D., associate director of Behavioral Associates, says this technique stops hyperventilation in less than one minute. And when we stop exhaling too much carbon dioxide, we stop the panic attack.

- The Phobia Society of America advises anxiety sufferers to count backwards from 100 by threes to keep your left-brain hemisphere active. If you become practiced at that, switch to counting back by fours or sevens. Word or math games can get you past those difficult moments, too.

- Most important, don't leave the situation you are reacting to until the panic is passed. If you do leave during the attack, and the panic subsides, you have just "rewarded" yourself for flight and increased the chances that an attack will reoccur.

- If you must leave, go back as soon as possible or anticipatory anxiety will grow and compound your problem.

If none of these measures is effective enough to help you turn your attacks down low, don't become discouraged. There are many effective therapeutic approaches to the management of acute anxiety attacks. Tranquilizers are sometimes given to temporarily block the symptoms of anxiety, but for long-term management try psychotherapy.

Behavior therapy uses gradual exposure techniques. The aim is to help you tolerate the attack and then extinguish it. This is done with techniques which give your mind and body signals that you are not responding to the urge for "flight or fight." If you don't use it, you lose it! Cognitive therapy uses psycho-education to help you understand and reinterpret your symptoms. Biofeedback helps you learn to adjust your breathing and heart rate as effectively as a tranquilizer could.

THE FOUR D'S

The most subtle but most frequent of the female stress symptoms I call the four *d*'s. They are cognitive symptoms, changes in our thinking behavior. They make us fear we have a brain tumor or Alzheimer's disorder. In fact, when we have the four *d*'s, we have a bad case of stress:

1. *Disorganization* seems to set in first. You know, the car keys were just in your hand, you haven't left the room, and now they are gone from the face of the earth. And even more worrisome is that when you find them, you discover that they were right in front of you. It is not your sanity which is in jeopardy, it is your ability to problem-solve which is on overload.

2. *Decision-making difficulties* become obvious next. The big decisions, those of a presidential magnitude, involving Mid-East economic policy, are no problem, but what to have for lunch can become a major obsession. If it's three o'clock and you haven't ordered yet,

consider that you may be on stress-overload. Or if you have changed your blouse four times and are now on your way from the car back to the house to change one more time before leaving for the day, skip ahead to the chapter on short-term stress interventions and try one minute of deep breathing or progressive relaxation, instead.

3. *Dependency-fantasies* begin to emerge if the stress is chronic. Because dependency needs are increased under stress, but usually denied, women begin to dream about situations in which they can legitimately be cared for. One woman told me she dreamed of a week in the hospital for nothing very serious—just a chance to rest, receive flowers, not receive visitors, watch television, ignore the telephone, and be very, very appreciated.

4. *Depression* is the final stage of cognitive change under stress. Not necessarily a clinical depression in which a woman can't eat or sleep, but a depression in which all we really want to do is eat and sleep. Expect that aches and pains will be magnified and your capacity to carry on will be diminished. Both your optimism and your energy will be worn out, and if the stress continues unabated, this symptom may become a state of mind.

WEAK LINKS AND OTHER THEORIES

How is it, you may be wondering, that a particular woman develops a particular stress symptom at a particular time?

One theory is that anxiety and stress aggravate problems that already exist because of our genes, prenatal environment, diet, or earlier diseases, damage, or accidents. These vulnerabilities are the *weak links*—symptoms waiting to happen.

Another, similar, theory hypothesizes that each organ and system has lowered resistance levels when the body is subjected to a high enough degree of anxiety or stress. When this happens, a virus, disease, or disorder is more likely to appear.

A third theory claims that a particular woman will develop a particular symptom because she has been reinforced or rewarded for it.

> Every time her husband gave her an angry look, Christine's stomach flip-flopped, her knees felt weak, her hands became clammy, and her heart raced. Without realizing it, she would clutch at her chest and press her hand over her heart. She felt all four symptoms, but her husband was only aware of the last one. His angry look would change to a look of concern whenever her hand flew to her heart, and a particular organ-response was thus reinforced. Soon both Christine and her husband worried about her heart rate when she was under stress.

Perhaps, however, each woman has a unique set of responses to each emotion. Five women could react physiologically with five different response patterns when experiencing similar stress. Each might call her own pattern "anxiety," but the different patterns would, of course, produce different symptoms.

Although there is not much research yet to support it, there is a theory that the fight, flight, or fright response is *not* as nonspecific as Selye described it. This suggests that there are subtle differences in the body's responses to different kinds of stresses. Fright situations could be stressing different organs or systems than fight situations, and so on. Thus, particular stresses might lead to particular symptoms.

Historically, many theories have tried to associate certain stress symptoms with certain personality profiles. Even the father of psychoanalysis, Sigmund Freud, agreed with this approach. In fact, he thought that both a particular personality profile and a particular stress symptom resulted from the same early childhood experiences. A woman with unfulfilled dependency needs, for example, might show more eating and gastrointestinal disorders than is usual, whereas a woman who has difficulty expressing her anger directly might have a tendency to develop sexual dysfunctions.

Two famous women explain female stress symptoms in yet another way. The psychiatrist Karen Horney and the anthropologist Margaret Mead both trace particular symptoms back to anxiety-provoking communications from mother to child—subtle messages conveyed during feeding, discipline, and emotional demonstrations.

The psychoanalytic schools would argue that a particular organ in a particular woman is affected at a particular time because it is symbolic of a particular conflict she is experiencing. In the following case history, for example, Robin had both a wish and a fear concerning pregnancy.

> Although she worried that she and her husband were not ready for parenthood and its responsibilities, Robin and her husband decided to try to start their family while he was in the Army and had excellent medical coverage. She became more and more excited about the idea of having a baby, and rationalized that she might never feel ready, so why wait? Soon after the decision, Robin stopped menstruating. At first, she assumed she was pregnant. Later it became clear that she was not. The symptom of amenorrhea (lack of menstruation) under stress conditions relieved her of the conflict by eliminating the fear and making the wish "safe."

Many theories about why women develop the symptoms that they do focus on the importance of individual differences among women under stress. It is as if each has her own threshold for psychosomatic reactions, and her own combination of variables that can push her over that threshold.

- The *amount* of stress needed before a symptom is produced can vary.

- The *number of times* the same or similar stress is experienced may affect women differently.

- The *physical condition* of each woman, and her *emotional state* preceding and during exposure to a stressful situation may influence her threshold.

- The significance of *age* to stress symptoms varies from

woman to woman, as does the *readiness* to cope or ca-
pitulate.

Every one of these theories attempts to explain why a specific
stress symptom appears in a particular woman at a particular
time. It is most likely, however, that the factors mentioned are
interacting to produce the various stress symptoms. As you
begin to understand your own stress patterns, bear in mind the
multifaceted nature of the Female Stress Syndrome. You can
learn to recognize your own physical and psychological vulnerabilities, your reinforcement history, your areas of conflict, your
reaction patterns, and your personality profile. You can sort out
the symptoms that have symbolic meanings from those that reflect physiological predispositions; and you can learn to differ-
entiate the symptoms you have learned from those you have
inherited.

One of the most alarming aspects of the Female Stress Syndrome
is that it starts shaping itself almost immediately after we are
born! In the next chapter, we will look at the world into which
girls are born and see how the groundwork is laid for future
stress patterns.

4
IT'S A GIRL . . .

IT'S TRUE THAT EVERY CHILD IS A UNIQUE INDIVIDUAL. IT'S TRUE THAT ANY individual boy can be passive, calm, quiet, and cuddly, and that any individual girl can be achieving, assertive acrobatic, and athletic. It's true that people—including baby nurses—cannot accurately guess the sex of a baby when it is wrapped in a yellow blanket. It is also true, however, that raising girls and raising boys is different. Ask any parent! Most will tell you that their experience suggests the following:

- Girls are more likely to be compliant than boys—more likely to run errands and help out.
- Girls seem more social and concerned with their appearance.
- Girls, although not passive, seem less aggressive than boys.
- Girls show more anxiety than boys.
- Girls use their intuition more.
- Girls speak and read earlier than boys.
- Girls are more emotional and more responsive to emotions.
- Girls have better fine-motor coordination.

Is this because girls are exhibiting genetic differences in their cognition, their physical capacities, and/or their emotional makeup? Might it be due to socially modeled and behaviorally reinforced differences? Or is it, perhaps, caused by an interaction of both?

Since the different expectations and perceptions that parents and teachers have of girls and boys strongly affects the messages, rewards, punishments, and models each child receives, the question of nature vs. nurture becomes hard to answer. To further complicate the question, children obviously affect their parents as much as parents affect their children. If parents do, indeed, talk more to girl babies than to boy babies, are they *teaching* girls to be better listeners than boys, or are they *responding* to a sex difference? Let's see what research can tell us.

NONASSERTIVENESS TRAINING

Socialization begins at birth. If girls are generally less assertive than boys, then training must begin early. In fact, the sexual stereotypes believed by the parents of a female child obviously *precede* her birth.

Consider the following statistics. H. Barry, M. Bacon, and I. L. Child, studying 110 cultures, found that 82 percent of the people they polled expected females to be *more nurturing* than males; 87 percent expected females to be *less achieving* than males; and 85 percent expected females to be *less self-reliant* than males! Another research team had similar findings: D. Aberle and K. Naegele concluded from their studies that fathers expect daughters to be pretty, sweet, and fragile, whereas they expect their sons to be aggressive and athletic. Are these valid expectations or self-fulfilling prophecies?

It seems that the way parents see their children is consistent with what they expect to see.

J. Meyer and B. Sobieszek showed men videotapes of seventeen-month-old children. When the men were told they were looking at a boy, they were more likely to describe the child as active, alert, and aggressive. When they were told they were looking at a girl, they described the baby as cuddly, passive, and delicate.

From perceiving girls and boys differently according to stereotyped images, it is only a short step for parents to create *different realities* for each sex. Research has shown that

- Most girls are treated more protectively than boys. This logically suggests to girls that they nust *need* protection.

- Most girls are complimented on their appearance before any other trait. People exclaim, "What a pretty girl!" but "What a big, strong boy!" This, of course, conveys to girls that their packaging is very important.

- Most girls are handled with more vocalization than are boys. Michael Lewis found that mothers of twelve-week-old girls speak and respond more to the babbling of their babies than do mothers of sons. F. Rebelsky and C. Hanks found the same was true for fathers! Being verbal, therefore, "works" for girls.

When it comes to nonassertiveness training, women and men—mothers and fathers—seem to work in tandem, perhaps reflecting their own training.

- As mentioned previously, in a cross-cultural study J. H. Bloch found that fathers emphasized assertion, aggression, achievement, and self-aggrandizement in their sons, while emphasizing *control* of aggression and assertion in their daughters.

- Researchers R. Sears, E. Maccoby, and H. Levin found that mothers of kindergarten children tolerate more aggression toward both parents and peers in their sons than in their daughters.

- Another team of researchers, Lisa A. Serbin and K. Daniel O'Leary, found the same was true with nursery school teachers.

Although it would be unlikely that *some* sex differences were not operating here, the influence of socialization on female behavior comes through loud and clear. Males may indeed have a higher activity level in general, and females may indeed have more verbal facility in general, and prenatal hormonal differences may indeed produce brain-hemisphere-dominance differences, as research suggests; but the *direction* these sex-related differences take is related to the Female Stress Syndrome.

EARLY ANXIETY

The results of nature and/or nurture are swift. By eighteen months of age, girls already show more control over their tempers than do boys. But this sort of control can have a price.

Anxiety that is not directly related to a specific external cause often stems from fear of one's own unacceptable internal impulses. If girls are treated as though their aggressive, assertive, and achieving impulses are unexpected and even undesirable, we can logically anticipate a high anxiety level in young girls as they struggle to control these natural impulses.

Indeed, girls *do* experience much more anxiety than boys. Shocking confirmation of this can be found in a wide range of studies of different groups (quoted in E. Maccoby). To mention just a few, anxiety scores higher than those of comparable groups of boys were found among

132 nine-year-old French girls
470 girls, both white and black, nine to eleven years old
64 nine-year-old American girls
1,249 high-school-aged girls
2,559 females aged thirteen through adulthood
149 college-aged women

Maccoby also quotes studies indicating that both teacher evaluations and self-reports show girls higher than boys on anxiety scales.

Although self-control can be an important ingredient in the development of mature coping strategies, the repression of strong impulses consumes energy and contributes to frustration, depression, and the Female Stress Syndrome.

> In high school, Lea had been a star. She was editor of the school yearbook, president of the Spanish club, and captain of the girl's basketball team. Her friends, parents, and teachers all told her that she was special—hardworking, social, and pretty.
>
> Off went Lea to college, where the entire freshman class, she soon learned, was special! Each member had also been a star. Without social, parental, or teacher feedback, Lea began to lose her confidence and her ability to cope. Once that happened, she felt that she was losing control over her ability to achieve and concentrate. High demands, low control, and no positive reinforcements: stress!
>
> Lea was in and out of the infirmary all that year. She had a free-floating fearfulness and kept pinning her sense that something was wrong on her body. Soon, in fact, she did develop mononucleosis and actually moved into the infirmary. This relieved her anxiety for a while, since she felt, again, as if she were home and under someone's watchful eye. Her impulses to quit school, be taken care of, or, at the very least, stop putting her energy into trying to be so special, were again safely under control. She had learned to perform for others when she was young, and now was on her own . . . passive and purposeless.

Lea's case is not uncommon. Society still sends girls a strong message: "Control yourselves!" And the message doesn't change when we grow up. Don't show tears at work—it's manipulative, we are told. Don't curse with the men—it's unbecoming. Don't shout—it's premenstrual. Don't cheer for yourself—it's competitive.

FEAR OF FAILURE VS.
NEED FOR ACHIEVEMENT

Fear of failure, like fear of success, is the legacy of nonassertiveness training. Fear of failure is the result of years of being
shamed or teased by boys, brothers, fathers, mothers, or teachers
whenever a public performance of athletic, mechanical, or com-
bative prowess was attempted. Fear of success is the result of
years of being warned against being "too smart" or "too strong"
or "too independent." Finally, there are some role models for
strong, assertive women in our culture. Some can be found on
the sports pages; there are a handful of world leaders to whom
we can look; occasionally one even hears about prominent
women in business, women producers in film and theater,
women fashion designers, professional women, or a barrier-
smasher such as astronaut Sally Ride. But these are still more
the exceptions rather than the rule, and generally a major component of the message we get about them is often how *unusual*
they are—a mixed message indeed.

Need for achievement, however, is built into all of us. It is an
extension of our earliest desires to explore, crawl, walk, and
run. It is a reflection of our ability to process information, formulate plans, and solve problems. It is an adult expression of
our need to gain some control over our environment and solve
some of its problems.

It's not uncommon for women to feel a mixture of fear of
failure and need for achievement. The head-on collision between
the two is what aggravates the Female Stress Syndrome.

The need for achievement moves women toward their goals.
Although looking back on television reruns it may seem that this
need was not explicit in female role expectations over the past
few generations in this country, it existed nonetheless. Middle-
class women achieved it through volunteer and community organization work, and settled for vicarious pride in children's
achievements, and identification with their husbands' careers.
Working-class women built their reputation through running

their homes, taking care of their families, and settled for jobs with less than equal pay in order to achieve a higher standard of living. Upper-class women tried to increase the power, prestige, and exclusiveness of the family by doing charity work, and settled for making large donations to various causes, and orchestrating social events. Need for achievement has always been a female motivation.

The fear of failure, on the other hand, moves women away from their goals. This fear is fed by many stereotypic female role expectations and myths.

> Women are the weaker sex, not suited to be fire fighters or linebackers.
> Women are too emotional for the business world; they cry in the office.
> Women will leave their careers for a man or the mommy track.
> Women are less logical than men; they work on intuition.

Sometimes women themselves buy into these generalities, and then fear of failure moves women away from their goals by involving them in excessive concern with the opinions of others. Failure then means shame, rather than just personal disappointment. Fear of failure requires constant collecting of excuses and a general defensiveness—both of which drain energy from directly pursuing goals!

The classic ring-toss game has been used to show how fear of failure operates. Subjects could stand anywhere they wanted while tossing the rings over the stake. Some walked right up to the stake. Others backed away to make the challenge more difficult. Researchers found that backing away was characteristic of people with high fear of failure. It was an attempt to provide an excuse in case of failure, under the guise of increasing the value of achievement.

Women with a high fear of failure will constantly handicap themselves and increase their own stress in order to defend themselves against failure with excuses. For example, they may schedule too many things at the same time. Or they may never start a task until the last minute.

Today more and more women *are* expressing their need for achievement. Unfortunately, their fear of failure hangs on from early childhood lessons. The vacillation between moving toward goals and backing off from situations involving the risk of failure creates a great deal of constant stress for the "new woman" of the '90s.

> Polly was torn by both her need for achievement and her fear of failure. She wanted a career in real estate and so entered a training course but stopped short of taking her final exam. Too many demands at home made studying impossible, she said. Besides, there's an economic recession so there are no clients anyway, she reasoned. But Polly was driven to pursue her career nonetheless. She applied for jobs in real-estate offices, but restricted herself to locations close to her home and to working hours that conformed to her teenaged children's school hours. She landed an apprenticeship, but found that family vacations, entertaining, doctors' appointments, and even volunteer activities interfered with her taking the broker's examination required for advancement. She stayed on, working on salary rather than receiving a broker's commission, talking incessantly about her career frustrations. Should she stay in real estate, handicapped as she thought she was, or move to another field? she asked constantly.

Sometimes women are not fully conscious of their ambivalence and the stress it imposes. Their nonassertiveness training has become so much a part of their way of being and their self-image that they don't even realize they are vacillating. At most, they may wonder why they feel so uncertain most of the time, or why they labor over making decisions.

RETRAINING YOURSELF

As in other areas of the Female Stress Syndrome, understanding the origins of a particular type of stress is only half the battle.

Reducing that stress is the very important other half. If you feel that vacillating between the need for achievement and the fear of failure or fear of success is a long-term, chronic source of tension for you, try to bring the problem under control using these techniques.

1. Gather *information*, rather than opinions, about a problem or situation. This will increase your capacity to assess things realistically, and decrease the anticipatory anxiety you may be feeling. The only important opinion will be your own, after you have processed all the information you can.

2. Similarly, look at all situations involving your goals through *your* eyes only; don't try to see yourself as others see you. Spectatoring (looking at yourself to see if you appear to have failed) will only hamper your ability to pursue goals and will usually produce inaccurate information anyway.

3. Try to experience falling short of a goal as unfortunate, or as a learning experience, or as a disappointment, rather than as a failure. This means you must *describe* your behavior, not judge it.

4. Avoid self-blame at all times. Try your best, but don't put yourself on trial. Be your own defense lawyer—not the lawyer for the prosecution.

5. Be task-oriented rather than a praise addict. Focus on finishing a job, not showing it off, and you will reduce your performance anxiety and fear of failure at the same time.

TAKING CONTROL

As your fear of failure fades, you can do even more to shift control of your life away from others and place it in your own hands:

Openly assert yourself. This is not the complete answer to taking control of your life, but in the areas of time and money it takes you a long way. Do not give others the power to control your time schedule or your money unless it is appropriate or to your benefit. Every time you give this power away, you will feel less like the grown-up that you are. In fact, you are probably older than your mother was when you were born!

Practice, practice, practice. These three steps will teach everyone around you that you can take control of decisions. Stop saying, "I don't care" when you are asked to choose a movie or restaurant. It teaches you that being responsible for selecting a bad movie or restaurant is not the end of the world. It is the beginning of the end of all that nonassertiveness training. From now on, your mistakes will be your own. So will your successes.

GIVING UP CONTROL

Being in control is not a goal for all times and situations. To hold on to our sense of control, we must learn how to let ourselves go. We have to let go of our lists and limitless plans for organization and reorganization. We have to limit our expectations for ourselves to one role at a time. We have to schedule relaxation and play instead of contaminating mental health days with chores.

We have to stop holding ourselves responsible for everyone else's moods. If you ask yourself, "What did I do?" or "What can I do?" whenever someone around you is upset, this tip is for you. Count to ten before you say "I'm sorry" to anyone about anything, because I suspect many of your apologies are unnecessary and will not help to make things better. Ask, instead, if the person would like to talk about whatever is troubling him or her, and if the person says "no," let it be.

We have to stop pursuing control when circumstances are beyond our control. Do you visit yet one more doctor after many sets of tests tell you the same thing? Do you call your ex-lover yet one more time even though the relationship is clearly over? If so, then you probably keep trying for control just to avoid the guilt or self-recriminations involved when you stop. Substitute constructive behavior to burn up your nervous energy: Paint a wall, reorganize your closet, put up shelves, take photographs, draw your feelings, go to the nearest playground and climb the monkey bars or ride the swings.

We have to stop thinking of the future as more of the present. Everything changes, and we can control and predict very little of it. Our children move away, our husbands grow up, grow out, grow old, or sometimes grow away. Even the people who work for us are not ours to control. We never know what they may be thinking or planning. If we try to base our lives on this impossible knowledge, we will always be losing our sense of control. You can have it all and get it all done—but sequentially, not simultaneously!

As you work at overcoming the nonassertiveness training you have had, and the female stress symptoms that accompany that training, it may help to remember that you are something of a role-model pioneer. You are on the forefront of social change, but you are not alone. You will be helping the next generation of women come up with some guidelines to aid them in expressing their own needs for achievement. And you will be helping the next generation of *men* establish more realistic and open-minded expectations for female achievement, as well.

5 THE NEW PRICE OF SUGAR AND SPICE

IT'S NOT YOUR IMAGINATION: LIFE HAS BECOME MORE COMPLEX. THE LIFE events that are supposed to be "difficult" are still difficult—the death of a spouse or a close family member, being fired at work, or getting a divorce. But now, events that are supposed to be "happy" can turn out to be enormously stressful, too. The economic crunch of the late '80s and '90s means that any kind of financial setback—like Christmas, a wedding, a vacation, or raising a child—ups the stress ante. And because any event that brings significant change can threaten your already overloaded sense of control, life events—positive or negative—can throw off the delicate rhythm we women use to juggle all our roles at once. The stress of being a woman is going up.

In the late '60s, two social scientists, Thomas Holmes and Richard Rahe, devised a scale that rated the stressfulness of life events based on a sample poll in Seattle and on a Navy study of twenty-five hundred subjects. The people polled considered the death of a spouse the most stressful possible event; it was rated 100 points. The other forty-one life events were scored in relation to that loss.

SOCIAL READJUSTMENT RATING SCALE*

LIFE EVENT	POINT VALUE
Death of spouse	100
Divorce	73
Marital separation	65
Jail term	63
Death of close family member	63
Personal injury or illness	53
Marriage	50
Fired at work	47
Marital reconciliation	45
Retirement	45
Change in health of family member	44
Pregnancy	40
Sex difficulties	39
Gain of new family member	39
Business readjustment	39
Change in financial state	38
Death of close friend	37
Change to different line of work	36
Change in number of arguments with spouse	35
Mortgage over $10,000	31
Foreclosure of mortgage or loan	30
Change in responsibilities at work	29
Son or daughter leaving home	29
Trouble with in-laws	29
Outstanding personal achievement	28
Spouse begin or stop work	26
Begin or end school	26
Change in living conditions	25
Revision of personal habits	24
Trouble with boss	23
Change in work hours or conditions	20
Change in residence	20
Change in schools	20

Change in recreation	19
Change in church activities	19
Change in social activities	18
Mortgage or loan less than $10,000	17
Change in sleeping habits	16
Change in number of family get-togethers	15
Change in eating habits	15
Vacation	13
Christmas	12
Minor violations of the law	11

*Thomas H. Holmes and Richard H. Rahe, "The Social Readjustment Rating Scale," *Journal of Psychosomatic Research* 11 (1967): 213–18.

In their sample poll of men and women, Holmes and Rahe found that people with scores over 300 points for one year had an 80 percent risk of becoming seriously ill or vulnerable to depression. Those with scores between 200 or 300 points still had an impressive 50 percent risk. Although these statistics cannot predict the risk for any particular individual, they do confirm the correlation between life-change stress and both physical and emotional health.

Now scan the life events scale again. Put in your own stress rating for each item and add items you feel are missing. Compare your ratings to the original ratings. Because you are a woman of the '90s, expect your scores to be different, and many items that you feel are important to be missing from the list.

This is what women across the country were asked to do. In my travels across the country, I polled 2,300 women in twenty states to see how they were affected by these same events. I also interviewed 238 women to see how they rate the life events, and to discover new events that have become important since the Holmes and Rahe study. I compared the new sample of women-only scores to the original scores and found more changes than similarities. Here are the results:

SOCIAL READJUSTMENT RATING SCALE

LIFE EVENT	NEW POINT VALUE	OLD POINT VALUE
Death of spouse	99	100
Divorce	91	73
Marital separation	78	65
Jail term	72	63
Death of close family member	84	63
Personal injury or illness	68	53
Marriage	85	50
Fired at work	83	47
Marital reconciliation	57	45
Retirement	68	45
Change in health of family member	56	44
Pregnancy	78	40
Sex difficulties	53	39
Gain of new family member	51	39
Business readjustment	50	39
Change of financial state	61	38
Death of close freind	68	37
Change to different line of work	51	36
Change in number of arguments with spouse	46	35
Mortgage over $10,000	48	31
Forclosure of mortgage or loan	55	30
Change in responsibilities at work	46	29
Son or daughter leaving home	41	29
Trouble with in-laws	43	29
Outstanding personal achievement	38	28
Spouse begins or stops work	58	26
Begin or end school	45	26
Change in living conditions	42	25
Revision of personal habits	44	24
Trouble with boss	45	23
Change in work hours or conditions	36	20
Change in residence	47	20
Change in school	36	20

Change in recreation	26	19
Change in church activities	26	19
Change in social activities	26	18
Mortage or loan less than $10,000	27	17
Change in sleeping habits	27	16
Change in number of family get-togethers	15	15
Change in eating habits	29	15
Vacation	43	13
Christmas	56	12
Minor violations of law	30	11

Your total:

THE BIG PICTURE

How is stress for women different in the '90s? There seems to be a lot more of it. In the thirty years between the two sets of stress rating, the average rating climbed a whopping 19 points. Some of the difference is attributable to the fact that the subjects of the original sample were both male and female, while my subjects were solely female, but it still looks like life in the '90s is much more trying for women than it used to be. Social and financial changes of the last decade, for example, have opened up vast new areas for female stress, and women now rank job and money changes on a par with family matters. Since women work outside the house, job and money related events are now ranked as high as the stresses of "women's work" inside the house.

But new stresses have not replaced the old stresses—just multiplied them. Have you noticed that after falls and fights your children still zoom past all other adults as they run for your hug? That before bedtime they still need a concentrated five minutes of backscratching from your nails only? That hair combing, shoe buying, food buying, clothes selecting, and entertaining seem to be your department, even though you are working late and Daddy may have offered? That school nurses, teachers and baby-sitters still usually call Mommy's office, not Daddy's? That friends still want your company on mammogram day, and *you* hear the midnight cough from the next room or the sounds of silence from the playroom? It's not that no one else is around in the '90s or never offer their services. It's not that we encourage our children's or friend's or family's dependency. It's that after liberation, employment, consciousness-raising and coparenting agreements, we are still the nurturers, and although 62 percent of men and 55 percent of women in a sample of 210 couples say they think the home responsibilities should be shared equally, according to social scientist Ivan Nye, women still do more of it all in practice!

Is it any wonder, then, that moving, or "change in residence," has jumped up 27 stress points? In the '60s, people polled by Holmes and Rahe gave moving a rating of 20; the women I surveyed scored it 47! Now, moving has never been a pleasurable activity, but if you have to move while you are holding down a job and maybe also taking care of the children ... expect even more relocation stress. And if you are a single parent without an extended family nearby, watch out. Cross-country or cross-town, moving means not knowing what comes next, and that means the four *d*'s again: disorganization, decision-making difficulties, depression, and dependency feelings—readjustment symptoms that don't end as the last carton is unpacked. In over seventy American cities, the average stay is less than four years. In Washington, D.C., over half the telephone book listings change each year! "Change in residence" has become part of life in the '90s.

Getting fired at work is also a big part of the big picture now. With over 90 percent of women working for income at some time in their life, it is no wonder that getting fired is given a stress rating of 83 points by women—up from 47 points for both men and women in the '60s. Women used to say that being asked for a divorce by a husband was like being fired. Now husbands still leave, grown children are moving back in bringing along their own children, and we are getting fired from our nine-to-five jobs, also. Beyond the ego damage are the practical considerations that bring stress: Can you find another job during a recession? Will you lose your support network when you are no longer around your coworkers? Will you stay friends with your work buddies? Will you have enough money to pay the rent?

For a clear look at the big picture of female stress in the '90s, here are the top ten stressors in order of new ranking:

TOP TEN STRESSORS

New Rank	Stressor	Old Rank
1	Death of spouse	1
2	Divorce	2
3	Marriage	7
4	Death of close family member	5
5	Fired at work	8
6	Marital separation	3
7	Pregnancy	12
8	Jail term	4
9	Death of a close friend	17
10	Retirement	10

DEATH OF A SPOUSE

It's interesting that some pieces of the picture don't change. The death of a spouse, which was given an average of 100 points in the '60s, is now given an average of 99 points by women and remains at the head of the list. In fact, 98 percent of the 138 women who were questioned in depth still gave death of a spouse 100 points. After all, the loss of a loved one is compounded by low probability of remarriage and the high probability that there will be severe economic and social consequences. What hasn't changed since the '60s are these statistics:

- No more than one in four widows can expect to remarry within five years (compared to half of all widowers).

- Almost 50 percent of widows must cope with a drop in income that is not offset by insurance.

- The majority of widows must deal with courts once the majority of men die without leaving a will.

- Most widows will not receive special social support, since widowhood is at epidemic proportions, and if her husband was older than sixty-five when he died, many will wonder why she is grieving for someone so "old."

DIVORCE

Like the death of a spouse, divorce has not lost its rank. Divorce still holds the second spot among the top ten stressors for women in the '90s and as a stressor shares much with the number one stress, death of a spouse. In both cases, loneliness is the aftermath. Even if you didn't like your spouse, he was still someone else around the house, someone who might have shared chores, someone who made the married life-style possible socially, sexually, and economically. And consider how long before the divorce the stress probably began. During the decision-making process, a woman must typically consider problems most men do not. If there are children, in most cases they will still live most of the time with their mother after the divorce. If she is a working mother, as most single parents are, she will have to do endless juggling to be the mother and breadwinner and maybe surrogate father. And imagine trying to parent for life with someone you couldn't live with, whom you sued, or by whom you were sued.

Even if there are no children, divorce can create stresses by changing your life-style: waiting to be called, battling the numbers that tell us there are more women than men available, competing with younger women for men of all ages, and being primarily reacted on the basis of your appearance. Or perhaps you will give up companionship altogether. Furthermore, if a woman looks to romance or marriage as an important component of her happiness, she must deal with all the above while shouldering a major disappointment, the failure of her marriage, freshly experienced.

A total of 51 percent of the women surveyed gave divorce 100 stress points; 75 percent gave it 90 or more points. And compared to divorce in the '60s, divorce in the '90s is up 17 percent, from 73 to 91 stress points. The shift probably reflects both the change from the two-sex sample to an all-female sample, and a change in the amount of stress associated with divorce. In fact, many women have told me that they'd prefer to cope with the death of a spouse than divorce, because divorce forces them to mourn again and again. For more on divorce, see Chapter 9 on "The New American Family."

MARRIAGE

Moving up from seventh place to third of the top ten female stressors of the '90s is marriage. That life event that young girls used to dream of would now seem to be moving toward the nightmare category for some. Only 17 percent of the women left marriage at the original 50 points. Almost 60 percent of the sample give marriage more that 90 stress points. Forty percent give it 100 points! The increase of almost 35 stress points moved marriage ahead of jail term, death of a close family member, and personal injury or illness. For more on marriage, see the "Happy Happenings" section of this chapter.

DEATH OF CLOSE FAMILY MEMBER

Death of a close family member has also moved up in stress points—21 points, from 63 to 84, from fifth place to fourth, ahead of marital separation. And one in four women gave this life event 100 points! Perhaps this is a reflection of women's capacity for empathy. Although both men and women can both feel sympathy (that is, feel sad that someone else is feeling sad), women seem more frequently to feel empathy (actually feel the sad feeling the other is experiencing). This means that women not only feel the loss of a close family member but also feel the sorrow of the children, spouse, or parents left behind. They then imagine what their own loss would be like if it had been their own immediate family member. They try to anticipate the needs of those grieving, and try to meet those needs—and do all this without missing a beat of their own drummer.

FIRED AT WORK

Isn't it interesting that being fired at work has moved up to the stress spot right below the death of a close family member? Along with pregnancy and Christmas, being fired at work was most greatly re-rated upward by women—from 47 to 83 stress points, a change of 36 points! In fact, the score most often assigned was 100 points, and more than 50 percent of women surveyed gave it 90 or more points. These results should be no mystery. A total of 88 percent of the women increased the rating of being fired above the original 47-point rating—about the same percentage of women nationally who had had to work for money at some time in their lives. But the loss of income is not the most stressful aspect of being fired. Those who quit and are unemployed suffer the same economic hardships with fewer stress symptoms. Being fired means a loss of your sense of control and is a violation of your sense of choice or your ability to predict what is coming next. And as choice, control, and predictability decrease, stress symptoms always increase: Adrenaline rushes keep us up at night or wake us up in the morning; food becomes our only consolation, or so tasteless that our weight drops; the pavement is now not only pounding, but maybe has kicked in, and it may take a new job before most of us will feel in control again.

MARITAL SEPARATION

Marital separation was the third top stressor a generation ago. Now marriage is number three, instead, and marital separation is below the death of a close family member and being fired at work. Why? Women tell me that marital separation is often less disrupting than marriage, the death of someone close, or being fired. The other three stressors involve permanent reorganization of our emotional and financial worlds: separation is often just temporary. Moreover, during a separation finances usually don't change—nor do names. Dating hasn't usually begun, and the hopes and hassles that are familiar haven't yet ended. But like our survey population, 30 percent of you would probably say that marital separation rates 90 or more stress points—and so it remains one of the top ten stressors for women in the '90s. After all, it is more often than not the beginning of many changes, for better or for worse.

PREGNANCY

Pregnancy, that blessed event, has gone up 38 stress points since the original rating in Holmes and Rahe's sample. This is the second-greatest increase among all the events and moved "pregnancy" from twelfth place to seventh place among the stressful life events. For those who have easy, successful pregnancies, this rating serves as a reminder that even happy events can be stressful if they involve change, and pregnancy involves change. It changes our bodies, our relationships, our finances, our view of ourself, responsibility, our future.

In part, the leap reflects the difference in the respondents of the '90s—they are all women. But the new rating surely reflects the pregnancy problems that are relatively new in the '90s as well. As a group, we women are trying to have our first baby later than ever before in human history. In June 1990, for example, the U.S. Census Bureau told us that half of childless married women thirty to thirty-four years old still plan to have a family, compared to only one-third of a similar group in 1975, and obstetricians tell us it is not unusual for women in their forties to plan to have their first pregnancy. Now everyone knows someone who had a "surprise" or "change of life" baby—an aunt or grandmother or sister-in-law. But these were rarely first babies. Most women today who are having their first pregnancies at a later age have spent money and time in *in vitro* fertilization programs, fertility clinics, or ovum-donation programs. Many are "last chance" pregnancies, and the next step is an expensive and complicated adoption.

Although the idealized pregnancy of the 1950s, complete with proud father-to-be and baby showers, seems still to be featured in television commercials, the pregnancy of the '90s is usually just the beginning of a string of stressors. The California State Joint Select Task Force on the Changing Family reported in 1991 that fewer than a quarter of Los Angeles households are married couples living with children. For women aged fifteen to twenty-nine, the Census Bureau reports, about 40 percent conceive out-of-wedlock, two of every five American women are not married while they are pregnant, and of these two-thirds will still be single when they deliver. This means that almost one-third of all first-time mothers will be relying on families, work, or the government for support—and worrying about it during the pregnancy. And if you live in an urban area, you can expect to deal with a child-care crisis, the rising cost of living, increased costs of pediatric care, and job scarcity. Urban or suburban, single or married, pregnancy is certainly a time for change. Call every change you choose "stimulation"; call every change you didn't anticipate "stress."

JAIL TERM

Jail term is ranked eighth among the top ten stressors, although most respondents say that if they actually had served time they might have ranked it number one. A total of 53 percent gave it more than the original 63 points, but almost 45 percent left the original score because they said they had no personal knowledge of the event. For women it means separation from children who may have been completely dependent on them. It sometimes means permanent separation if the children become wards of the state or are put in foster care. And unlike the "macho" status that can be awarded men who serve jail terms and thus enhance their status in some circles, women who are convicted are more often labeled unfeminine. They lose time, status, earning potential, and all sense of control over their lives.

DEATH OF A CLOSE FRIEND

The death of a close friend has moved into the top ten from seventeenth place—perhaps because all respondents are now women, and because women now need each other more since extended families have contracted or completely disappeared. Women in the '90s more than ever look to each other for humor, practical suggestions, information, networking for jobs, physicians, child care, recreation, permission, and feedback. The death of a close friend reminds us, of course, of our own mortality, and when it is out of phase, coming earlier in the life cycle than we expect, it is a double shock. Although 20 percent still give this item 37 points, none give it fewer, and 25 percent give it 90 or more points.

RETIREMENT

Last among the top ten life events that women find stressful is retirement. When the original population of men and women in Seattle rated this event, both women and men were probably thinking about the retirement of the man in the house—and of what it was like to now have him around the house full time. Then it was ranked tenth. Now women think of their own retirement when they respond to this item—and it is still ranked tenth. But although the rank remains the same, the number of actual stress points increased by 23. During interviews, many women differentiated between forced and voluntary retirement. Voluntary retirement was associated with going on to other useful activities. Involuntary retirement was associated with leaving behind friends, money, and routines. Involuntary retirement is also associated with lowered sense of control, choice, and predictability—ingredients for stress. And when women think about their husbands' retirement? Forced or voluntary, most women smile and say 100! "He's looking over my shoulder all day." "He won't go anywhere without me." "He is gaining weight and losing interest in life." "He's depressed and bored—he's making me depressed, too!"

THE CHANGES AMONG LIFE CHANGES

Let's group life events according to increases in stress points. When we do, we see that daily issues and life-style events have increased the most in stress ratings:

EVENTS	POINTS
Christmas	+44
Pregnancy	+38
Fired at work	+36
Marriage	+35
Spouse stopping/beginning work	+32
Death of a close friend	+31
Vacation	+30

This is ominous news, since, like taxes, most of these events (except vacations) are here to stay. The second group of events that show the greatest increase in stress points are associated with our jobs and money:

Change in residence	+27
Foreclosure of mortgage or loan	+25
Retirement	+23
Change in financial status	+23
Trouble with boss	+22

Until the economy changes, the status of women changes, and the divorce rate changes, these life events are also here to stay. What to do about these inevitable stressors? Be aware; remember, knowledge is power! Know that each is a sign not of personal punishment or failure, but usually of the rhythms of life. Keep dancing until the melody changes—it always does. And take care of yourself, really take care of yourself, during and after the life change. You will be using up extra stores of emotional and physical strength during each change and will feel depleted after the crisis if you don't.

Curious about the areas that changed the least? They seem to be family factors:

Death of spouse	−1
Jail term	+9
Change of health in family member	+12
Change in recreation	+7
Change in church activities	+7
Change in social activities	+8

And which items have been rated as less stressful than in the '60s? The following events' stress rankings have declined:

Son/daughter leaving home—down 9 places

The empty-nest syndrome has become an empty threat in the '90s. When children leave, according to the American Board of Family Practice survey released in 1991, it's a time when parents become more involved with caring for each other, a new spouse, or old parents. Even the middle-age crisis seems to be disappearing. We have babies in our forties, face-lifts in our fifties, and 29 percent of those seventy-five or older still call themselves middle-aged. It's not, then, when our children leave that we become upset. It is when they return, after their college or divorce—and often with their own children in tow, hard won after lengthy court battles. The real signs of middle age, according to twelve hundred people nationwide, are not being able to identify the new music groups, being called "sir" or "ma'am," needing more than two days to recover from strenuous exercise, and thinking more about the past than the future! If none of these applies to you, I guess you're not middle-aged yet.

Outstanding personal achievement—down 8 places

The stress of personal achievement may have been revised downward because our culture is less competitive than it used to be—but I doubt it. This change probably reflects the difference between the original population surveyed, which included men, and this one—all women. The stress of outstanding achievement involves the resentment of others, the added pressure of visibility, of higher expectations for performance in the future; in other words, leaving the ranks of "team players." Women were not usually allowed to join the team anyway. Their achievements can only help their cause for equal pay and equal say.

Trouble with in-laws—down 6 places

As in-laws have gotten younger and marriage shorter and extended families rarer, the spector of the mother-in-law has faded. Now, women say, they have become more of a resource for child care and information than a source of stress. The greatest in-law problem today is their scarcity when a baby-sitter is needed, and not one woman gave this item 100 points!

Change in number of arguments with spouse—down 6 places

A change in the number of marital fights from 19th to 25th place not because they are less upsetting than they used to be, women say, but because so many other events have become more stressful. Taking on a new mortgage, moving, change in work, and even Christmas have become so much more stressful in the '90s that they have been reordered ahead of a change in the number of arguments with spouse. Not surprising.

Although the original life events scale was an important tool for measuring the effects of change on stress symptoms, the list of events left women wanting more . . . more events on the list, that is. Six years ago, women in Iowa, Tennessee, Florida, California, and Colorado began to write in stressful events they felt belonged on the list. Some seemed unique or unusual, but others seemed to ring true for most of us or for those women we love. So I began to request that the groups of women attending my stress management seminars develop their own lists of stress life changes, not mentioned on the original Holmes and Rahe list. Here they are:

THE STRESSORS MOST FREQUENTLY ADDED FOR THE '90S

STRESSOR	PERCENT OF SAMPLE MENTIONING THIS ITEM
Parent's illness	59
Husband's stopping work	58
Child's illness	58
Spouse's illness	55
Chemical dependency	31
Remarriage	29
Commuting	27
Crime victimization	26
Depression	23
Raising teens	22
Husband's retirement	22
Infertility	19
Single parenting	18
Abortion	17
Son/daughter returning home	15
Own retirement	14
Parenting parents	12
Loneliness of singlehood	11
Disabled child	7
Friend's illness	7
Adoption	6
Sexual discrimination	5
Racial discrimination	4
Honeymoon	3

Here's how respondents rated the stressful demand for adjustment created by twenty of the new items:

STRESS RATINGS FOR NEW ITEMS

STRESSOR	POINTS
Disabled child	97
Single parenting	96
Remarriage	89
Depression	89
Abortion	89
Child's illness	87
Infertility	87
Spouse illness	85
Crime victimization	84
Husband's retirement	82
Parenting parents	81
Raising teens	80
Chemical dependency	80
Parent's illness	78
Singlehood	77
Moving	76
Adoption	74
Son/daughter returning home	61
Own retirement	58
Commuting	57

Isn't it interesting that although most women now work at some point during their lives, most of our major stresses still focus on the family: trying to have one, trying to care for family members, trying to raise children alone, trying to juggle the needs of children with the needs of elderly parents and needs of our spouse. After all, you are still the mom, also.

STRESS RATING OF LOSSES

STRESSOR	POINTS
Death of spouse	99
Divorce	91
Abortion*	89
Infertility*	87
Death of close family member	83
Marital separation	77
Jail term	72
Death of close friend	68 (up 31 points)

*New item, not included in original survey

You can (if you're in a grim mood) see life as series of losses. When you're born, you lose the comfort of the womb. As you grow up, you lose the innocence of childhood and the protection of your parents. If one of your parents dies when you're a child, you may lose your sense of safety. If a marriage fails, you may lose your hopes for love. If you have an abortion, you lose a potential child. If you can't become pregnant, you lose your fantasy of a child. When your spouse dies, you lose companionship and security. And when a close friend dies, you lose a great deal of intimacy.

One of the ways great tragedies—like an untimely death or major earthquake—affect us is that they shake up our view of how the world is supposed to be. Most of us walk around thinking that tomorrow is going to be pretty much like today. When we turn on the stove, we expect that it won't blow up in our face.

But if we get a phone call in the middle of the night saying that our husband has been killed in a car accident, then this view of the world as a benign place is shattered. Some people stop believing in God. Some people become terrified to step outside. Some get consumed by massive anger. The pain of a child dying, for instance, is so strong that some therapists estimate that 90 percent of couples who experience this tragedy risk getting divorced.

Even small losses, say some pyschologists, bring up painful feelings from previous losses. By this line of reasoning, when you mourn the end of one relationship you are, to some extent, mourning the end of all your previous relationships because emotions create echoes and ripples from the past.

You might have noticed the large jump in rated stressfulness for the death of a close friend. I believe that as more women remain or become single, they rely on friends as surrogate family members. Also, at least one study has shown that married women tend to compensate for lack of intimacy in their marriage by becoming close to other women. In both cases, the loss of a close friend becomes similar to the loss of a close family member.

JOB AND MONEY CHANGES

STRESS RATINGS FOR JOB AND MONEY CHANGES

STRESSOR	POINTS
Fired at work	82 (up 35 points)
Husband stopping work	79
Retirement	67 (up 22 points)
Change of financial state	60 (up 22 points)
Spouse begins or stops work	57 (up 31 points)
Foreclosure of mortgage or loan	55 (up 25 points)
Change in line of work	51
Mortgage over $10,000	59
Change in responsibilities at work	46
Trouble with boss	45 (up 22 points)
Change in living conditions	41

Money may not buy happiness, but it certainly can bring peace of mind. Survey after survey has found that the more money you have, the less likely you are to feel stressed.

If the '70s and the '80s were the eras for the getting and spending of money, now many people are running hard just to stay in the same place. In 1988, the average family income, adjusted for inflation, was only 6 percent higher than in 1973, although close to twice as many wives now work. According to one estimate, the number of hours a family must work to maintain a middle-class life-style has increased by 50 percent—with most of the extra hours put in by working wives. The costs of many middle-class "necessities" has skyrocketed. In the past twenty-five years, in real dollars, the price of housing has jumped 56 percent and college tuitions have soared 88 percent. The Congressional Joint Economic Committee says that the typical thirty-year-old man buying a middle-range house in 1973 incurred carrying costs that made up 21 percent of his income. By 1987, those costs had increased to 40 percent.

Little wonder then that money matters and job concerns have become more important stressors for women in the past thirty years, often being on a par with family problems. And, although the women I interviewed found that performing their jobs could cause stress (if they had trouble with their bosses, or experienced a shift in job responsibility), they rated financial changes, especially negative ones, as more stressful. The key stresses in the financial area include: being fired, a husband losing his job, a change in a money situtation, and—a real '90s phenomenon—having a mortgage foreclosure.

FAMILY STRESS

STRESS RATINGS OF FAMILY EVENTS	
Stressor	Points
Child's illness*	87
Spouse's Illness*	85
Parent's illness*	78
Son/daughter returning*	61
Marital reconciliation	57
Change in health of family member	56
Sex difficulties	53
Gain of new family member	51
Change in number of arguments with spouse	45
Trouble with in-law	42
Son or daughter leaving home	41

*New item

As we noticed earlier, in the '90s women may well become very invested in their jobs, but still take responsibility for the well-being of others. Illness in the family—whether it happens to a child, a spouse, or a parent—is seen as a seriously stressful crisis among the women I studied. Other research has shown that women are much more likely than men to become distressed by troubles occurring to those in their social networks. You may not be getting divorced, but if your best friend is, odds are you're taking on some of her pain and anxiety. You may not get bullied as you walk down your sidewalk, but if your son is you're probably feeling an enormous amount of concern for him.

In the family realm, there's one way in which the '90s are very different from the late '60s: grown children are returning to the "nest." Once upon a time people worried about the middle-aged women who faced an "empty nest" when their children grew up and left home. Presumably these women felt cast adrift because they'd lost their function in life. These days some women clearly feel that having children leave home is a big stress. But a bigger stress, in many women's eyes, is having grown-up children return home! The stress ratings for the "refilled-nest syndrome" are higher than those for the "empty-nest syndrome." I'll talk more about these two issues in a later chapter.

CRIME VICTIMS

Five years ago, after Sally broke up with her live-in lover, she quickly moved into a cheap apartment in a fairly dicey neighborhood. The first Saturday morning after she moved in, she went out grocery shopping. As she walked into her building, loaded down with packages, she noticed a man behind her. Politely—and stupidly, she now thinks in retrospect—she held the door open for him. The two were in a small foyer between the inside and the outside door when the man pulled out a gun, pointed it at her head, and said he'd "blow her brains out" if she didn't give him her money. With shaking hands, she pulled the money out of her wallet and handed it over to him.

When the police arrived, they advised her to move out of the building, and one policeman in particular had a sympathetic reaction. Her friends and relatives told her what mistakes she'd made (like being laden down with packages), or recounted their own crime tales.

Crime is becoming a daily fact of life for many Americans. The women I've interviewed gave being a crime victim a stress rating of 84, a slightly higher score than being fired from a job, and women in their 30s and 40s, from the New York, New Jersey, and Connecticut area rated being a crime victim as their number one most stressful life experience.

The stress of being the victim of a crime doesn't end with the incident. Many crime victims suffer from posttraumatic stress disorder (PTSD), a severe and lingering emotional turmoil often associated with Vietnam veterans. The turmoil, which can last for years, involves a large number of symptoms, including flashbacks, troubled sleep, angry outbursts, agitation (or the opposite, listlessness), and a feeling of estrangement from other people.

PTSD still afflicts more than half the rape victims three months after the crime, and 15 percent of people who have been assaulted, according to a study of crime victims at the Medical College of Pennsylvania.

Victims of any violent crime are more prone to PTSD if the crime happens in a place generally considered to be safe, like one's home or neighborhood; if you feel your life was in danger, expect to be even more prone to PTSD. As with untimely deaths and earthquakes, trust in your ability to make sense of the world when it feels shattered.

"People who deal with traumatic events in a straightforward way—talk about it with other people, get angry, and cry—may have less PTSD," explains Edna Foa, a psychologist involved in the Pennsylvania study. When you push the event away from your memory and try not to deal with it, you are more likely to have longer and stronger emotional echoes. So, if you've been the victim of a rape, or are having a strong reaction to another crime, run—don't walk—to counseling. Most cities offer free victim support services. If not, ask your local mental health clinic for a referral.

DAILY HASSLES

Major life events are relatively rare ocurrences. "It's the garden-variety type of stress that generally harms peoples' mental health on a day-to-day basis by exacerbating daily hassles," notes Dr. Ronald Kessler, a sociologist at the University of Michigan. If you work full-time, for instance, and need to arrange a move, you may find that the time to do it just isn't there, but you manage to move anyway. Or, you have to arrange a wedding and the tension between you and your mate is now going sky-high. This is because one of the daily hassles that most disrupt our sense of well-being, according to Kessler's research is overload, too much to do in too little time.

For many women, this is a way of life.

OVERLOAD

STRESS RATING OF CHRONIC OVERLOAD

STRESSOR	POINTS
Having a disabled child*	97
Single parenting*	96
Infertility*	87
"Parenting" parents*	81

*New item

> Cynthia had just finished a major report, and decided to slide
> at work for a while. She scheduled that long-put-off gum sur-
> gery. She started working on throwing a surprise party for her
> sister's thirtieth birthday. She finally made an appointment to
> get that carburetor looked at. But then her boss called her into
> his office. Congratulations! He said. He liked her report so
> much, he wanted her to do another. The only catch: She had
> five days to do it. From the tips of her toes to the top of her
> head, every muscle in Cynthia's body started to tense up.

Cynthia just entered the very common realm of overload. For
many of us, overload comes in spurts. On the first day of the
spurt, most of us feel overwhelmed. The odd thing is that by
the second day most of us become habituated to the overload,
according to Kessler's research.

Sounds like good news? It isn't. Once we habituate ourselves
to this higher level of busyness, we then permit ourselves to
overload even more. Even if we like having too much to do, our
body becomes exhausted from too much adrenaline stimulation.
Soon there is no room on our daily list of "must-dos" for real
emergencies and certainly no time for time-outs. One traffic jam
and we can no longer predict how our day will go. Our sense
of control is gone, our digestion is in shock, and the Female

Stress Syndrome is in full swing. Expect those familiar four *d*'s: disorganization, decision-making difficulties, dependency feelings, and, eventually, depression.

In Cynthia's case, she had gone for stress management training the previous year, so she knew what to do for herself. She realized she had to unload some of her tasks in order to write her report in time. She canceled (once again!) her dental and auto appointments. She delegated part of the job of her sister's party to her sister's best friend. But she never stopped going to exercise classes for that week.

With a little help, most of us can cope with spells of overload. But chronic overload—overload that has no end in sight—is a different matter. The women I interviewed gave very high stress ratings to a number of situations that are guaranteed to wear anyone out: having a disabled child, single parenting, and "parenting" parents. Infertility can also be seen as a chronic overload if it becomes a full-time preoccupation—involving frequent trips to the doctor, operations, sex on schedule, and constant monitoring. All these situations cause not just time pressure but also usually call forth feelings of guilt and/or inadequacy.

The women I interviewed who had a disabled child rated it as one of the most stressful possible situations, with a score of 97 (out of 100). Unlike more normal children, disabled children aren't likely to become totally independent as they grow up. A mother may spend her time (and money) taking the child back and forth between specialists and specialized programs. She may feel guilty for ignoring her other children at the "special" child's expense. One way to cope with this situation is to stucture in breaks, find other parents in similar situations and form a co-op. Chip in and hire help, and give each other permission to have some time for herself. Hospices that take in special children for a few days are available. It's amazing how resilient you can be when you get a break from stress.

The same advice holds true for single parents and those who take care of their own parents. In my study, single parenting was given a very high stress rating: 96. And other studies that have toted up the stress of different occupations almost invariably place "single parent" in the top 10, up there with air traffic controller and newspaper editor. Women who take care of their parents are also prone to feeling overloaded; these women rated the stressfulness of their situations as 81.

Although it's less obvious, taking a break can also help relieve some of the stress of trying to conceive a child. The biological time clock can probably be ignored for two months, and a hiatus may help you put the matter in proper perspective. What's more, as I said in an earlier chapter, there is some evidence the stress may be a contributing factor to infertility. Reducing your stress levels may even improve your chances of becoming pregnant.

HAPPY HAPPENINGS

More surprising—and as troubling—as all we've seen so far is that seemingly sought-after experiences have become major stressors for women. Getting married is now seen as more stressful than getting sent to jail! Apparently, being incarcerated may sometimes be less complicated than dealing with the hassles of staging a nuptial event. Note the following:

STRESS RATING FOR "HAPPY" EVENTS

STRESSOR	POINTS
Remarriage*	89
Marriage	84 (up 34 points)
Pregnancy	77 (up 40 points)
Adoption*	74
Christmas	56 (up 44 points)
Vacation	43 (up 30 points)

*New item

On the eve of her second wedding, Rose-Marie remembered what her first wedding had been like. Twelve years earlier, Rose-Marie's mother had taken care of everything: contacting the minister, renting a hotel space for the reception, hiring a caterer, finding ushers, tossing a rehearsal dinner, and picking out flowers, and her father picked up the expenses without complaining.

Twelve years later, the situation was different. By 1990, Rose-Marie had a high-powered job, worked fifty to sixty hours a week, and lived about two hundred miles away from her mother. Rose-Marie's parents had divorced, so Rose-Marie and her fiance Mark, picked up the tab themselves. Mark, who'd never been married before, wanted a huge wedding. Rose-Marie wanted to keep the guest list down (the caterer charged by the head) and had no interest in turning her wedding into a networking event. Mark wanted Rose-Marie to take his last name; up until the last moment, Rose-Marie was undecided which way to go.

In the weeks before the big day, Rose-Marie's boss was complaining about how little she was working—her sisters were concerned there would be a lot of friction between her mother and her father's new wife.

The wedding took place, with only minor disasters (the wrong number of corsages showed up, the caterer forgot to bring a salad, the ex-parents were cool but not openly hostile). Exhausted before the event, Rose-Marie still became a radiant bride. She and Mark stopped bickering long enough to say "I do." And Rose-Marie got a fantastic honeymoon: Her mother picked up the cost of a two week vacation to Ireland.

Still, the couple started their marriage ten thousand dollars in debt due to the cost of the wedding.

The reality is that unless you're paying for the party yourself, eloping, or have been through this at least once before, you cannot possibly realize all the choices—and compromises—you'll have to make, all the control you might have to wind up sharing. This may mean that you'll feel like a kid again, just when you want to feel most like an adult. It may even mean disagreements, just when you wanted everyone to love each other. But if full control over all the wedding decisions is not realistic, don't waste your emotional energy fighting for it. Try thinking of the wedding as a clan gathering in your honor and let everyone share in shaping the day.

After all, the wedding ceremony does have a societal meaning as well as a personal one. A wedding is a "rite of passage," and unlike your first kiss, this passage will be public. So will your choice of mate. You may have always pictured yourself walking down the aisle, but you couldn't have pictured your groom, since you probably didn't know him yet. What will your friends and family think of him? What will his family think of you? Is it any wonder that some brides react self-consciously during the reception festivities?

If you catch yourself becoming a spectator instead of a participant, stop. Close your eyes and shift your focus to inside looking out rather than outside looking at yourself. Then open your eyes again. You will now be in the center of your own wedding activities again—where you belong.

Remember that weddings, like marriages, are package deals: some fun, some frustration, some choice, some compromise. If you find that you are feeling some wedding stress, it's not a dire foreshadowing of things to come; it's just a consequence of a unique situation: a public event that marks a private decision to change your legal status by means of a formalized ceremony, attended by two families who do not yet know each other but will now be associated, perhaps forever, through you! Whew! And you wonder why there may be some tension mixed in the excitement?

Things you can do:

- Consider the bigger picture when disaster looms. Don't call off the wedding because your new sister-in-law hates the hat you choose for her.

- Keep in touch with your friends, especially those who have been through wedding whirlwinds, so you'll know that you alone have not been singled out for stress.

- Keep in touch with your sense of humor, as well. Tears will only make your eyes red; laughter will make them twinkle!

The key to keeping the fun in the planning is to remember what you are planning: It's a celebration. Put aside family politics and performance pressures and get ready for a *party*!

Another happy event that can create a stress crisis for women is Christmas. We look forward to the Christmas we used to have as children—and seem to forget each year that now *we* have to make it happen. We set it up and clean it up, and all on borrowed time. We shop between work and dinner. We wrap when everyone else is sleeping. We cook when we are half asleep. We return gifts when everyone else is returning them, too. And we forget how difficult our sister can be or how inept we feel around Aunt Eve.

Last year, Christmas not only overwhelmed Jackie, it also terrified her. Two weeks before Yuletide, her husband, a salesman, lost his job. On her lunch hour Jackie looked longingly in department store windows, afraid to charge the presents she knew her children wanted. For the first time in her life, Jackie wanted Christmas to go away. It was the first time she didn't find *It's a Wonderful Life* uplifting. This year, she knew, no one was going to chip in to solve her financial problems.

If Christmas or other holidays are your seasons to be panicked, try these stress strategies:

1. Don't let the holiday sneak up as if you've never seen it before. Plan ahead for the work and the stress. Delegate tasks. Stick to your regular routines as much as you can. Don't skimp on sleep or exercise—particularly exercise. Don't suddenly increase your drinking or eating, or you will pay as you go through the holidays.

2. If you are alone, plan ahead. Don't wait for invitations or withdraw. Create your own small dinners, brunch, or caroling party. Reach out to others to distract yourself from your own plight. Or give yourself permission to dislike the holidays. You are not the only "Scrooge."

3. Don't expect your family to be perfect. Do expect recreation of sibling rivalries, regression to some childish

feeling, and some trampling of feelings in general. Set some limits on relatives—the number and the amount of time. And if the family is reconstituted, don't compete with ghosts of Christmases past!

4. Schedule some breaks from the throngs of relatives or crowds—for you and for your children. Naps, baths, and even old movies make great breaks.

5. Take your time cleaning up. A *Parents* magazine survey in 1991 reveals that 56 percent of us say taking down the decorations is our most unpopular holiday activity. Shopping is also a cause of stress, as are the bills in January. So be smart: Use cash, or buy throughout the year. And since 71 percent say receiving presents is the best part of Christmas, include yourself on your shopping list.

HOW'S YOUR STRESS LIFE?

As we've seen, life events always involve stress. This is obvious if the event is an unexpected death, an unwanted divorce, or an incapacitating illness. It's less obvious if the event is a change for the good. But as we've seen even good events, such as moving to a bigger home, changing to a better job, or having a long-awaited baby, can create stress by necessitating reorganization of time, energy, and expectation.

Did you test yourself on the revised version of the 1960s life events scale? Add up the indicated points for every life event or change that you have experienced in the past year, bearing in mind that the average rating for a life event is 19 points higher than in the past.

Remember, in the original life-events scale, Holmes and Rahe found that people with scores of over 300 points for one year had a 90 percent risk of becoming seriously ill or vulnerable to depression. Those with scores between 200 and 300 points still had an impressive 50 percent risk. Although these statistics cannot predict the risk for any particular individual, they do confirm the correlation between life-change stress and both physical and emotional health.

The list of the stresses women struggle with today does not, of course, end here. You have probably thought of a few of your own that are not yet mentioned. These items were the ones most frequently experienced by the women who were surveyed or interviewed. But if you want the complete list of female stresses for the '90s, add these, too. These are the ones that were less frequently mentioned but that seem no less stressful.

Automobile accident or breakdown on the road

Teen in trouble with the law

Finding a therapist, starting therapy

Needing glasses, getting glasses, losing glasses

Stopping cigarette smoking

Finding a nursing home, taking a parent or grandparent to a nursing home

Joining a recovery group

Coworker conflicts

Cost of college, loans, payments, college shopping, acceptances and rejections

Forced separations because of military duty

Sexually transmitted diseases

Gaining weight, dieting, gaining weight back, dieting

Teenager getting car, teen driving

Beginning or ending a love affair

Rape: date rape, "black out" (drunken) rape, marital rape, anonymous rape

Dealing with stepchildren, weekend parenting, reconstituted family holidays, in-laws

Friend moving away

Bills: receiving them, writing checks, mailing them

Children becoming sexually active

Natural disaster

Parents' divorce and/or remarriage

Fixing meals, cleaning up after working in an office

Cohabitating: moving in, moving out

Car radio stolen, tires stolen—entire car stolen
Husband's sexual difficulties
Illness of grandchild
Finding child care; losing child care
Helping adult children; housing adult children
Unwed pregnancy
Nontraditional relationships: older woman, younger man;
    interracial; interfaith; older man, younger woman
Celibacy

It is not always the most frequently mentioned life events which are the most stressful. Do you have more items you would add to this stress list? If so, you probably also have symptoms of the Female Stress Syndrome.

6 NEW WOMEN, NEW STRESSES

BACK IN THE '50S AND EARLY '60S, MILLIONS OF AMERICANS THOUGHT OF *Ozzie and Harriet* as portraying the perfect American family. Ozzie Nelson was the family breadwinner; his wife, Harriet, stayed home to raise their two strapping boys—and all family conflicts were resolved in thirty minutes (less time out for commercials). But in the '90s, the breadwinner-husband/wife-at-home-with-the-kids families have become a minority. And marital stress is now often resolved through divorce.

The '90s have ushered in the New Woman. She:

- Works. From choice or necessity, in 1990, a total of 58 percent of women aged sixteen and older were part of the labor force. During the peak ages of labor force participation—from forty to forty-four—78 percent of women were workers.

- Has a higher-status position than a typical woman of earlier generations. As of 1988, women made up 39 percent of all people holding managerial, executive, and administrative jobs. In 1978, that figure was 26 percent.

- More often regards work as a career rather than merely a job. In 1990, for the first time, a majority of women with full-time jobs felt they had a career.

- May be divorced. It's estimated that one-half to two-thirds of women who married in the '80s will divorce.

- May never have married. An estimated 20 percent of baby boomers will never marry. In previous generations that figure was 6 percent.

- May not have children. By forty, a growing percentage of American women, both married and unmarried, are childless.

- Is less dependent on men. Back in 1970, 66 percent of women believed that for a woman to be truly happy, she had to have a man around. In 1990, that figure dropped to 31 percent.

THE DILEMMA OF THE NEW WOMAN

Few women now have the life they expected they were going to get when they were growing up. Most of us thought that the *Ozzie and Harriet* life-style was at least an option, if not our first choice. But in the '90s, all bets are off. A woman may wake up at thirty-eight and conclude that she may well never have children. A woman who wants to stay home with her kids discovers that the economic realities of the '90s make that totally impossible. A high-powered career woman realizes she can't work full-time *and* be a wife *and* be a mother; when she quits her job, she wonders if she'll ever get back on the fast track. A thirty-five-year-old single woman suddenly decides that she prefers the unmarried life. A twenty-six-year-old mother who never planned on a career is forced to go to work when she gets divorced.

The dilemma of the New Woman is that life in the '90s is totally unpredictable. "One day the *Ozzie and Harriet* couple is eating a family meal," says social historian Barbara Dafoe

Whitehead. "The next day, they are working out a joint-custody arrangement."

DUAL ROLES, DUAL STRESSES

Although married women have entered the labor market in record numbers, research backs up women's own observations that they are still expected to execute their traditional roles at home as well as their duties at work. Working women carry out dual roles in response to their own expectations as well as their husband's expectations. We have learned our roles through custom and culture, through models and reinforcement, and we are no less hard on ourselves than are those around us. We run from board meetings to PTA meetings, monitor ticker tape and supermarket receipts, deal with demanding supervisors and recalcitrant repair people, and rarely question our dual responsibilities. We are stressed and resentful, driven and guilt-ridden, and we are convinced that's the way things are supposed to be.

While being a full-time homemaker has its own stresses, in some ways it is the easier side of the coin. Compare the role of wife or parent to that of a working woman. As a wife or parent:

- No exams, prerequisites, or previous experience are necessary.
- There is no need to submit a résumé for the job.
- Failures are usually not observed, analyzed, and judged in public. They can be hidden in the privacy of the home.
- There is no competition on the job. The laundry is all yours!
- There is no competition for the job. Your children are all yours!
- There is no time clock. Your schedule is yours to structure—no doubt it's filled beyond the waking hours, but it is still all yours.

- You are your own supervisor and boss. This is not to say that you are not your own severest critic and slave-driver. On the contrary, at home you probably assume more responsibility than if you did have a boss. It is a different kind of stress trade-off, however, than that involved in working under a boss.

Working women who are wives and/or mothers often live with a sharp conflict between their roles inside and outside the home. Many mothers who work feel guilty that they were away from home during the day. When they come home, they begin to compensate rather than relax. They put in extra effort and activity at home, as if they had been playing all day.

Of course, arriving home after a hard day at the office, women can feel resentful of children's and husband's demands—and then feel distressed by their own resentment!

The '90s have brought a disenchantment with the idea that a woman can "have it all," unless "all" means all the symptoms of stress! Since the mid-'70s, a majority of American women have said that the ideal life combines marriage, career, and children. But preference for this kind of life, which increased from 1974 to 1985, has since declined, according to national polls taken by Virginia Slims. From 1985 to 1990, the proportion of women who say they prefer the "have it all" life-style dropped 6 points, to 57 percent. In 1990, among women who actually do it all— wife, mother, full-time job—61 percent say that the conflicting demands of family and job put them under stress. And 56 percent say they feel guilty that they don't spend more time with their families, according to the Virginia Slims poll.

BUFFERS AGAINST DUAL STRESS

Although juggling a lot of roles always puts a woman in a time crunch, some women seem to thrive with very filled lives. In "Women and Depression," a 1990 report from the American Psychological Association's National Task Force on Women and Depression, the authors argue that the quality of the roles is as important as their quantity. That is, either a good job or a happy

marriage—preferably both—can protect women from stress.
The report cites a study that ranked women from least depressed
to most depressed, starting with the least depressed:

1. Employed wives with a combination of low marital
   strain and low job strain.

2. Employed wives with low marital strain but high job
   strain.

3. Unmarried women with low job strain.

4. Nonemployed wives with low marital strain.

5. Employed unmarried women with high job strain.

6. Employed wives with high marital strain and low job
   strain.

7. Nonmarried, nonemployed women.

8. Employed wives with high marital strain and high job
   strain.

9. Nonemployed wives with high marital strain.

The happiest women are those who are pleased with both their
jobs and their marriages. The least happy women—they have
five and a half times the risk of depression as the first group—
are housewives with troubled marriages.

What does this mean? Marriage can either protect a woman
from stress or be a major cause of stress, depending on its quality.
Women with happy marriages are much less affected by job
tensions than those with unhappy marriages or those who aren't
married. On the other hand, work—whether it's satisfying or
not—can help protect a woman from becoming depressed. Of
course, it's better to have a satisfying job than an unsatisfying
one, and in a later chapter I'll tell you how you may improve
your work life.

Clearly, working and a lower risk for depression are related.
Can we argue that a woman who's less prone to depression is
more likely to work? Of course. But any therapist can tell you
that working also reduces depression. Why? Because despite all
the stresses involved in working, its benefits are enormous. An

important antidote to the Female Stress Syndrome is the kind of support system most work environments offer—the network of coworkers. This support system serves many functions on many levels, described in detail in Chapter 7, "Stress and the Working Woman: Nine-to-Five Plus."

THE MOMMY WARS

If the '60s and early '70s were defined by the feud between hippies and rednecks, the conflict that defines the '90s is that between working mothers and stay-at-home moms, *Time* magazine recently said. Neighbors, instead of offering the support that can help them both survive stress, may feel that they have to prove *their* way is the right way.

Faced with stresses peculiar to their different situations, the two kinds of mothers are increasingly eyeing each other with suspicion—and resentment. Working mothers, often concerned that they're not spending enough time with their offspring, may feel that stay-at-homes have it easy. "People think you're eating bonbons all day," one resentful stay-at-home complained to a national magazine. "I had a baby, not a lobotomy!"

For their part, the stay-at-homes, who have often given up needed income in order to supervise their kids as they grow up, may feel that working mothers are selfish. They may watch for signs that the children of these women are neglected, or for indications that working moms are shirking crucial obligations. One working mother reports that her stay-at-home neighbor keeps a tally of how many of her son's soccer matches she misses!

These women-at-war are failing to understand that neither way of mothering is necessarily right. What's important to find is what's right for you. Several studies have found that depressed mothers raise unhappy children and that this unhappiness can persist for a lifetime. The ideal mother is the mother who chooses a life that keeps her stress to a tolerable level.

TIME TENSIONS

Even in this recession economy, nearly two of three New Women say they would prefer having more personal time than having more money, according to the 1991 Bristol-Meyers' Keri Report, "The State of American Women Today." The Keri Report surveyed over a thousand women and found that the women of the '90s experience serious time shortfall:

- Only one woman in three (33 percent) agrees strongly that she has enough energy to get through the day without feeling exhausted.

- Although women, on average, now spend over six hours a day taking care of others (spouse or partner, children, parents, and/or friends), only one in four makes her own exercise a priority, and less than half the women surveyed make their own nutrition a priority.

- Women with children under eighteen get only seventy-eight minutes of the two hours of personal time women say they need daily.

- Although slightly more than half of the women interviewed say that making time for themselves is very important, two of three (67 percent) still don't make it a point to find time alone.

Some things, unfortunately, have not changed. We are still spending more time taking care of everyone else than we are spending taking care of ourselves. We are putting ourselves last on our priority list, and we are feeling out of control. Confirmation comes from the Keri Report:

- Fifty-two percent of women surveyed say they feel their finances are out of control.

- Fifty-seven percent say they don't feel in control of their job or career.

- Fifty-one percent don't think they have a handle on their relationship with their parents.

And three of four women surveyed could not say that they were capable of managing all the stress in their lives! The 1991 Keri Report finds that women who allot enough time for exercise, grooming, and nutritional needs feel more in control of the rest of their lives, too. And the extra time it takes, says the report, is just twenty-one minutes a day!

No one is suggesting that we stop doing the nurturing we enjoy, or shirk our responsibilities as we see them. I am suggesting, however, that you put yourself on your own list of loved ones. Don't wait until you are so sick or so exhausted that even your children give you permission to take time out. Make a date with yourself before it's too late. Women who give themselves the gift of time give themselves an important stress management tool. Time increases your ability to plan your day, week, and life, increases your ability to handle the unexpected, increases your opportunities to neaten up, freshen up, put your feet up for five minutes, and make a phone call that will make you laugh. Treat yourself to some time and request more time from those who love you. Both will teach everyone around you that you are entitled to time and are worth it.

STRESS AND THE SINGLE WOMAN

"Study says that women over forty have a better chance of getting hijacked by terrorists than of getting married," blared headlines across the country a few years back. Panic swept through America's offices, koffee klatsches, health clubs—anywhere single women gather. The study, since widely disputed, struck a raw nerve. Single women in their forties believed their situation was hopeless. Single women in their thirties saw a deadline they weren't sure they could meet. Even single women in their twenties looked ahead to a grim future.

By and large, society believes that unmarried women are unhappy women. They are perceived as flawed in some major way. After all, women are still raised to attract men—and if they haven't succeeded, how valuable are they? People assume a bachelor man *could* get married if he wanted to, but that the bachelorette either has a dearth of suitors or is too picky. Make that too picky, too ugly, too angry—or a lesbian.

At the same time, singles are one of the fastest-growing segments of the American population. People living alone—the bulk of single people—are now almost 10 percent of the population, according to the 1990 Census. In the past 20 years, the number of these single people has grown 112 percent; 61 percent of them are women.

Women over thirty who want to get married are at a disadvantage. There really is a man shortage in this country. In 1985 there were 119 unmarried men twenty-five to thirty-four years old for every 100 women the same age. But past thirty-four, the odds go against women. And by the forty-five-to-sixty-four age bracket, the number of single men plummets.

Many women react to this shortage by becoming obsessed with finding a mate. The push to marry comes from both inside themselves and from outside.

At thirty-two, Suzie is vivacious and attractive—but also unmarried, with no prospects. Focused on her career, she has a wide circle of interesting friends and is most often satisfied with her unattached status. But not always. Put her around her large extended family, and she falls apart. "Any sense of achievement I feel in my life evaporates when I see my cousins and their numerous children. My mother nudges me and says, 'Now, wouldn't that be better than a career, dear?' I've stopped going to family events like seders, which I used to love, because I can't handle the comments I get."

Like Suzie, many single women feel outside pressure to act "normal" and get married. Like Suzie on a bad day, many single women feel internal pressure to prove that they're desirable.

The biggest mistake single women make is that they stop living their lives, waiting for the moment that they become married. Women don't move out of cramped apartments, thinking that they'll waste energy because they'll be hooked up soon. They don't buy a new couch because they're afraid it will clash with Mr. Right's furniture. They don't take a trip to Europe because they don't want to travel alone or because they'd rather go with a lover than a girlfriend. They won't make plans far in advance with friends because they're afraid someone will ask them out for a date that night. Meanwhile, the years pass and they live in an apartment they hate, rarely have good vacations, and spend a lot of time home alone. They could have enjoyed the freedom that comes with singlehood—instead of letting it slip by.

Don't wait to find a mate. Take that trip, buy the new sofa, move to the new apartment. Enjoy your life *now* instead of postponing your pleasure to the future.

THE SINGLE CAREER WOMAN

Talk to a few single career women and you will probably hear stories similar to Mickie's:

> Mickie was single, successful, and sexual. She was twenty-nine years old, however, and beginning to feel alone. Not lonely, she explained: *alone*. She wanted a partner. She wanted to meet a man who could join her and share in her life. Perhaps marry. Perhaps have children.
>
> But Mickie was having a hard time. She found men she could "adopt." Men who would make great "wives." Men who would "take care" of her. Men who truly believed she wanted to be "dominated." And men who truly believed that she wanted to "mother" them. What she could not find was a man who believed her when she said she wanted a partner.
>
> She was successful and loved her work. This made many men feel competitive. She was sexual and yet discriminating. This made many men feel anxious about "performance." She was mature and intelligent. This made many men feel self-conscious. She was self-supporting and financially secure. This made many men feel inadequate.

Mickie's story has a happy ending. She met a man who enjoyed her just as she had wanted to be enjoyed. Her independence was a bonus to him, not an escape from responsibility and not a threat. They are still living happily ever after, arguing about politics rather than about her achievements.

Not all such stories end so well, however. An achieving woman who harbors both fear of failure and fear of success tends to find herself devastated by male rejection, great or small. She blames herself for unsuccessful affairs. She retreats before her partner can. She "obsesses" so much about past problems and future fantasies that, often, she cannot let things be. She may sabotage the relationships herself in order to explain possible failures or to avoid the responsibility of success.

Not all men in the '90s fear successful women. Some women report that potential mates check out their assets to make sure *they* earn enough. In the 1990s, when it takes two decent incomes to support a middle-class life-style, some men are afraid they'll be burdened with a woman who can't support her economic weight. In a *Time* magazine survey taken in 1990, some 86 percent of American men aged eighteen to twenty-four said they are looking for a spouse who's ambitious and hardworking. A quarter of those men want a partner who has a high-paying job.

THE BIOLOGICAL TIME CLOCK

The clock strikes thirty-five (or thirty-nine, or twenty-nine), and suddenly a woman starts getting motherhood yearnings. Even if the moment's not just right—her finances aren't great, or her career isn't where she hoped it would be—the woman, for the first time, is willing to make the necessary sacrifices. The problem is that the man she's keeping time with may be marching to a different tempo. Or worse yet, the woman may be partnerless.

Once the motherhood yearnings start, a woman who feels her biological clock is running out may overreact to the deadline. She may put too much pressure on a husband who's not ready to have children. She may scare away potential suitors by raising the issue of kids on the first date. She may make a poor match by marrying the first semisuitable man who comes along. She may get pregnant "accidentally on purpose" so her boyfriend will walk down the aisle with her. She may hastily use donor sperm and then worry at leisure about what to say to the child when he or she asks, "Who's my daddy?" She may obsess about all the bad choices she made in life that got her where she is today.

On the other hand, some women react to the biological time clock stress by becoming very focused. In looking for mates, they may find themselves suddenly preferring nice, stable men over exciting, unavailable men. Or they may enter into therapy to help clarify their life goals. Or they may realize that the realities of motherhood—as opposed to their fantasies about it— are not what they really want. Or they may sadly resolve to express their nurturing needs by mothering their nieces and nephews rather than having their own children. Alternatively, they may decide they want children so badly that they are willing to join the ranks of women who are single mothers by choice.

The great news is that it is now possible for some women to become pregnant after 35 years through in vitro fertilization techniques, and to be pregnant after 40 years through ovum donation techniques. In fact, in a current report in *The Lancet*, Dr. Daniel Navot et. al., conclude that although female fertility does decline as we get older, the uterus can sustain pregnancies even when our reproductive potential is artificially prolonged into our late forties.

So contrary to conventional wisdom, the rate of infertility is going *down* in this country. Older first-time mothers are becoming increasingly common. Between 1980 and 1988, the birth rate for unmarried white women aged thirty to thirty-four jumped sixty-eight percent; the rate for those thirty-five to thirty-nine surged 69 percent. In addition, the rate of first births among all women in their thirties, both married and unmarried, has doubled in the past ten years. Among women who are 40 to 44 years of age, it's gone up 50%. And the recent Bureau of the Census population report expects that these trends are likely to continue. Later marriages, longer education, larger career goals, and new, improved contraception means delayed childbearing.

Does this mean problems for their babies? Probably not, say epidemiologist Gertrude Berkowitz, Ph.D. and Richard Berkowitz, M.D., Chairperson of Obstetrics, Gynecology, and Reproductive Sciences at Mt. Sinai School of Medicine in New York City. Their news-breaking research concluded that there was no evidence that older mothers have an increased risk of having a premature delivery, a low birth-weight baby, or a baby more likely to die perinatally. Even though older women having their first child (primiparas) are themselves more likely to suffer some complications (pregnancy-induced hypertension, diabetes, and placental problems, for example), their babies are as likely to do well as the babies of younger women.

So where is the problem? New and improved fertility techniques means more sense of choice, and more choice usually means less stress, doesn't it? Not when we can't predict what will happen next, and that is one of the stresses associated with increased fertility options. More fertility options means many more months and years of monitoring ovulation, intercourse on medical command, hormone therapy and its emotional and physical side effects, watching for conception, worrying about miscarriage, and wondering about one more program, one more doctor. Couples themselves must set limits on how much time, money, and energy they have to spend pursuing pregnancy, and how old they feel they can be and still provide the kind of parenting they would want any child of theirs to have.

If you feel stressed by your biological time clock, my advice is: Don't panic. Advances in infertility treatment have made it more likely than ever that an older woman can conceive. Ovum donor programs have made it possible for even postmenopausal women to bear children. (A donated egg is fertilized with the husband's sperm, then implanted in a woman's uterus.) And private adoption, though difficult and expensive, is still a possibility at any age.

THE NEVER-ENOUGH WOMAN

In the '80s, we worried about the Type A woman. In the '90s, we worry about her sister, the never-enough woman.

You know the type. If there's a soupçon of flab beneath her leotard, it ruins her day. When she gets a raise, she starts plotting her next promotion. No matter when her child learns to read, it's never early enough. No man is ever Mr. Exactly Right—not rich enough, not smart enough, not something enough.

During interviews around the country, psychologist Colette Dowling, author of *Perfect Women*, found an enormous number of women who are driven to achieve but who never feel satisfied when they succeed.

"The drive to achieve stems from a need for approval. These women need feedback so they can feel good about themselves," says Dowling. But the effort is doomed to fail because it's based on external events—which are transitory and unpredictable—rather than on a stable sense of self-worth.

Women have long been perfectionists. What's different now is that the New Woman has so many more realms to achieve in. For many '90s women, it's no longer enough to succeed as a wife, or a mother, or a worker. Now they must succeed as all three!

The dilemma of the New Woman is that life in the '90s is terribly unpredictable. Her fatal flaw is that she may be basing her self-esteem on events over which she has little control. The inevitable result? Stress, stress, and more stress.

In the next four chapters I'll talk about how women can gain a sense of control in their marriages (as well as divorces and remarriages), with their children, and at work. (For more on control and giving it up, see Chapter 4).

7 STRESS AND THE WORKING WOMAN

IT'S THE '90s AND YOU ARE PROBABLY A WORKING WOMAN.

It has been estimated that about 90 percent of the women in this country have worked or will work for pay at some time in their lives. In 1991, 54 million of us are employed—almost 60 percent of all women over sixteen, and 75 percent of that amount work full-time. Most of us work because we have to— either because we are single and self-supporting, or because we are married and one paycheck will not stretch to cover the house or apartment, edible food, decent clothing, the phone, the lights, and an occasional vacation. But a substantial number of us say we would work even if we did not have to. That's because we've come to know the other benefits of working besides the money: the social network, the change of pace, the chance to achieve, better self-esteem, less depression, and, for some, money to have under our own control.

But work is called work for a reason. Now that the number of women entering the work force has peaked, we have learned something that men have known for a long time: Work can be stressful as well as rewarding. Sometimes work is *more* stressful than rewarding—for example, when:

- You have a lot of responsibility but very little control.
- You have a lot of work but not enough time.

- Your chances for advancement are limited but you want to get ahead.
- Your boss is incompetent.
- You are not being paid enough for what you do.
- You are often interrupted.
- The work is boring and repetitive more often than it is new, exciting, challenging, and stimulating.
- You are discriminated against or harassed sexually.

It is not surprising that studies tell us that the most stressed-out women employees are clerical workers; in the course of a day they have to deal with most of the stresses on the list above. The woman executive may be in slightly better shape—39 percent of the jobs that the U.S. Labor Department classifies as executive, administrative, and managerial are held by women. As a boss a woman has more control, a chance to structure her own day, more of an opportunity to be noticed and praised, more interesting work to do—but she may still have to deal with pressures that men do not have to face: sexual discrimination and family responsibilities.

TYPE A WOMEN

Given the special stresses that working, career, and professional women are subject to, it is no wonder that they experience female stress symptoms. Given the special drive and character women must have to compete successfully and even to excel in the working world, it is no wonder that they suffer "executive stress" symptoms as well.

In the 1970s, cardiologists Meyer Friedman and Ray Rosenman told us that achievement-oriented male executives were paying for their personality profile with high blood pressure and/or heart disease. They warned that the same characteristics associated with career successes are also associated with excessive levels of norepinephrine, making men with these characteristics susceptible to psychosomatic diseases. These characteristics include:

- competitiveness
- aggressiveness
- secret, chronic anger
- impatience and irritability
- perfectionism
- concern with others' approval

Friedman and Rosenman labeled this profile the Type A personality, and America started worrying about the personality profiles of its men.

By the early 1980s, new evidence suggested that only one component of the Type A personality was linked to heart disease: secret, chronic anger. But the other components were not declared benign. By creating stress for the Type A, and everyone around the Type A, all the characteristics were still seen as dangerous. Stress was more and more being linked to lowered resistance to cancer, infections, depression, viruses, and accidents. Stress was more and more linked to increased risk of infertility, divorce, and drug abuse.

By the middle 1980s, we women were worrying about Type A behavior also. We were working outside the house and inside the house. We were now executives and secretaries. We were smoking more, rushing more, and still we earned less than men. We tried to be assertive without being aggressive. We tried to watch out for ourselves and be a "team player" at the same time. We still looked for men to save us but no longer really expected that they would. And although Meyer Friedman's new book *Treating Type A Behavior and Your Heart* told us that men who modify their Type A behavior reduce their risk of heart attacks, no one was telling women what to do.

When a man exhibits Type A behavior, physicians and family become concerned. "Get a thorough checkup," they say. "Take two weeks' vacation." However, this advice is not as readily applied to Type A women, most of whom have family and social responsibilities they can't easily escape—or that they *feel* they can't easily escape, which amounts to the same thing. Too often they simply find themselves settling for the notion that everything will look a lot better after a good night's sleep.

By 1990 it became clear to me that women have as much potential for developing Type A personalities as men do. It also came to the public's knowledge that heart disease, not cancer, was the number-one killer of women. If there was any link at all between Type A behavior and heart problems, women wanted to know about it. The link, it seems, is this: Time urgency and free-floating hostility often lead to eating on the run, smoking, drinking, loss of sleep, loss of humor, loss of libido, and loss of friends and family.

All of this means that if your behavior is Type A, your body is probably being constantly bombarded by noradrenaline, which constricts your blood vessels and pushes up your blood pressure. Stress also means your adrenal cortex will secrete extra cortisol to mobilize fatty acids. These fatty acids are metabolized by muscles in fight-or-flight situations but are left circulating when there is more anxiety than action. Eventually they may convert to cholesterol. Although cholesterol is used by the non-stressed body for mending membranes and composing certain secretions, when it stops circulating it can cling to arterial walls, catch blood clots, or even block vessels.

All of this also means physical symptoms. A Gallup survey sponsored by the Upjohn Company found that among working women, job stress was experienced almost daily as

- muscle strain or pain in back, neck, arms, or shoulders
- headaches
- trouble falling asleep or staying asleep
- stomach, digestive, or appetite problems
- unusual weight loss or gain
- unusual menstrual difficulties
- shortness of breath
- palpitations with normal physical activity

More than 50 percent of the working women surveyed also felt emotionally drained from job stress. Another 30 percent said they had difficulty getting started in the morning, and 31 percent said they frequently felt anxious, nervous, or tense.

If you are thinking that this review is not for you, now is the time to take my Female Type A Quiz. Give yourself one point for every description that is sometimes true for you and two points for every description that is usually true for you:

———— *I am perfectionistic.*
If you stretch the phone cord so you can straighten the picture on the wall while you are talking, this is you.

———— *I am impatient with others who don't do things as well or as quickly as I do.*
If you try to hide it, add an extra point.

———— *I am never satisfied with my achievements.*
If you started jogging to reduce stress and now you feel guilty when you don't, give yourself at least one point.

———— *I overschedule myself.*
If even one traffic jam throws your whole day off, there is surely no room for pleasure or relaxation.

———— *I am a closet competitor.*
If your neighbor bakes cookies after her board meeting and before her mammogram, and you then add cookie baking to your list, too, you are a closet competitor.

———— *I am a stimulus junkie.*
If you say "the more I have to do, the more I get done," you get points on this one.

———— *I am polyphasic.*
If you do at least two things at once, such as talk on the phone while you cook dinner and open the mail, you are polyphasic.

———— *I have telephone tension.*
If you do not assume it's the lottery calling when the

phone rings, but suspect it's one more problem for you to handle, give yourself points.

_____   *I hate to wait*!

If you find you finish sentences for everyone else, you hate to wait!

If you gave yourself even *one point* on this quiz, you are a Type A. And if you gave yourself more than one point, you just got an A+ on this exam—Type A+, that is.

The following is a list of ways to cut down on your Type A stress:

- Do one thing at a time. When you read, eat, or speak on the phone, concentrate on that one activity only.

- Catch yourself when you use quantity rather than quality adjectives in your thoughts or speech. Try to describe the beauty of an object or location without referring to its cost.

- Read books that are purely recreational for you, not occupationally or professionally relevant. Concentrate on the form as well as the content; look up new words in the dictionary as you encounter them.

- Walk, eat, and talk more slowly. Drive in the slow lane to avoid pressing the gas pedal with every urgent thought and to become accustomed to a steady, moderate driving pace.

- Pick days to leave your watch at home. How often do you find yourself looking at your wrist that day?

- Record one of your own phone or dinner conversations and play it back to yourself. Note whether or not you speak rapidly, ask questions, or listen to answers. Do you try to speed up your conversation by supplying the endings of sentences for your partner? If you recognize a Type A speech pattern, rerecord as you practice your listening and Type B conversation skills.

- De-stress yourself before you deal with home, after the office. Read while you have a cup of tea in a diner for ten minutes, pop into a church or synagogue for five minutes, or ask your husband to watch the children while you take a fifteen minute bath or shower before you start dinner.

- Get on the *longest* supermarket line to practice waiting without agitation. Discover how you can make the time pass pleasantly. Speculate upon the lives of those around you. Review pleasant memories. Plan a lovely future.

- Check your face in the mirror at least twice a day for signs of annoyance, tension, or fatigue. Get to know these expressions so that you can *feel* them without the mirror.

- Practice smiling and laughing. Do this by deliberately thinking of a delightful memory or funny incident. Don't wait for smiles and laughter to come to you—make them happen.

NOT JUST ONE OF THE GUYS

Unfortunately, sexual discrimination is alive and well in the workplace. A young woman newspaper reporter in New York—supposedly one of the most liberal, least discriminatory places in the world—found out that her older, male boss had an amazingly archaic attitude when she told him of an upcoming change in her life.

It was during a discussion on an article that Sylvia happened to mention to her editor that she was planning to get married in a few months. He replied, "Oh, will you be leaving us?" She was shocked silent for a moment. Then she informed him that she would be staying. She now has two small children and draws a part-time salary from the same newspaper, though she feels she puts in close to a full-time week.

By now, the differences in male and female salaries are well known, but not everyone is interested in doing anything about it. A woman who worked in an Indiana electronics company is an example. She noticed that the men she trained as part of her job were soon making more money than she was. She asked her supervisor for a raise. He told her that she did not need a raise, since her husband had a good job. She told him she did not need to work for a company with an attitude like that.

Many managerial women cite another sexual barrier: the "glass ceiling," the invisible shield that blocks their ascent up the corporate hierarchy. The glass ceiling is real: According to the U.S. Department of Labor, only 1 or 2 percent of senior executive-level officials are women. In one survey, more than two hundred chief executive officers admitted that stereotyping, preconceptions, and a reluctance to take risks with women in line positions were reasons why they did not promote women more often.

The only treatment worse than this is outright sexual harassment—the requests for service that go beyond the scope of the job (taking shoes to the shoemaker for resoling, or scratching someone's back), the unwanted arm around the shoulder or pat on the bottom, or the office pool party in which the secretaries are told to wear bikinis!

Control is the antidote to stress. Some ideas:

- Complain if you object to someone's sexist remark. Start gently; the person may not realize how bad the remark sounds. If you get no results, get advice from the Personnel Department.

- Find out how to file suit if you are a victim of serious sexual harassment, and then proceed if you don't get satisfaction.

- Raise your children with equality in mind. Teach your children to respect other people. Sexual harassment is a combination of disrespect for a woman's feelings and a desire to be superior to her, to put her down.

- Comment on bad examples and be a good example yourself. Children learn sexism from their parents and the world around them. "I don't like the way that man is treating that woman," you can say when you see something objectionable on television. If you yourself are being treated badly at home, knowing that your children are learning from your example may give you the push you need to make a change.

ON THE JOB AND PREGNANT

Working pregnant can mean working with nausea and fatigue, not to mention a whole range of emotions: euphoria, anxiety, optimism, and fear. And just when you need an office ally to talk these things over with, you may be trying to keep everything secret for a least a few weeks more. Even after the word is out, the people around you can be surprisingly unsympathetic, particularly colleagues, both men and women, who have no children of their own and are resentful or do not understand how it feels to be pregnant.

Besides job performance, pregnant workers have other things to worry about as well—for example, the possible effect of stress on pregnancy. One study found that pregnant women in high-stress jobs secrete more catecholamines, the fight-or-flight hormones, than women in lower-stress jobs do. Some experts suspect that these hormones can cause premature labor and delivery. Others say that the evidence is not so clear and that an otherwise healthy woman can work long days in a stressful job with no effect on her unborn baby.

But we do know that specific jobs may be bad for the baby's health. Though studies have so far failed to prove definitively that spending hours in front of a video display terminal can cause early miscarriage, staying on a job that involves chemicals or radiation definitely risks the health of the baby. In fact, if you are *thinking* of becoming pregnant and have this type of job, check with an obstetrician.

Another stress is the worry of wondering whether the job the pregnant woman left at the beginning of her maternity leave will be there when she returns. In about half of our states, the law says that a woman who works for a company with more than fifteen employees can take up to four months' leave and still have a job when she comes back. If you are pregnant and your supervisor seems skeptical about your return, you can tell him or her that 50 percent of working women who become pregnant are back on the job by the time their children are three months old, and 72 percent are back when their children are one year old.

THE WORKING MOTHER

The drain on energy and efficiency does not end after pregnancy. The working mother may have recovered from the pregnancy and birth, but each night when she gets home, there is now a child to consider, plus a house, plus a decent dinner, plus mending, plus . . . the "second shift," it has been called. If you are not a working mom, just walk into an elevator in a busy downtown office building at 9:00 A.M. and look around—you will have no trouble spotting a woman who is. She is the one who looks as if she has been up since 6:00 A.M. (she has!) and has no hairstyle to speak of because the last person she had time to take care of was herself.

Working mothers live a delicate high-wire balancing act, and the slightest adverse breeze can topple the entire structure of their day's schedule. A child is sick and cannot go to day care. The school system announces a snow day. The husband goes out of town on business and cannot take the children to their after-school program. The au pair baby-sitter quits with no notice. A managerial mother may be able to get away with disappearing from the office for a few hours or coming in late in order to deal with a domestic crisis, but less autonomous employees often end up using their sick days and vacation days to take care of family business. Mothers can be and have been fired for taking too much family time. If they are not actually fired, bosses and coworkers may respond with resentment when a working mother becomes less dependable because of family obligations. *Some* bosses are sympathetic. That is something to keep in mind when you are job-hunting. As you interview, remember that mothers are often presumed to be less reliable and less available for after-hours work than other employees, regardless of whether it is true.

SUBDUING WORK STRESS

Although 42 percent of the working women Gallup surveyed said they coped with job stress by walking, exercising, or meditating, most used "remedies" that eventually *increased* their stress:

- Forty-two percent say they work even harder.
- Forty-two percent say they do more things at once.
- Forty percent act as though things are okay, and keep their problems to themselves.
- Thirty-two percent think of changing jobs or retiring.

Before you write your resignation letter, see if some simple stress-reducing ideas make a difference.

On the very practical side, here are some suggestions from other working women:

1. Buy more clothes and underwear to avoid the need for frequent laundry and cleaning trips. Include dark soil-resistant suits and lots of extra blouses. Give yourself permission to stock up! You save time for every penny you spend.

2. Hire help, as much as you can afford. Find a cleaning service. Let the tailor fix your hems, the laundry do your shirts. Have a fashion consultant identify a few types of clothing that always look good on you to simplify your shopping. Or use a professional shopper if your department store offers this service. Use caterers or waiters and bartenders for parties. Teenagers and college students are good sources for many of

these services. Don't overlook a tax accountant and a travel agent. In the long run, these services are cheaper than the doctor's bills that may follow too much stress.

3. Schedule escape. Read a novel in the bath, on the bus, or at lunchtime. If your body can't go to a faraway island, at least your psyche can!

4. Find private time. One half hour after everyone else has gone to sleep or before everyone else has awakened can be *your* time for indulgence, contemplation, or fun.

5. Play. If you enjoy games, take a crossword puzzle to breakfast, or backgammon to dinner. Psychologist Constance Freeman and her associates have relaxed during ongoing lunchtime Scrabble games for years!

6. If you have a mate who works, establish a policy of "equal flexibility," Each of you must be able to take it for granted that your goal is to share the total load of household work equally, and that both your schedules and energy levels may vary unpredictably. For example, once you have this understanding, whoever had the easier day or who got home first would prepare the dinner. If neither of you has the time or energy, you might go out, order in, or even eat separately.

   Practicality is the key. It is important that working couples not let practical tasks such as cooking and cleaning become symbols for other things, such as loving and caring. When both partners have equally heavy schedules, let meals be for nourishment and count on conversation, sex, consideration, and the like to demonstrate your love and caring for each other.

7. Determine the healthiest diet for you and make sure you have the right foods on hand. Do you need a protein snack at 4:00 P.M.? Does your favorite diet call for only cottage cheese at breakfast? Again, stock up! You will be much less stress-prone if your body has

the nutrients it needs, and you have the satisfaction of sticking to your diet. Make it easy for yourself.

8. Keep lists. Whether in the form of a small notebook or pocket calculator that is always in your purse, or a more elaborate categorizing technique taught by some of the time-management courses, such a system will enable you to trap thoughts, names, addresses, dates, and so on as they come to you and to get things done efficiently. Again, taking control of your environment lowers stress.

9. Self-hypnosis and other special relaxation exercises can be great helps in relieving tension.

10. Get a message machine. In this way you can screen out junk phone calls, whether at the office or at home.

11. Get the best-quality child care you can find. If this means paying a professional instead of taking advantage of a mother or sister who has been doing the job for nothing, make the switch—it will be worth it.

MAYBE I SHOULD QUIT

For the first time since the U.S. Labor Department began keeping track in 1948, the percentage of women in the work force is down. The peak came in the first half of 1990, at 74.5 percent of women aged twenty to forty-four. Part of the reason may be the recession—there are fewer jobs to go around for everyone— but there are other reasons, too. As Lily Tomlin once said, "If I'd known this is what it would be like to have it all, I might have been willing to settle for less." Having it all can be too much—too much stress!

We cannot stand the thought of having one more baby-sitter quit on short notice. We suspect we may be missing out on life's most precious moments. We are not paid enough, or our jobs are not interesting enough, to make all the sacrifices worthwhile. We can no longer work the "second shift" alone.

In spite of our begging, threats, and appeals to fairness, statistics say the man of the house still is not doing a fair share of housework and child care. He often thinks he is really pulling his weight if he feeds the cat, takes the junk mail out for recycling, puts one child to bed, *or* leaves the newspapers he has just read in a neat pile instead of all over the couch as usual. Men say they are willing to share the second shift, but they usually need to be shown what to do and reminded to do it—another management job for the woman of the house.

PART-TIME OR AT-HOME

Working your way up from the bottom rung of the ladder as quickly as possible—the standard male-style approach to conquering the hierarchy—is not the only way to run a career. Millions of women (and men, too) are satisfied with the detours they have discovered.

> Rhoda works part-time as a lawyer in a firm. She is not sure what effect this will have on her chances of becoming a partner, but she is sure that she values the extra time.
>
> Deborah writes magazine articles while her five-year-old son is in school. She earns about half of her former salary. She has also held office in his co-op nursery school, been on school field trips with him, and spent countless hours at the playground and pool, time she values more than the money she has given up.
>
> Ellen left a public-relations company to start her own business: She felt her gifts lay not only in creativity but also in management, and there were too few positions in the upper reaches of her old company for her to aspire to. She now has three employees and plans for more.

The downside of working part-time, working at home, or having one's own business: You are spread thin and find excellence in any one field to be elusive—whether it is excellence as a parent, homemaker, employee or specialist. You may risk chances of advancement because any employers you encounter may be unwilling to invest in someone who is available only half the time or from a distance.

But the benefits are many; for example, you may have fewer meaningless meetings to attend, you waste less time fielding miscellaneous phone calls (isolation has its virtues!), and you avoid the time and expense of dressing for success every day.

THE BENEFITS OF WORKING

Hard as it may be to believe, despite all the stresses associated with working, its benefits are enormous. An important antidote to the Female Stress Syndrome is the kind of support system most work environments offer—the network of coworkers. This support system serves many functions on many levels.

- Working can provide social contacts and a sense of belonging. Spending almost half your waking life during the week with any group of people is bound to facilitate ties. Spending it sharing goals, hard work, anxieties, and victories can make for very strong ties. Sometimes lifelong friends are made at work. Sometimes the friendships are unique to the workplace. Either way, the relationships can be valuable and supportive. Either way, you are part of a team: a department, a company, an industry, or a profession. A fundamental need for belonging is to some degree filled.

- Working can provide different points of view. There is never one reality or one view of reality. Talking about problems with your work network can broaden your perspective on any topic. It can help you understand another's behavior in a less personalized way. It can help you reinterpret last night's domestic fight or this morning's news bulletin. It can bring you into conversation with men and women from other backgrounds, generations, and businesses. It can exasperate you and fascinate you and help to make your thinking more flexible.

• Working can provide humor. Heard any good jokes lately? If so, and if you work, you probably heard them at the office. Office jokes travel by word of mouth, by phone, and even by photocopies. Cartoons are posted. Gags are pulled. Office war-stories and office histories are shared. Tense tales become comedies in the retelling, and looking at the light side is an important fringe benefit of the working life.

• Working can provide resources. Your workmates may have ideas, information, and know-how that you do not, and vice versa. Pooling resources, in fact, has become almost a ritual in many work situations involving women. Sometimes the aim is career information and opportunities; sometimes more personal needs are met. Either way, the more information and knowledge you can gather, the more control you will have. And the more control, the less stress!

• Working can provide confidantes. Who understands your work frustrations and elations better than someone who is also on the job? Who would be safer to talk to about family problems than someone who is *not* in the family? In both cases, a workmate can be a valuable ally. Have you noticed that it is sometimes easier to unburden yourself to a semistranger about a personal sorrow than it is to those close to you?

• Working can provide cushioning and escape valves for anger. This can work in two different ways. First, work can provide an opportunity to use constructively the adrenaline generated by anger. You can tear into your work instead of into your mother-in-law. You can beat a deadline instead of a dead issue. You can argue for a proposal instead of arguing against your husband. You can leave your desk phone instead of your boyfriend.

Second, anger that feels inappropriate at home may be entirely legitimate at the office. You may not feel it is constructive to get angry at a spouse or child for performing poorly, but you can do so constructively and systematically at the office, where grievance and evaluation procedures are formalized.

• Working can provide sympathy. The communal expressions of sympathy for sorrow that you get from the office are a unique source of support. Your workmates are a semipublic group, wider than your family yet not as impersonal as strangers or polite neighbors. The larger the group, furthermore, the more likely that you will find others who have experienced the same sorrow. You can see why retirement means far more than separation from work. It means separation from a network as well.

• Working can provide adult conversation and intellectual stimulation. Do you spend most of your time talking with children? Do you spend most of your day hearing *Sesame Street* and Mister Rogers educating infants? Do you consider the verbal exchange at the gas station the most adult conversation of your day? Then you will understand how important this aspect of working is. Many women take part-time jobs or volunteer their work just to spend at least part of their day with other adults. For most women, who work because they must work, intellectual stimulation is not the aim, but it is always an important fringe benefit.

• Working can provide a source of praise and reassurance. Too often, good or extra work at home is taken for granted or goes unnoticed altogether. Although this is possible on the job, too, more often you will be told if your work is good. Promotions and paychecks are tangible proofs of performance. Even women who enjoyed being homemakers for its own sake are thrilled with their enhanced sense of worth when they return to work in their later years. They enjoy feeling that they can contribute to the family in a financial way. They enjoy the power that accompanies any position. They enjoy putting their many skills on public display.

- Working can provide objective feedback. Your own family, appreciative or otherwise, can't really be considered objective. In the workplace, you and your work are evaluated often, by many people who have no interest in you other than how effectively you are doing your job. You can base further actions and decisions on impartial data, which increases your sense of identity and control. A great stress reliever!

In the past, the extended family helped to prevent stress buildup by serving all these functions. Now, in a way, we must each create our own extended "families," our networks, our support systems. Whether you work outside the home or not, think about each of the ten network functions mentioned. Are there some that you're not getting through your work, friends, or family associations? If so, actively seek people to add to your support system who can help provide what you need. The quality of your life may depend on it.

The benefits of working go far beyond networking. Entering the marketplace with your skills means negotiating a price tag for your work. For most women, an increase in salary or commission means an increase in self-esteem. A paycheck is a tangible statement of work, a source of pride and some degree of independence.

Raised in an era when girls were taught "you are who you marry," women in their forties and fifties often find that working at a career or profession helps them reaffirm their identity. Women at workshops tell me that working outside the home finally provides them with an answer to that perennial cocktail-party question, "And what do you do?" Many women choose to work as homemakers for many years, then move on to their next commitment. Many others have not yet married or have decided not to marry. For these women, work is even more primary to their identity. For still other women, work and love (with or without marriage) are equally vital. The key is to know yourself and what you want; to be aware of both the problems and the benefits inherent in your choice; and to seek to reduce the stresses in the ways suggested here, as well as in any other ways that work for you.

8 LOVE, SEX, AND STRESS

IT ISN'T A UNIQUELY FEMALE ADDICTION. IT HAS HIT US ALL. "IT" IS AN altered state of consciousness that makes us say everything we feel, mean everything we say, and believe everything we hear. Call it infatuation, or passion, or lust, or falling in love—it is the same. It is a temporary psychosis, a passing insanity. We're walking on air, not sleeping, not eating, and feeling no pain. And it's no wonder, because our brain is flooding itself with pain-killing endorphins, amphetaminelike phenylethylamine, energizing norepinephrine, and antidepressant dopamines.

While we are "drugged" we see him as the essence of attractiveness and irresistible to others.

While we are drugged we know we can overcome any obstacle and overlook any differences.

While we are drugged we bestow enormous power on the object of our interest: His approval becomes necessary for self-approval; his disapproval leads to our self-blame.

While we are drugged we are sure our feelings will never change, and we say so . . . we swear so.

And then infatuation ends. Like all peak emotions, it must pass. The body must get back to eating and sleeping. The mind must be able to concentrate again. The color of his eyes didn't predict his capacity for commitment. The debates on dates became tedious arguments at home. The aggravation you thought was passion turned out to be just aggravation. Love is not blind after all—infatuation is!

FALLING IN LOVE

Ask any woman "Who falls out of love more easily . . . and in?" and she is likely to recite the facts of romantic life as passed on from mother to daughter:

- "Women fall in love more easily."
- "Women hold on to hope longer."
- "Women are less likely to initiate separations."
- "Women suffer more after breakups."

If you believe that women fall in love more easily and that men fall out of love more easily, you are wrong. In fact, if you believe any of the statements above, you are wrong!

> Marcy is now in her fifties. She had three wonderful romances before she married and loves to remember each. The first raised her spirits when her father died. The second made her sexually aware of herself. And the third helped her get "bastards" out of her system. She was the one who ended each romance when she felt ready to move on, and married "a good man" who gives her a "good life." "I enjoyed my affairs," Marcy says, "but I never confused falling in love with learning to love."

We may watch more soap operas, read more gothic novels, light more dinner candles, and see sentimental movies more often, but we are not really an easy touch for Cupid's bow. It is true that we are romantic in our fantasies, but our behavior is very down-to-earth. In my research on love and infatuation, I surveyed hundreds of men and women and found that most women do not suffer from the happily-ever-after syndrome or believe in Doris Day. We have practical reasons for our affairs!

> Bobbie wasn't ready to get married. She had just moved to Chicago and wanted to live on her own for a while. She also

wanted to have some wonderful lovers, but felt very guilty about "recreational sex." So Bobbie shared sex with a man only when she was "in love." And, she confides, she was "in love" quite a few times when she first moved to Chicago!

Sometimes falling in love provides the intimacy that is missing from a high-achieving woman's life—with built-in obsolescence to eliminate any possible long-term drain on career time or career energy:

> Laurie loved working in television. She was an assistant producer now but planned on running the show soon. She needed to focus completely on her job during the day but wanted to cuddle at night. Ted was the perfect answer. He was romantic, over-worked, and lived two hours away. When he spent the night during the week, he left early enough for Laurie to dress alone in the morning. When she was tired, they spoke on the phone instead of spending the night. She had Ted on weekends and no children or grocery shopping during the week. When Ted began to speak of children and groceries, Laurie asked for time out of the relationship. And she stayed out.

Falling in love can also let us feel less responsible for our behavior:

> Susan had spent fourteen months standing by her man as he went through a bankruptcy. The marriage was not in jeapordy, but Susan felt like her sanity was. She knew that she needed to have someone to listen to her, care about her, and even care for her. She felt like she needed to take a little before she could give any more. So she fell in love for a while. The affair would have felt too cold and calculated if she had not felt "in love," Susan admits. Now that it's over, she sees it as part of her private life, part of the past.

Who says women are masochists looking for love in all the wrong places? Not the statistics. Social psychologist Zick Rubin, Ph.D., conducted a two-year study at Brandeis University, in Waltham, Massachusetts, asking over a thousand college students if they would marry someone with all the qualities they desired but with whom they were not in love. A total of 76 percent of the women said yes; 64 percent of the men said no.

> Larry really liked Cathy. She was a loyal friend and good company. But Susan made his head swim. He wanted to show up at parties with her and pictured her walking downtown, their daughter-to-be walking next to her, two beautiful blondes—both his. He romanced Susan for two years until she said "yes." He is still friends with Cathy and still in love with his wife.

Since most men expect to be a breadwinner, they can afford to choose a mate who strikes their fancy or their fantasy. In fact, more men than women in my survey reported that their marriages began as infatuation and more women than men reported that their marriages did not begin as infatuation. This means that women, not men, are more likely to end a love affair. They end it, once again, for practical reasons: to find more security, greater fidelity, or permanence.

> Henry is seventy-two years old and often remembers Renée. He was madly in love with her during World War II. It did not end well between them. She would not leave France and her family to marry a young American, and he was brokenhearted. He still remembers the affair with affection. In fact, surviving his broken heart makes him as proud as earning his Purple Heart.

Although the women I surveyed said they thought men fall out of love more easily and leave for other women, men knew better. Men said they were dropped more often than they did the dropping (90 percent of men had been jilted, 61 percent of women) and that they rarely left for another woman—but liked having another woman around.

> Fred and Marsha hadn't had a long talk in two years because they were so tired of ending up in a fight. Fred and Marsha both knew that Fred was more needy. He was jealous after parties and resentful of the time she spent with her sister or mother. He tried to become more independent by joining a ski club and a therapy group. He began to spend time with a woman he met

and soon started coming home later and later. Marsha became even less giving, and Fred became even more resentful. Marsha finally suggested that they separate. Fred moved in with his new friend rather than be alone.

Does all this mean that women don't fall in love at all? Of course not. We do, and we enjoy it.

- In every age group except for the thirty-to-forty-year-old divorcées, women say that falling in love was a more positive than negative experience—regardless of its consequences!

- In every age group women agreed that their infatuations are more intense than men's infatuations because women have less control over the outcome. They have to wait for calls, dates, and proposals. But they love to have that adrenaline flowing.

- In every age group there was agreement that we never outgrow our capacity or need for romantic experiences. Younger women reported love affairs lasting months. Women over fifty reported infatuations lasting years!

THE NEW MRS. ME

Unfortunately, some young women find themselves marrying in order to grow up. Even if she is still daughter, student, or in her late teens, a woman has "adult" status once she is married. She is now a wife. She is Mrs. Somebody. A new name, a new home, and a new adult life. But the teenage wife usually pays a high price for this instant new self-definition. She may bypass the identity confusion of these years, but she can become confused and overwhelmed by the responsibilities of marriage instead.

At first Judy said no to Jack's proposal of marriage. She had wanted more in a husband—more maturity and more security. Jack was not quite tall enough, smart enough, or old enough to suit Judy's fantasies. Even his car was secondhand. But then she began to think about marriage in general rather than marriage to Jack. Married, she would not have to live at home nor ask permission to borrow the car. Married, she could give advice, not receive it. Married, she could dismiss forever the anxiety surrounding dateless weekends. Married, she could have a baby—dress it, take care of it, and show it off. Married, she would no longer feel her own life was secondhand. Judy said yes to Jack.

Judy and Jack married. They set up home in a walk-up apartment. Soon Jack quit community college to work as a retail salesman. Both Judy and Jack wanted more for him, but a baby was on the way, and they needed money. The baby and the baby blues arrived at the same time. Judy was constantly tired and lonely. She longed for the days of clubs and dates. She longed for her parents' home and the hot meals that she didn't have to prepare herself. What had she been thinking, she asked herself, when she had said yes to Jack?

As both statistics and clinicians tell us, the act of marriage generally changes even the longest premarital live-in relationships. The factors that seem to be responsible can be labeled the four *r*'s.

1. *Regression*. Moving into a marriage may spark new plans for home life, but it also activates memories of our parents' marriage and home. With childhood memories come childhood feelings and behaviors. Since these old behaviors are often more practiced and familiar than new, adult perspectives and behaviors, they may keep popping up when least expected. Husbands become confused with daddies and wives may act like daughters, much to their own horror.

2. *Re-creation*. Women may also find that despite their best intentions they are re-creating and perpetuating stereotypical, sexist behaviors, For example, they may find themselves displaying learned helplessness—imitating dependent behaviors that they observed to have worked for their mothers. They may find that they are suffering from the "Cinderella complex"—waiting for

the handsome prince to change their lives from emotional rags to riches. They may be acting out "little woman" passivity—living in fear that they will be deserted if they become their own women. Or they may be slipping into nagging aggressiveness—sounding exactly like the women who most repelled them when they were young.

3. *Reaction*. To their surprise, some women find that they *react* more than they act. That is, they monitor their mate's moods and needs, trying to be perfect for him rather than being themselves. They watch every word to make sure that they are giving appropriate, justified responses. They hesitate to initiate plans, conversations, even sex, to avoid the responsibility that goes with self-assertion: Plans may not work, conversations may become arguments, sexual overtures may be rejected. They soon feel like spectators of their own lives, and their sense of control erodes until the Female Stress Syndrome surfaces, inevitably.

4. *Recollection*. Memories that may be confusing, unsettling, or stressful are often locked away through repression—a kind of motivated forgetting. This makes our daily lives easier. Marriage, however, can trigger the reappearance of recollections of our parents' marriage—of scenes, screams, and secrets. This, of course, makes coping more difficult. We may find that we are suffering from nightmares, unpleasant daydreams, mood swings, and a free-floating anxiety.

THE HERE AND NOW

Fritz Perls, the originator of Gestalt therapy, popularized the phrase "here and now" and warned us not to use the present to master the past. He observed that many of us re-create our most upsetting relationships of the past again and again to try to gain mastery of the past situation through the present reenactment. Even if we should gain mastery in the present, however, it would not count because the original situation in the past would not have been settled—so we would be bound to set up the challenge once again. If you are having trouble moving out of the past and into the "here and now," try the following:

1. Look for evidence of the four *r*'s operating. Acknowledge to yourself which are causing you the most trouble.

2. Raise your awareness of them until you can recognize them as they are actually happening. Recognizing their dynamics after they have played themselves out will enable you to make only apologies, not changes!

3. Remind yourself that your increased awareness will permit you to make behavioral choices. Take yourself off automatic pilot and take control of your interactions.

4. If you find it hard to believe that the present can be different from a replay of your past, just try behaving *as if* the present is different from the past. This will set up a positive, rather than negative, self-fulfilling prophecy! Both you and those around you will have a chance to try new actions and new reactions. You may be contributing to the very outcomes you fear most, simply by expecting those outcomes and behaving defensively and dejectedly before the problem has begun.

The four *r*'s are not the only sources of relationship stress. Females in this culture are often taught that they are the "weaker sex," but they may be rebelliously uncomfortable with emotional dependency. Since young women are often warned that men might want to use them as sex objects, they may be particularly wary of turning their sexual pleasure over to their partners. Since women in this culture often perceive that they may be traded in for a younger model in later years, they may be particularly focused on security. And since women in this culture are often warned that career is primary and marriage secondary for a man, they may deny feelings of rejection by fortifying themselves with anger and adopting a distant, "I don't care" attitude.

Stress can also stem from a bad meshing of the expectations that a couple usually brings together. Think of it this way: Every relationship involves at least four sets of expectations—the woman's expectations for herself; the woman's expectations for her partner's behavior; the man's expectations for himself; and the man's expectations for his partner's behavior. Since role expectations are learned through imitating behavior that seems to work for others, we imitate those whom we see the most: our parents, our siblings, our teachers, and our friends. Thus most role expectations are learned within one's own family and subculture, and identical matches between both partners' expectations would be rare—even impossible! There must be constant adjustment and communication of expectations in an ongoing relationship. And the stresses do not stop there.

- Add the problem of a woman who cannot meet her *own* learned self-expectations. She is likely to bring guilt, self-blame, and feelings of inadequacy to the relationship.

- Add the problem of multiple role conflicts, particularly prevalent in marriage. That is, a woman often finds that her roles as mother, daughter, and friend conflict with the behaviors expected of a wife.

- Add the problems of women who preferred their fathers to their mothers as role models in many areas. Such women are usually well-adjusted, high achievers, but they are unlikely to fit into a conventional role.

- Add the special problems of those women who did not have adequate or acceptable female role models at all. They must discard the old and evolve the new simultaneously!

Unfortunately, there is no second chance at childhood. To make relationships work without excessive stress, we must parent ourselves in those areas where our parents were inadequate. We cannot expect our partners to make up for the past.

Go even one step farther to take control over your daily life by giving yourself permission to develop your own set of relationship expectations. When you do, be realistic; know both yourself and your mate. We are all package deals! Take the bad with the good, the weaknesses with the strengths—develop roles that take both sides into account. Remember, your relationship is made up of you and him—nobody else. It is shaped by who the two of you are, not who you *should* be.

FIGHTING FAIR

Psychiatrists, psychologists, poets, and philosophers all agree that loving relationships involve a degree of "letting go," accepting vulnerability, and sharing control—admitting that you care about and can be affected by your mate's behavior. But if couples struggle against dreaded feelings of vulnerability and struggle for a sense of control, they will create fights to serve both functions. Through fights they try to convince themselves that they "don't care," that they can upset their partner, that they can hurt more than be hurt. Through fights they avoid close, intimate moments and warm, caring feelings, which might be so desperately needed that the thought of losing such a bond becomes worse than pretending the bond doesn't exist in the first place!

If the real point of a fight turns out to be reducing the stress of vulnerability and/or loss of control, rather than solving the issue at hand, one or more of the following manipulation tactics will appear. Check yourself on this inventory.

MANIPULATION TACTIC	DEFINITION	YES	NO
Mind-reading	Telling your mate what he thinks or feels, despite his protests to the contrary.		
Sleuthing	Collecting clues and evidence consistent with your own fears and dire prophecies.		
Grab-bagging	Reaching into the past to grab at insults and injustices you have saved up for fights or flights.		
Name-calling	Teasing and taunting your mate in a way that ensures that anxiety-provoking issues will not get faced squarely.		
Running scared	Behaving in ways you think will protect you from disappointments that have not yet happened (and may never happen!).		
Replaying	Rerunning and reviewing upsetting or frightening memories again and again to keep yourself on guard against being vulnerable to your mate.		

Fights that rely on manipulation tactics are a sign of stress. But, as with all stress, trying to deal with the symptoms alone has at best only short-term benefits. Dealing with the underlying dynamics of the relationship will have long-term consequences, since these dynamics can either aggravate or ease relationship stress. Let's look at some of them.

DYNAMICS THAT AGGRAVATE RELATIONSHIP STRESS

Women have spent two decades trying to recreate men in the female image—to no avail. Men have feared that women would learn to think like men—little chance. Mothers and fathers tried to raise androgynous children, and found to their amazement that boys will usually still be boys.

But here it is in the '90s, and many of our differences are still causing stress. From a large survey by David Buss, Ph.D., at the University of Michigan, comes this list of male behaviors which most stress women:

- Sexual aggressiveness, which makes us feel used or coerced.

- Condescension, which makes us feel ignorant or unimportant.

- Unfaithfulness, which makes us feel gullible or humiliated.

- Inconsiderateness, which makes us feel neglected or insulted.

If you're wondering how we, in turn, stress men, the list is shorter: We bother them when we are sexually withdrawn, fussing about our appearances, or moody. We may be equal, but we are certainly not the same.

PROJECTION

A man who flies into a rage if his partner procrastinates on a commitment may be fighting his own embarrassing tendency to procrastinate at the office. A woman who panics or sulks at the least sign of her mate flirting may secretly feel that she herself could take a flirtation too far. In such ways, partners may "project" their own unacceptable thoughts, feelings, and impulses onto the other. They may be hypersensitive to just those habits in their mates that they are least tolerant of in themselves.

This style of handling incidents on a daily basis can greatly increase the stress level of the relationship. Take the case of Jim.

> Jim had had a bad day at the office, an annoying drive home on the crowded freeway, and an upsetting conversation with his accountant. When he finally reached home his regular parking space was occupied. Jim would feel much better if he could let off some steam, if he could find someone to blame for his day, if he could yell a bit. Jim knows, however, that this "fight" impulse is "unacceptable." In reality, there is no one to blame for his unfortunate day. He would, in fact, feel very guilty if he took out his frustrations on his wife and equally innocent children.

Solution? Perceive his *wife* as starting a fight! He searches for a look on her face that might suggest dissatisfaction or demand, and, of course, he finds it. Jim gets to have his fight and lets off steam without feeling guilty or consciously responsible. The price, however, is steep.

DISPLACEMENT

By definition, displacement involves reducing potential guilt by redirecting a feeling from its original source toward a safer person or object. Have you ever kicked your cat after talking to your mother? Slammed the door while your baby was crying? Honked at innocent motorists as you mentally replayed your most recent romantic squabble? That's displacement.

Taken further, displacement can put stress on relationships. "You always hurt the one you love" can be more accurately stated as, "You only dare to hurt the one who loves you." A man who appears mild-mannered to the outside world may be touchy and quick-tempered with his mate. A woman who rages at her partner when he asks her to do something she considers excessive may not be able to raise her voice to her boss when he makes unreasonable demands on her.

DEPENDENCY

Although dependency can be healthy and a strong bond between two people, it can also be destructive and undermining. Confusing a mate with a mother or father encourages childlike reactions and muddles the present with past memories. Remember, to avoid falling into a dependent relationship that leaves one partner a child, both people must understand that there are no second chances at childhood. You can't make your mate into the parent you didn't have. Caring is, of course, different from care-taking. The former is a form of loving; the latter is manipulative and can be destructive.

AGGRESSION

The important distinction between aggression and assertion is its intent. During assertion, we move ourselves *toward* another; during aggression, we move ourselves *against* another. Assertion is vital within a relationship. Aggression is not.

It's difficult for women to be assertive when they have been raised with the notion that they should spend their days doing office work or housework, but act like the weaker sex. Many of us fear displeasing others, fear abandonment, fear appearing too independent. The truth is, reports indicate that both men and women enjoy a partner who is assertive. Such a partner eliminates the need for second-guessing and mind-reading. Such a partner gives his or her mate implicit permission to be similarly assertive. Aggression, however, often evokes more aggression—thrusts, parries, and strategies for defense.

PASSIVITY

Passivity and evasion are not simply nonactivities that have no results. Rather, they are very manipulative and are used to seize power within the relationship without assuming the responsibility for it.

Passivity can be an aggressive act. A familiar example is the man or woman who, with an outward show of cooperation, does not accompany his or her mate to a party ("You go ahead, dear, I'll be perfectly fine here at home"), or who goes but sits passive and uninvolved. Either way, the couple is deprived of having a good time *together*.

SEXUAL WITHDRAWAL

Sexual withdrawal can be seemingly passive yet is powerfully manipulative. Although most sexual dysfunctions are related to anxiety or guilt, avoiding sexual intimacy can also be an expression of disapproval or anger. Through sexual withdrawal a partner can be saying "I will not give to you, nor will I put my pleasure in your hands. I no longer feel comfortable letting you know that you can have an effect on me."

There are many problems with this dynamic. First, it sets up a pattern of bringing nonsexual problems into the bedroom. Second, it is indirect and does not effectively address the real cause of the anger. Third, it deprives *both* members of the couple, not just the partner being punished!

Sexual problems are so common among women under stress that it would be unrealistic to attribute them all to relationship stress. Some of them must be attributed to the Female Stress Syndrome as well.

TO FIGHT OR NOT TO FIGHT

If you're confused about the consequences of fighting or not fighting when you're angry, that's no surprise. Popular advice for decades has been all about sharing our feelings with the "significant others" in our lives. If they love you, givers of this advice conclude, they will understand and take your tongue-lashings as a sign of deep caring. So you practiced yelling and tried out the "new honesty" approach—and found that there were few people around who respected your anger or took it as a sign of deep caring. More likely, you found that your angry outbursts led your loved ones to defensiveness, withdrawal, or angry outbursts of their own.

If we look at carefully controlled research rather than popular notions, the answer to whether it's better to fight or not to fight is clear. The main outcome of fighting is called the *practice effect*, which means yelling once serves as practice for a second shouting match, and a second fight increases the risk of a third, and so on. Each time you let it all hang out, you *lower your threshold* for doing it again. You also act as a model for those around you, and have lowered their threshold for fighting, too. Furthermore, you probably provide them with an excuse for focusing their day's frustrations with commuting, working and conforming on you! In the short run, then, fighting may feel good—but in the long run, fighting only leads to more fighting.

If you grew up in a household with parents who fought routinely, you probably didn't need that last paragraph to help you come to the same conclusion. Warfare rarely solves marital problems (or any other kind), because the adrenaline released during battle triggers the "fight or flight" response, not a logical thought response. The fight response can lead to physical abuse, and the flight response to walk-outs and separations: all difficult or impossible situations to mend. Unfortunately, if you were raised in a fighting household, you're at high risk for becoming a fighter yourself.

Am I suggesting that you swallow your anger or bottle up your furies instead? No. But what I do suggest is that the expression of all-out rage is a *self-indulgence*, a luxury that should be reserved for your private moments alone. If you want to grab a pillow by two corners and beat the bed with it, do it! If you feel like writing a scathing letter and then ripping it into little pieces, do it! If you need to run, walk, pedal, swim or chop wood until you've used up the adrenaline that poured out when your fight or flight button was pushed, do it!

Then, after you've privately vented your impulse to *destroy*, begin to form a *constructive* plan. Search your psyche until you can honestly explain your anger to yourself. Most of us will find that our anger means we've been *insulted* by someone who matters to us; we've been *criticized* about something we often criticize ourselves about; we've been *ignored* by someone we care about, or we've been *frustrated* by unexpected demands.

Try to review the situation in an objective fashion without *personalizing* it. See, instead, what you can learn about yourself from the conflict—and about your "rival" as well. Then, start to formulate the communication you want to express. Here are some suggestions on how to start:

- Use sentences beginning with "I" rather than ones that begin with "you." Most husbands, lovers, and family members will care very much about how you feel. "You" sentences usually accuse, attack, or attempt to mind-read the other person. Mates and dates will then become defensive, withdrawn, or too angry themselves to care about *your* feelings. For example, "*I* feel so unattractive when you flirt with other women" is very likely to inspire your partner to give you reassurance and more attention next time the situation comes up. On the other hand, "*You* never pay enough attention to me because you make a fool of yourself and me by flirting all the time" is more likely to begin a rebuttal and counter accusation—in other words, a fight!

- Tailor your communication for the particular person you're angry with. Speak to them in language they can understand. Don't assume your husband and your best friend will hear you the same way, or that they're sensitive in exactly the same way that you are sensitive. If *you* find that you're always sounding off with the same complaints and phrases, your communication is clearly not effective.

• Decide *before* you get involved in a discussion that can lead to a fight exactly what you want from your partner. Then find the words to ask for it. Your aim, presumably, is to make yourself feel better after the discussion. If a hug, an answer, or more time together is what you need, don't wait for the process of mental telepathy to be perfected. Tell him what you need! To test his love by expecting him to read your mind is to invite a fight.

• If all else fails and you find yourself yelling anyway, promise yourself that you'll try not to stray from the issue at hand or say things that both of you would prefer to be forgotten afterward. When you stray to old grievances, you add fuel to the fight fire, and if you think things said in anger can later be forgotten, think again. You probably remember hurts for what seems like forever—and so does he. And although it's a possible alibi, temporary insanity is a difficult defense to prove—and an undesirable label to ask for.

The final word on fights? If deep down your aim is to make things between you better, not worse, don't use your fighting skills on your friends or lovers. Use your abilities to negotiate, clarify, request, and assess instead. That way you'll all come out ahead.

SEX AND FEMALE STRESS

Before birth control technology, unwanted pregnancy and life-threatening abortions were the feared consequences of sexual affairs, teen sex, and even marital lovemaking. Then came the terror of herpes, and other sexually transmitted diseases which silently attacked our fertility. Now, the emerging individual and global sexual stressor for women is AIDS.

AIDS ANXIETY

For the single woman, AIDS means the stress of negotiating safer sex. While each of us has control over our own behavior, we can't control our current or prospective sex partners, or know everything about our partners' past sexual behavior. This is even more of a problem for the woman who is married or in a long-term relationship but suspects that her partner is not monogamous. The fear of HIV infection can precipitate an open accusation where before there was only hidden suspicion. An even worse situation prevails for women who were raised to avoid contraception or to keep sexual matters a silent secret.

While we are all appalled by the spread of AIDS, Robert Benjamin, M.D., the Director of Communicable Diseases, Alemeda County, California, says that pediatric AIDS seems to be a tragedy which affects women the most deeply. But prevention of pediatric AIDS can only be accomplished through primary prevention of HIV infection in women. In fact, in a world wide sense, says Dr. Benjamin, spread of HIV infection can and should be seen as a woman's health issue.

Most women I interviewed felt this way about all sexually transmitted diseases. Since infection and scar tissue can be hidden in the female reproductive system until permanent damage has already been done to the fallopian tubes, ovaries, and uterus, primary prevention is the prescription. Protect yourself now, and you will be reducing stress in the future. Say "No" to unsafe sex.

MYTHS ABOUT FEMALE SEXUALITY

In his book *This Was Sex,* Sandy Teller quotes an eminent physician at the University of Pennsylvania.

Undoubtedly man has a much more intense sexual appetite than woman. . . . With a woman, it is quite otherwise. If she is normally developed mentally, and well bred, her sexual desire is small. If this were not so, the whole world would become a brothel and marriage and family impossible.

It is certain that the man that avoids women and the woman that seeks men are abnormal. Woman is wooed for her favor. She remains passive. This lies in her sexual organization and is not founded merely on dictates of good breeding.

> Joseph Richardson, M.D.
> (and seventeen other authorites)

Although this statement was made in the year 1909, American women are still often expected to be sexy but not sexual, enticing but not forward, and available but not eager. American humor paints the picture vividly.

"What does the French wife say when she is made love to?"
"Oooo, la, la!"
"What does the Italian wife say when she is made love to?"
"Mamma mia!"
"What does the American wife say when she is made love to?"
"Frank, the ceiling needs painting!"

Is this stereotype true? Not usually. Women share with men the capacity for sexual fantasy, desire, arousal, and satisfaction. Female orgasms involve contractions of the pubococcygeus muscles every 0.8 second, just as male orgasms do. In fact, women seem to have little or no refractory (unresponsive) period after orgasm, have greater sexual stamina, and are more likely to experience multiple orgasms.

Why, then, is the American woman presumed to suffer more from headaches than from desire? One reason may be male defensiveness. That is, if a man can believe that women have a low sexual drive, his own performance anxiety may be relieved. "She doesn't enjoy it anyway," he can think. "She's just going along with sex for my sake," he may want to believe.

Patricia Schreiner-Engel, Ph.D., President elect of the Society for Sex Therapy and Research, points to another possible problem, which is that women, unlike men, do not have external signs of arousal to distract them from preoccupations and worries. Men see their own erections, label themselves aroused, and turn their attention to sexual pleasure. Women, however, are frequently unaware of their vaginal lubrication or genital swelling. In fact, both clinically and in her research, Schreiner-Engel finds that women often do not know how physically aroused they actually are!

SEXUAL CONFLICTS

Low sexual desire can be a female stress symptom for various reasons. Sometimes the stress is created by gradual life changes that have crept up over long periods of time. Sometimes the stress is related to unresolved anger and resentment toward a partner or toward men in general. Sometimes the stress is a crisis situation. Most often, chronic low sexual desire results from fears and anxieties left over from past learning.

Women in this culture seem to have been raised amid conflicting sexual messages. They face at least four different sexual dilemmas.

1. *The fear of saying "yes" vs. the fear of saying "no."* To say "yes" involves taking responsibility for birth control, protection from sexually transmitted diseases, monitoring male methods of contraception, or risking an unwanted pregnancy, herpes, or even AIDS. To say "no" can involve risks ranging from rape to angry rejection.

2. *Performance anxiety vs. castration concerns.* If a woman absorbs advice from her mother and the media on "how to please your man," she may become a spectator during her own sexual encounters and suffer from performance anxiety severe enough to inhibit her own sexual response. If, on the other hand, she absorbs advice on "how to maximize your sexual pleasure," she runs the risk of frightening off men who may see re-

quests as instructions, advances as aggression, interest as promiscuity, playfulness as manipulation, and passion as competition.

3. *Fear of discovery vs. fear of frustration.* Young women, older women, married women, religious women, daughters, mothers, and grandmothers all seem to be potentially embarrassed by their sexuality. There is someone, in almost every case, from whom they would prefer to hide their sexuality. Frequently, even husbands can be unaware of their wive's capacity to masturbate or fantasize. Frustration, however, is an unsatisfactory alternative, particularly since current research assures us that women, like men, have sexual needs. To deny or hide these needs may not only add to the Female Stress Syndrome, but deprive women of a natural stress antidote—satisfying sex!

4. *Dyadic duet vs. do your own thing.* Humans seem to be a bonding species, and women, particularly, find themselves looking for long-term partners. Too much emphasis on finding a husband and defining oneself in terms of his success, however, has led this generation to a reaction among women against the "Cinderella complex." Too much emphasis on going it alone seems to be equally unsatisfying, however. The trick will be to find new ways of working with men to build and rebuild lives, rather than bailing out of bonding altogether. Finding a balance, then, is an ongoing problem. And ongoing problems contribute to female stress and low sexual desire.

SEX AND MOTHERHOOD

Sometimes female sexuality becomes a victim of motherhood's stresses:

less time
less privacy

more distractions
fear of another pregnancy
self-consciousness about body changes
concerns about adequacy as a mother

To make matters worse, a mother's own sexual desire can become a victim, too. She may feel that she no longer should be either sexy to her husband, or sexual in her own interests. Too often, her husband may feel the same way. He would feel guilty if he allowed himself to have sexual feelings about a "mother," so he experiences a mysterious loss of desire or arousal instead—the Madonna Complex.

As sex fades from a couple's life, stress grows. An important expression of adult affection has been lost. An important source of physical pleasure has been lost. An important type of stimulation and punctuation of a routinized life has been lost. An important aspect of love has been lost. An important stress antedote has been lost. Such a couple must rediscover each other as *people*, remind themselves that they are entitled to sexual pleasure—entitled to each other!

RELATIONSHIP-STRESS MANAGEMENT

Here are some ideas for managing the stresses inherent in relationships. Some are new, some recapitulate what we have been talking about up until now. What they share is an emphasis on realistic expectations to help reduce chronic frustration or disappointment—realistic expectations for yourself, your mate, and your interactions.

1. Remind your mate and yourself that you are a team— both on the same side, that of the couple!

2. Communicate to be heard, not to win.

3. Realize that it is not your job to teach your mate right and wrong; teach your children, if you have them.

4. Don't confuse compliance with caring, nor lack of compliance with lack of caring.

5. Principles are rarely more important than people. Most women can find room for both!

6. Make requests, not demands. Requests are flattering and usually fulfilled. Demands are challenging and often resisted.

7. *Ask* for what you need. Don't wait for your partner to develop mental telepathy! In the meantime, work on communication and speaking your mind. This will give your mate implicit permission to do the same, and no one will be forced to play Twenty Questions.

8. Develop imaginary role-reversal skills. They add empathy and sympathy to relationships. Put yourself in his place and help him understand how you see things. You will be less likely to take his behavior personally if you do.

9. Acknowledge that perfect fits do not exist; go for compromise and points for effort.

10. Recognize jealousy; it is a common human reaction. Can a father be jealous of his own children? Can a mother be jealous of her own husband? Of course. Don't deny these feelings or they will operate autonomously—treat them as real and you can give them perspective and limits.

11. Try to be self-centering. View yourself through your own eyes. Give yourself permission to relax, speak for yourself, and be good to yourself. Know yourself as you *are*, not as you think you should be. Do as Rita did:

Rita came to therapy with a list of her husband's complaints about her. She wanted help with her efforts to diet, since Don preferred her slim. She wanted help with her efforts to stop smoking, since Don couldn't tolerate cigarette butts. She wanted help becoming more organized, since Don prized efficiency. She wanted help reducing her enormous anxiety when she expected guests, since Don wanted to entertain more.

Rita had given Don the power to make her dissatisfied with most aspects of her marital functioning. Her view was off-center; it was outside-in. She was seeing herself only through his eyes.

Rita left therapy with information about how she felt about her weight, smoking, level of organization, and hostessing. She decided to give up smoking for her own sake, lose some weight as a "gift" for her husband, learn to live with the differences between her style of organization and her husband's, and to entertain whenever her husband wanted to—but by inviting guests out to a restaurant for dinner. She was pleased to be more self-accepting and surprised that Don was more accepting of her as well!

12. Try to be your own parent. It's a chance to raise yourself the way you would have wanted to be raised. Don't look to your mate to compensate for your parents' inadequacies; and don't try to parent him.

13. Permit yourself the vulnerability that comes with normal bonding. Know that you can put yourself in your partner's hands, both literally and figuratively. We bond to produce friendships. We bond to produce families. We bond to produce love.

Sometimes, no matter how much effort you put into trying to understand the dynamics of a relationship, you will not be able to alter behaviors and expectations that are firmly entrenched or operating on automatic pilot. If the problem seems to be unyielding, remember that you can always turn to professional counseling, either for yourself alone or for the two of you as a couple. A marriage counselor, sex therapist, or psychotherapist may be just what you need to help you pinpoint the sources of stress and heal a troubled relationship.

PASS THE PARACHUTE

How do you decide when enough is enough? When being alone is better than being in a flawed relationship?

You've probably heard the statistic that there were more than one million divorces last year in this country. Now add in the marriage separations, the live-in-relationship breakups, and the meaningful relationship terminations and the number of people deciding to opt out of a relationship that seems to be floundering becomes enormous. "Is it better to leave?" ask many of our readers. "Or is it better to stay?"

If you look for the answer from your friends who've been through it, you'll probably hear lots of stories—many conflicting:

"It was my only road to independence and personal growth."

"It was the worst mistake I ever made. Things are no better now, just different."

"Before we split up, I had the job, the housekeeping, and the children to look after—with no appreciation. Now I have the job, the housekeeping and the children to look after—with no appreciation *or* money."

If you look for the answer from your parents, you'll be speaking with a generation whose bias was to stay in marriages and work out relationships. Your parents will probably be practical and remind you that two incomes are often a necessity today, and if you have children, they'll probably be concerned about how the kids' lives will be upset. If you don't have children, your parents might—subtly or not so subtly—express concern that they'll never have grandchildren unless you get married instead of separated from your current boyfriend, or unless you stay married to your current spouse. In any event, they are almost certainly apt to ask you to wait a while before you choose.

If you're the one faced with that difficult decision (or if you're helping a friend or relative through it), start by examining two sides of the situation. First look at the relationship, and then the potential separation. When considering the relationship, ask yourself some hard questions:

1. Is the person you're with special to you in his own right, or is he just filling a role: as husband, boyfriend, escort, company? If he's special in his own right, this is a point in favor of staying and working things out.

2. Are you in the relationship or marriage to give yourself an identity? Some people enter into a live-in arrangement to act out fantasies of being a grown-up, to move out of their parents' house or college dorm, to break out of religious or social conformity, or to become Mrs. Somebody. If you think this is true for you, you may be considering leaving because you still feel like the old you inside. But don't rush to trade your situation for another try at the same plan with someone else. First, work on solving your identity needs yourself.

3. Did you marry or mate on the rebound? When we need to be needed, we often create a trap for ourselves. After rejection, our self-esteem may be low. We then may respond to someone who makes us feel like we're better than they are, vital to their very survival. Soon the rebound hurt has healed, and we're left feeling tied to a partner we resent as being beneath us, needy, or desperate. If this is your scenario, try couples counseling before you decide to bolt.

4. Was the ticking of your biological clock to blame for the disaster that's your marriage? If you married your husband to have a baby, you may have given more attention to your spouse's availability than to his personality. Now you're noticing every quirk, and they're driving you crazy! You're trying to get to know him and your baby at the same time, and what you need is a breather.

   Take some time out with your husband before deciding whether you must move out. If you're not yet pregnant, wait a few months before trying to conceive to see first if you have a marriage. If you've already had a baby, see if one of the grandparents will help out while you spend time with your husband to get to know the person you married.

After you've gone through this list of questions about the relationship, then go through the following list of considerations about separation before opting to stay or leave:

1. If you're thinking about the pluses of leaving without giving equal time to the minuses (and the pluses of staying), do it now—on a piece of paper. Consider your age and position regarding having a family. Consider your chances of remarrying or starting a long-term relationship again. Calculate your financial position—including legal fees and moving costs. List the number of daily changes the break-up will entail. List your partner's good points and bad points—from your point of view only. It doesn't matter if he's chronically late or messy unless it really matters to *you*.

2. If you're leaving because you think you've gotten a better offer from someone else, remember that some people find us most attractive when we're most unavailable. And sometimes we see forbidden fruit as tastier, too.

3. If you're thinking about separation during a time of high anxiety unrelated to the relationship, wait. It's too easy to blame stress on our partner when the real crisis may lie with our career, our health, our parents, our finances or our concerns about aging.

4. If you're weighing separation from a marriage or a long-term relationship without first trying counseling you may be rushing things. Unless mental or physical abuse requires that you seek safety immediately, get help first.

After reviewing these options, ask yourself the bottom-line question: "Even if I never meet anyone else to share my life with, would I rather live it alone than with my partner?"

If your answer is a clear "yes," try separation to see if you're being honest with yourself. If your answers to any of the questions about your relationship or separation have given you pause, or if your answer to the bottom-line question is only "maybe" or "no," your best bet is to stay for now. Tales of finding perfect personality matches are often just that: fiction. After all you have shared, you may have a far better chance of working things out together than you would with a blind date or some other "second try." And if it *still* doesn't click, the option to leave will still be there.

LEAVING

Sometimes the only option seems to be leaving, and leaving always produces stress. I'm sure you've noticed we humans are a bonding species; we get attached to each other. That means our lives will be filled with separations.

Leaving Mom on that first day of school, leaving the family for college or the city, or just leaving when a relationship is over— It's as hard to do as being left. So here are some tips about what to not do when your relationship is through:

1. *Sabotaging.* Whether you are a teen or a spouse, don't escalate the worst just to prove that leaving is best.

2. *Setups.* Beware of trying to avoid guilt by making your family throw you out instead of taking responsibility for leaving.

3. *Sudden pullouts.* Sneak attacks ruin your credibility forever. You save a few days discomfort for yourself but create everlasting hurt for someone else.

4. *Scapegoating.* We all know that it's easier to go away angry than just to go away. So beware: Don't create "bad guys," and you'll have a reasonable chance of a successful separation.

My best tip? Don't ever be less considerate to someone you are leaving than you would be to someone you are just meeting.

JUST UNHITCHED

Whether it's your husband or your live-in lover who is now gone, expect stress. Even if you are thrilled about the separation or divorce, expect stress. Because, as you know by now, change, even change for the better, is stressful. Change throws us into situations that are uncertain, unpredictable, and unfamiliar. Change demands adjustment and readjustment. And divorce involves change! Think about it: Maybe he was no bargain, but you're used to having *someone*.

- With divorce comes a change in your socializing patterns. You may be returning to dating and dealing with new messages, mixed messages, and mixed-up messages about sex. You worry about new disasters, new diseases, new disco steps, new baby-sitters, and old wardrobes.

- With divorce comes a change in your parenting patterns. Not only are you probably making more decisions unilaterally about your children's life, but you are probably feeling the responsibility of those decisions. You might be sharing joint custody long distance, or feeling lost on those weekends when the children are with their father.

- With divorce comes a change in your financial status. Seventy-five percent of divorced women in the United States are working outside the home. As alimony and child-support laws change, divorced women find they must deal with work at home and on the job.

- With divorce comes a change in your home life. Even if you do not miss the man who was your husband, you still may miss having a husband! You may miss having another adult around, miss being escorted to the movies.

Every one of these changes is experienced as much by women who wanted a divorce as women who did not. Although the first group has the advantage of facing divorce with a sense of choice, both groups face the same realities: Unlike men, we cannot start families again and again; unlike men, we usually do not divorce our children; and unlike men, our laugh lines and life lines are not seen as sexy, but rather as wrinkles!

What to do about postdivorce blues? First, check for those four *d*'s, again, the signs of transition trauma: disorganization, decision-making difficulties, depression, and dependency feelings.

After you have checked for these, focus on the *p*'s that will bring out your emotional best. Set up *positive prophecies* for the future; they tend to be self fulfilling! Give yourself *permission* to be less than perfect, to be a *package deal. Practice* separating your past from your present. Replaying old scenes will neither change them nor allow you to move on. *Pace* yourself; give yourself time to understand the divorce and *plan* for your future. After all, there is life, *your* life after divorce.

9 THE FAMILY, '90s-STYLE

THE AMERICAN FAMILY JUST ISN'T WHAT IT USED TO BE:

- Some 50 percent of American marriages now end in divorce. For remarriages (nuptials the second, third, etc., time around), the figure is even higher: 60 percent. Many divorces involve people with children.

- In 90 percent of divorces, mothers have sole custody of the children. Even with joint custody arrangements, children generally spend only about 30 percent of the time with their fathers.

- It's predicted that, during this decade, almost 60 percent of American children will live in a single-parent home before they reach adulthood.

- Five out of six men and three out of four women remarry after divorce, often creating steprelationships. Women with children are much more likely to remarry than those without them.

- Some thirteen hundred new stepfamilies are created each day.

- During the 1990s, almost 35 percent of American children will live, at least for a short while, in a stepfamily. At any given moment, one of five children under eighteen years are part of a stepfamily arrangement.

- Of those children, 4.5 million live with a mother and stepfather; an additional 1 million live with a father and stepmother.

- Children from stepfamilies are likely to be better off economically than those from single-parent homes.

The new American family is very complicated. It's as if its members started out on a two-lane road and suddenly ended up on a six-lane expressway—without a road map!

The new American family includes women who are single because of widowhood or divorce; single parents who head a household; simple stepfamilies, in which only one adult has children; and blended families, in which both partners bring children into a home. The extended families can involve ex-in-laws, step-grandparents, mutual children (the offspring of a couple with stepchildren), half-siblings, and even joint-custody dogs. Former spouses can be so friendly—remaining business partners, for instance—that no one understands why they ever got divorced. Or they can be so hostile that they make the Hatfields and McCoys look like pacifists.

Odds are you didn't grow up wanting to become a stepmother, a divorcée, or a single parent. Although these novel arrangements usually turn into a positive experience, they're formed because of some kind of trauma—a death or a divorce. And so the transition period—the time before you've adjusted to your new situation—is almost invariably filled with tremendous amounts of stress. In fact, in the Female Stress Syndrome survey (see Chapter 5), divorce and remarriage were cited as two of the most stressful possible life changes.

But if you know what to expect, and prepare for it, you can find the positive side of family stress—how it may even change you, and your life, for the better.

MOTHERING IN THE '90s

Imagine this: a fourteen-hour workday. A seven-day work week. No minimum wage, no pension plan, no expense account, no promotion, no lunch hour, no drinks after work, no paid vacation guaranteed, low status, and no prestige. Men need not apply.

Sound familiar? Despite its appalling job description, American women sign up for motherhood at the rate of about 347,000 per year. It is the fringe benefits they are after: participation in creation, touching life and lives, loving, sharing, and caring. For these payoffs they think they are willing to pay the price. Too often, however, the price is steeper in stress than they bargained for.

The Female Stress Syndrome is probably as old as motherhood itself. What is new is the size of the problem. Rates of both depression and anxiety reactions have been climbing among urban, suburban, and rural-dwelling homemakers since the 1940s. Furthermore, record numbers of women are choosing to postpone motherhood, forgo motherhood, or pursue a full-time career during motherhood, an option that carries its own brand of stress. Why?

SAGGING SUPPORT SYSTEM

Although kitchen technology has freed the homemaker from hours of physical labor, progress has created problems too. Harriet's experiences are common.

Harriet left the small Ohio town where she had grown up to attend Boston University in Massachusetts. Through her new roommate, she was introduced to Alex, a New Yorker attending Harvard Business School. They dated through his remaining two years at Harvard and then married. Alex became an account executive for a national corporation and was asked to locate in Atlanta, Georgia. Within thirty-two months of leaving her home, Harriet had moved, married, moved again, suspended her education, and was now pregnant. She did part-time work during her pregnancy to save extra money for baby costs and found little time to meet her new neighbors or continue her education. By the time the baby arrived, Harriet was feeling alone and stressed.

Separated from her extended family and hometown, Harriet was separated from an important mothering support system. Years ago, motherhood was shared by many generations, and a new mother was helped by her own mother and even her grandmother. Now, however, families are usually split into units small enough to move to locations that offer jobs.

Instead of turning to her mother and grandmother for advice, today's mobile young homemaker must turn to the "experts." Unfortunately, when she does, she gets too much information. "How to" books are everywhere. Child experts speak from car radios, television sets, and cassette tapes and write newspaper columns and magazine features.

The mass media have replaced grandmother! But whereas grandmother's advice was consistent, today's myriad experts offer myriad opinions. The young mother is soon completely confused, lacking the traditional support system.

THE WORKING MOTHER

Fifty-one percent of the women in this country, many of them mothers, held jobs as of 1979. Some were married, and some were divorced, single, or widowed. Most were working, because the American dream of "getting somewhere" had been replaced by the reality of working hard to avoid falling behind.

Working may help women relieve the family budget squeeze, but it also contributes to stress. Often working mothers must deal with sexism—and not just sexism at their place of employment, either. Many women report that as working mothers they are discriminated against by their children's teachers, school committee members, and neighbors, and within their own families by critical parents, in-laws, or even husbands.

Betti-Anne and Joe had four children. They both agreed that the children needed Betti-Anne at home full time, but as Joe's salary increments fell behind cost-of-living increases, Betti-Anne had to take a nine-to-five job. Soon after starting work, Betti-Anne was called to school by the teacher of her oldest son. The teacher reported that the boy seemed to be having difficulty concentrating on his classwork. She suggested that Betti-Anne's new job and schedule might be upsetting her son and interfering with his ability to concentrate.

Feeling upset and guilty, Betti-Anne called the boy's grandparents and received two versions of what she calls the "mother's place is in the home" lecture. Her husband suggested that they increase discipline and not indulge the boy. Betti-Anne's best friend disagreed and suggested family counseling.

Things did not improve until a statewide intelligence test given in school showed that Betti-Anne's son was extremely gifted and probably very bored in the classroom. His classroom problems coincided with his mother's new job, but were not caused by her working. He was skipped a grade, Betti-Anne kept her job, and all was well. Or was it? Betti-Anne learned how quickly her working could be held responsible for her family's problems. She also learned how ready she was to do the same. Would she feel less guilty the next time a problem came up?

The alternative seems to create stress as well. That is, a mother who chooses to stay home runs the risk of feeling that she is not doing her share to relieve her husband of the economic strain of these times. Furthermore, her sense of dependency is heightened even as she clips coupons, buys on sale, and pinches pennies. It seems that mothers in the '90s are likely to feel stressed and guilty if they do work outside the house, and stressed and guilty if they do not.

Divorced, single, and widowed mothers, of course, usually have very little choice about whether they work. The cost of raising a child from birth to about eighteen years on a moderate budget has been estimated to be at least $50,000, excluding childbirth and college costs; and since the cost of a well-educated mother not working during those same years is *at least* $75,000 in lost income, it is obvious that money stress is considerable in single-parent households.

A different kind of stress is created for modern mothers by what I'll call "Dana's dilemma." Dana is a friend who confided recently, "I'd be much happier at home than I am working." Since financial considerations were not the motivation for Dana's job, I asked why she did not remain at home. "I feel that being a wife and a mother is my thing, but I don't have any friends to do my thing *with* anymore," she replied.

It seems that most of Dana's friends left the PTA and the A&P to return to school or pursue careers. In fact, they scolded Dana for not doing the same. Social pressure on women to "do their own thing," Dana claims, apparently does not encompass staying home and mothering!

"A MOTHER'S WORK IS NEVER DONE . . ."

Current popular social pressures on women to reject the conventional sex-roles often mean that mothers and homemakers feel the stress of low status. Since women need no experience, no entrance exam, no prerequisites, no courses, and no degrees to become mothers, the role is frequently thought to be low in prestige and exclusiveness—and not just by men. Compare our culture to New Guinea, for example, where Margaret Mead found that men so envy and value motherhood that they hold ceremonies in which they pretend to give birth! Similarly, the Kung nomads of the Kalahari Desert have considered child care as a joint male and female activity for more than a thousand years.

Here in the Western world, however, we see things differently. The average homemaker spends between fifty and seventy-five hours a week on housecleaning and other physical labor: bending, pulling, pushing, zipping, wiping, catching, patching, lifting, lugging, and hugging. Since when has physical labor added to the attractiveness of a social position?

BEYOND HOUSEWORK

Beyond household duties are the stresses that include loss of freedom, some isolation, and much monotony. Not that these problems are exclusive to the mother—the secretary, executive, and cabdriver may have the same complaints. An important difference, though, is that the secretary, executive, and cabdriver have other adults around; the full-time mother usually does not. She waits all day for her husband, who may be too tired to talk when he returns home from work.

The list of stresses associated with mothering goes on and on. Listen to the mothers who meet with me weekly to discuss stress management.

> "I feel like I am always "on duty.' "
>
> "I am always trying to be the *perfect* mother!"
>
> "I worry about accidents all the time. If the children are late, I think the worst."
>
> "When I am on vacation, I don't miss my children. Is this normal? It makes me feel guilty."
>
> "Saying no is hardest—even when I know that I am right."
>
> "Coordinating everyone's time schedules drives me crazy."
>
> "I resent the fact that I'm running the family, but am letting the children think that Daddy is in charge!"
>
> "Having to have answers for my children wears me out."
>
> "I hate being responsible for discipline every day. I'm always the bad guy."
>
> "If my children don't stop fighting with each other soon, I'm leaving home!"
>
> "I don't mind the housework—it's balancing the checkbook I hate."
>
> "I'm always afraid someone will ask me what I 'do for a living' at a party; I'll have to say "nothing' when I really do *everything*!"
>
> "My husband thinks relaxing means watching television at night. Where does that leave me?"
>
> "I don't think I exist for the world. All the mail is for my husband!"

MOTHER'S STRESS CHECKLIST

Nine-to-five hours? Call in for a sick day? Maternity leave from maternity? Not a chance! High risk for the Female Stress Syndrome? Without a doubt!

If you are a mother, fill out this mother's stress checklist and see how high a risk you're running. To the left of each item, write your points according to the following scale:

0 NEVER TRUE
1 RARELY TRUE
2 SOMETIMES TRUE
3 FREQUENTLY TRUE
4 ALWAYS TRUE

ACTIVITIES

_____ I can completely lose interest in social activities and hobbies; the effort seems too great.

_____ I find it difficult to know what I would like to do with free time.

_____ I forget what chore I have started and don't follow through with plans.

_____ I start more projects than I can possibly finish.

_____ I feel the house must be spotless and run with complete efficiency.

_____ I find myself feeling overwhelmed and out of control because there are too many demands on me.

_____ I find it hard to say no to my children or husband, even when I think I am right to say no.

SELF-CONCEPT

_____ I feel that my appearance doesn't really matter to me or anyone else.

_____ I feel that there is very little time for me in my day.

_____ I think other people's opinions are more valid than mine.

_____ I feel unappreciated by my family.

_____ I fantasize about what my life would be like if I could start again.

_____ I find I exaggerate and boast to friends.

_____ I feel a sense of resentment and anger that I cannot really explain.

_____ I find that I often look for compliments and praise.

APPETITE

_____ I feel too aggravated or tense to eat.

_____ I crave coffee or cigarettes to keep me going.

_____ I binge and then regret it.

_____ I need chocolate and/or other carbohydrates when I feel tired or down.

_____ I suffer from nausea, cramps, or diarrhea.

_____ I snack too often.

SLEEP

_____ I have trouble falling asleep.

_____ I awaken earlier than I need/want to.

_____ I have nightmares.

_____ I do not feel rested even when I have a full night's sleep.

_____ I fall asleep earlier than I want to in the evening.

_____ I seem to need a nap in the afternoon.

_____ I awaken during the night.

OUTLOOK

_____ I feel like I've lost my sense of humor.

_____ I feel impatient and irritable.

_____ I cry without knowing why.

_____ I relive the past.

_____ I am pessimistic about the future.

_____ I feel numb and emotionless.

_____ I find myself laughing nervously, too loudly, or without reason.

_____ I ignore things that would upset me.

_____ I am sorry that I chose motherhood.

_____ TOTAL

If your score is between *1 and 40*, congratulations! You are at *low risk* for the Female Stress Syndrome, since you seem to have a sense of control and are managing your maternal career well.

If your score is between *41 and 75*, you are probably *mildly stressed* by mothering and may experience some transient stress symptoms.

If your score is between *76 and 110*, you are running a *moderate risk* for the Female Stress Syndrome. Use the self-help advice in this book to lower your stress levels.

If your score is between *111 and 148*, you are in the *high stress* range, and this book is particularly important for you!

MANAGING MOTHERHOOD

What to do when a mother is burned-out blue? What to do when she feels taken for granted, tired, unappreciated, and unattractive? What to do if that mother is you?

Begin by reexamining your role honestly. List the advantages of motherhood for *you*. Perhaps it is nurturing, perhaps feeling needed, perhaps being in control, perhaps being an authority figure, perhaps shaping decisions, perhaps being in the center of a family, or perhaps enjoying children's activities yourself. As your sense of choice about motherhood increases, stress stimulated by resentment will decrease.

Then reexamine your expectations for yourself as a mother. Are you realistic? How closely do your priorities match your routines? Which of these elements needs adjusting? (Often this is not an easy question to answer, so give it a lot of thought.)

In addition, every mother must become her own sympathetic permission-giver. Do you usually feel that you must be overworked and overtired before you let yourself rest? Do you feel that you have to justify time off to your husband, your mother-in-law, and the rest of the world? Was your hospital stay after the birth of your last child your last morning in bed? *Why?*

Take some two thousand mothers I've spoken to on my lecture tours last year: Don't wait to be rescued! They assure me rescue always comes too late. Intervene *before* you are too tired to relax or too ill to enjoy.

As I often tell my patients, be the understanding, sympathetic, supportive mother to yourself that you had when you were young, or always wanted to have. Give yourself the type of mothering that you are also trying to give your sons and daughters.

- Give your children important information about the value you place on yourself by appreciating yourself openly. Give yourself pats on the back and praise yourself openly. It's a far more pleasant way to encourage feedback than through angry demands, chronic complaints, or depressed sighs and sulks.

- Don't forget to have fun. Instead of sending your children out to play, join them. Instead of resenting your husband because he's out jogging, go jogging with him. Fun will help prevent you from contaminating extra time with mothering jobs that may not be necessary, immediate or exclusively yours.

- Don't use yourself as cheap labor if you want to survive the realities of mothering. Teach everyone in the house how to do all chores. You're not indispensable when you're the only one who knows how to use the dryer; you're exhausted and harassed!

- Reexamine the extra chores that end up as yours. Some you may be able to drop or redesignate. Some you will probably want to keep because you are more practiced or have more of an interest in them. Some you might opt to do yourself. But take an I.O.U. from your husband on them.

By reviewing your routines, you are increasing your sense of choice about their contents. And whenever choice is increased, resentment is decreased. It's easy to grumble when you're in the kitchen while the rest of the family is watching Sunday sports on TV. If a reexamination reminds you that you hate watching sports on TV and enjoy cooking, the grumbling may change to humming. If, however, you find that you hate cooking as much as television sports, get yourself out of the kitchen! Don't be a martyr, be a mother.

DIVORCE, AMERICAN-STYLE

Stress begins long before a divorce. During the decision-making process, a woman must typically consider problems most men don't. If there are children, in most cases they will reside with her. If she is a working mother, she will have to do even more juggling, since she will then be breadwinner, mother, and sometimes surrogate father. Most likely her income will drop; in the year following a divorce, the woman's standard of living declines, on average, 73 percent. (A man's rises by 42 percent.)

Even if there are no children involved, the woman's life-style will be drastically changed. She will give up her attached status for a round of dates and all the anxiety that involves: waiting to be called, battling the numbers that tell us that there are more women than men available, competing with younger women for men of all ages, and being reacted to on the basis of her appearance. Or perhaps she will give up companionship altogether, depriving herself of support. Furthermore, if she looks to romance or marriage as an important component of her happiness, she must deal with all of the above while shouldering a major disappointment, the failure of her marriage, freshly experienced.

For those women who wanted a divorce very much, stress will still be produced by the life changes involved in the breakup. Their world becomes less predictable, and their future is again full of unknowns. According to William J. Goode in *Women in Divorce*, the most frequent symptoms of divorce stress among the 425 women he surveyed were:

- difficulty in sleeping
- poorer health
- greater loneliness
- low work efficiency
- memory difficulties
- increased smoking
- increased drinking

Most interesting is the fact that he found the time of highest stress was the point of actual physical separation—the moving out—not, as he expected, the point of filing for divorce or getting the decree. Although the legal steps involve psychological changes, it is the process of moving out that most changes a woman's social status and relationships to her family and his, and has an impact on friends and children, on eating and sleeping patterns, on living arrangements, and so forth: life-change stress at its most intense.

The general rule of thumb is that it takes two to three years to recover from a divorce. During that period you may feel angry, sad, lonely, jealous, scared, and rejected. These are all normal parts of the mourning process, and to become healed you need to let yourself feel them. You also need to share them, if not with friends, then with a support group or a therapist.

It's destructive, though, to focus on feelings of failure. Many of us have parents who come from a generation where getting divorced was seen as symptomatic of a moral defect; that attitude can lead to unnecessary self-flagellation. Instead, tell yourself that your marriage was something that was appropriate at one time but now no longer serves your needs. Or was a state you enjoyed for as long as it lasted—or he lasted—and now you must find a new state of being.

That analysis means that you have to figure out what would serve your needs now. And that's where a divorce can turn your life into an exciting adventure.

If you're freshly divorced, this may be hard to believe, but many women veritably bloom once they recover from the trauma. They realize they have much more energy now that they're not struggling with a draining marriage. They take up activities they've always wanted to. They develop a new social life composed of single people. They make career shifts their husbands would have disapproved of. They often go into therapy, and become much more at ease with themselves.

And they often become much more attractive. One woman, for example, lost fifteen pounds by accident because she was so depressed after her divorce. One day when her fog lifted, she looked in a mirror and realized she had a good figure. She grew out her severe short haircut, began to exercise, and used a personal shopper to buy a new wardrobe.

Now, I can't guarantee you that a divorce will make you look great, or even help you lose weight, but if you take advantage of the opportunity handed you, then you have a chance at a new start, and that doesn't happen too often in life.

DIVORCED WITH CHILDREN

Carol and Frank got divorced when their son was sixteen and their daughter was thirteen. Their son chose to live with his father and their daughter chose to live with her mother. It all seemed so civilized: The two households lived in the same town, and both parents saw both children frequently.

But Frank remained involved in his daughter's life to an oppressive degree. He argued with Carol over whether the girl should have braces or bonding. Whether she should go to camp or get a summer job. Whether she should go to public school or a private one. Frank even wanted a say in who his ex-wife was dating. Recently, five years after the divorce, Carol said, "It would have been easier if Frank had died instead of divorcing me."

It's been said that when you have children, you never really get divorced. Or, as *New York* magazine recently put it, "If war is hell, then divorce is purgatory."

Unless your ex-husband is one of those fathers who totally disappears after a divorce, you can expect to deal with him for the rest of your life. This means that a relationship that didn't work in the first place has to be renegotiated so the two of you can cooperate on child-rearing. If you *can't* cooperate, then you're subjecting your children to the same kind of conflict they went through when you were married.

In her book *Divorced Families*, a report on a ten-year study of "binuclear" (two-household) families, sociologist Constance Ahrons found five types of arrangements former spouses reach, ranging from extremely friendly to extremely hostile:

- Perfect pals—the ex's as the best of friends
- Cooperative colleagues
- Angry associates
- Fiery foes
- Dissolved duos—the hostility is so high that the two ex-spouses have no connection to each other

These categories are fluid, of course. People who are downright hostile at first may learn to cooperate. And ex-spouses who are *too* connected—perfect pals—tend to become cooperative colleagues when one remarries.

The biggest category in Ahron's study was cooperative colleagues, and these are the ex-spouses who have the best chance for working out a viable "coparenting" arrangement. According to Ahrons, about half of all divorces are functional, which means that the children adjust well to the change.

How can you turn an ex-spouse into a coparent? The first rule is to put your anger behind you, or at least hide it from your children. Easier said than done, but it helps to look at your ex-mate in a different light. He's no longer your partner for life, but simply your partner for parenting. Does he eat crackers in bed? Does he stay out late with the boys? Does he make you feel unloved? If you're not—thank God—married to him, none of those matters. What matters is how he treats your mutual children.

Even if you can't get beyond your anger, try not to criticize him in front of your children. He's your ex-spouse, but he's their father, and the only biological one they'll ever have. Children often feel torn after a divorce, and you're only adding to their confusion if you force them to take sides.

The second rule is to communicate with your ex-spouse. If you can't agree on consistent rules—such as for bedtime—from one household to the other, at least you can tell each other what you're doing. Children often play one parent off the other. "Daddy lets me stay out till midnight," one boy insisted to his mother. Once she asked, she found out it wasn't true. Ideally, you and your ex-spouse end up with what one woman calls "an executive parenting committee"—a group that negotiates rules and boundaries.

WIVES-IN-LAW

Roseanne couldn't believe how well her life was turning out. At age thirty-two, when she was despairing of ever meeting Mr. Right, she was introduced to John, a prominent doctor in his late fifties. John had been divorced for about two years and had three grown-up children. The children looked upon Roseanne as someone who was making their father happy. When Roseanne and John quickly had two of their own children, John's first children doted on the little ones. The only glitch in her happiness came from an unexpected corner: John's first wife, Louise.

Although Louise had wanted the divorce, she had few suitors and was having trouble adjusting to life alone. And so, oddly enough, she started focusing her energy on John's new children. Louise, John, and Roseanne traveled in the same small suburban social circle, and Louise would tell everyone in earshot what Roseanne was doing wrong in raising her children. When Louise saw them on the street, she'd politely tell them they were inappropriately dressed. She did research on what after-school programs they might attend, and called up Roseanne with the results. Often she told mutual friends, "Roseanne is awfully sweet, but she is, well, rather dumb."

John had never figured out how to deal with Louise's controlling tendencies when he was married to her, and when he wasn't married to her he fared even worse. He left it to Roseanne to deal with the dilemma. Roseanne was too afraid of this overbearing older woman ever to confront the situation directly. The problem was resolved only when Louise decided to move a thousand miles away. John and Roseanne threw her one of the biggest going-away parties that their county had ever seen.

The word is "wife-in-law." She's the ex-wife of your current spouse, or the current wife of your ex-spouse. She's been married to the same man you've been married to, though hopefully not at the same time. The wife-in-law may share your last name, share some of the same friends, some of the same property. She may have slept in the same bed with your husband. She's sat through some of the same jokes, discovered the same mole behind your husband's knee, and heard the same snoring sounds at night.

There are over 14 million wives-in-law in the country. An estimated 1.5 million women become wives-in-law each year.

It's possible for wives-in-law to become the best of friends, sharing amusing anecdotes about the foibles of their mutual man.

But don't bet the ranch on it.

Almost to a woman, ex-wives feel that the current wife has a better deal than they had. Almost to a woman, current wives feel that the ex demands too much from the husband, according to Ann Cryster, who looked into the situation for her book *The Wife-In-Law Trap*.

You can't count on the husband to referee between the wives-in-law: They tend to leave it up to the women to resolve their differences. The situation usually improves when the ex-wife remarries or becomes seriously involved. But barring a remarriage, all you can do is try to look at the situation with humor. Think of how great a character *that woman* would make on a TV sit-com, or feel sorry for your current husband that he was ever married to *her*.

SINGLE MOTHERS, THE ALL-PURPOSE PARENT

There are now millions of single mothers in this country, and their ranks are growing quickly. Unfortunately, study after study has found that being a single mother is one of the most stressful possible "occupations," up there with air traffic controller and newspaper editor.

A single parent is both mother, father, and, usually, breadwinner for her children. Unlike a working mother with a partner, there is no possibility of having another adult around who can reliably relieve the burden. Single mothers who work are particularly prone to feeling guilty about spending time on the job. And they are reluctant to take time off for themselves.

If you are a single mother, you are in an especially difficult situation, and you need to learn to take care of yourself. You may feel like you can't afford time off from your various responsibilities, but any break will make them easier to handle. The happier you are, the more quality time you'll be able to give your children. In the chapter on working women I gave some time-saving tips that may help lighten your load a bit.

Because they are exceptionally busy, single mothers are prone to becoming isolated from other adults. This is a mistake, for a variety of reasons. For starters, isolated women tend to be unhappy women. Even if you adore spending time with your children, their company is no substitute for that of friends who can laugh and sympathize with you. Second, isolated mothers often "spousify" their children. That is, they treat their children as a confidant or confidante or as a partner rather than as a child. Children who've been spousified tend to grow up too fast. They are burdened not only with their own problems but also with those of their parents. They often feel responsible for their parents' happiness.

If you are a single mother, take a night or two off a week from being the all-purpose parent. Join a bridge club. Take in a movie with friends. Attend Parents Without Partners meetings or find a similar group at your local Y. Have a date or two. Get involved in local politics. In other words, treat yourself kindly.

STEPFAMILIES

Stepfamilies are not more trouble-prone or less satisfying than traditional nuclear families. But they are different.

In a stepfamily, one morning a group of strangers wakes up under the same roof and discovers that they're all related. It's an instant family, and like any social gathering, it takes time for people to get used to each other. Family therapists say it takes two to five years for the new unit to achieve "familydom"—a sense of wholeness.

Unless the children are so young that they don't remember

their biological parent, they are going to have multiple allegiances. Thus the hallmark of a stepfamily, even a well-functioning one, is that it is less close-knit than its traditional counterpart. This isn't good or bad; it's just different. In fact, children who grow up in a well-functioning stepfamily learn a very profound lesson: There is more than one "right" way to trim a Christmas tree, or bake corn bread, or decide on a movie. Stepchildren, in short, can acquire a sense of tolerance more traditional children don't need to have.

In a new stepfamily, the key is for stepparents to realize that they are not replacement parents. Rather, they are additional adults in the life of the children. A stepmother is more like an aunt than a new mother. She's trying to get to know the new children and helping the biological parent enforce rules rather than assert her authority.

It may be hard for women who are raised as nurturers to subdue their mothering tendencies, but it will help ease the transition to familydom. The new stepmother already risks being perceived as an interloper; if she asserts authority, she's doomed to fail.

The same advice holds true for new stepfathers. They won't succeed if they try to become the family's disciplinarian.

What this means is that stepparents have to get beyond the sexual stereotypes of who's the boss in any household. At least when the family is new, children will accept discipline from their biological parent only. It's often up to the stepparent to support those decisions—not an easy task for women who always dreamed of being mothers, or men who believe their manliness depends on acting authoritarian.

Some children respond better than other children do to stepfamilies, according to a variety of studies. Girls, for instance, seem to resent stepparents more than boys do. That's because the mother/daughter bond tends to be stronger than the mother/son bond, and the daughter resents having her place filled by a man. Boys tend to react better to a stepfather because they usually have a lot of conflict with single mothers. A new father acts as a buffer.

A difficult time for parents to get remarried is when the children are in early puberty. Younger children are more dependent on adults and are likely to accept the new situation. Older children are preoccupied with their friends, with sex, and with school; they're halfway out of the house anyway. But during the prepubescent period, children may react violently to a change. One reason: "They often don't like to think of their parents as sexual because that's an issue they're struggling with," says James H. Bray, a clinical psychologist at the Baylor College of Medicine in Houston. Another reason is that these children have gotten used to responsibility while they were part of a single-parent family.

Here are some ways to ease the transition:

- Let the children decide what they will call the new stepparent. If children develop a special name for the new adult, they can still call their biological parent "Mommy" or "Daddy" and retain those ties.

- Sympathize with what your children are going through—without offering to change the situation. If your kids complain about a stepparent, tell them, "It must be hard having a new person in the house—it's one more change that you didn't ask for." But don't let them bad-mouth your new spouse's personality.

- When starting a new household, make sure that each child and spouse have something they can call their own—a piece of furniture, a decision—on wall paint, a special photograph. When people alter their environment, they feel more at home and less like intruders.

- If you're a stepparent, prepare to hear a child at some point yell, "You're not my *real* mother!" How to answer? Say, "You're absolutely right, but we're going to have to learn to live with each other."

- Don't expect miracles. It takes time and effort for a new family to feel comfortable. "People need to understand that there's not going to be instant love and respect between children and stepparents," says Bray. "But there can be courtesy."

DON'T BRING THE KIDS ON YOUR HONEYMOON

Ultimately the success or failure of your stepfamily depends on the success or failure of your new marriage. "It looks like people can have very good relationships with their spouses and terrible relationships with their stepchildren," says Bray, who studies children in stepfamilies. "That's something you don't see in non-divorced families."

But if the new marriage falls apart, you're back to square one.

This means you should avoid the temptation to focus completely on the children when you're first remarried. Any relationship takes a lot of work and a commitment to communication; one under a great deal of stress, even more so.

So don't take your children on your honeymoon. Leave aside time for romance so the two of you can get to know each other. Even if your new household has turned into a battleground, remember why you wanted to connect with someone new in the first place.

And the ultimate connection—a new child—has an almost magical way of bringing a new stepfamily together. Sibling rivalry will, of course, rear its head, but suddenly, for the first time in its history, there is someone in the family unit who's related to each and every person.

NEW WORDS FOR NEW FAMILIES

It's hard to understand the new family without a scorecard. The following list includes terms that have arisen in the past few years to describe the new forms the family is taking:

binuclear family When a child's family unit is made up of two households—the mother's and the father's.

blended family   A merged household into which each parent has brought a child.

cohabitation   Living together in an intimate, sexual relationship without legal marriage.

coparental divorce   An arrangement in which divorced fathers take legal responsibility for financial support, while divorced mothers continue the day-to-day care of their children.

coparenting   When ex-spouses act like a team to raise a child.

extended family   Three or more familial generations, often including relatives along with parents and children.

familism   The valuing of the traditions of family life.

family   Any parent-child relationship or any intimate interpersonal relationship, in which people live together with a commitment.

familydom   The feeling that a family is a strong unit; it's the goal for which stepfamilies strive.

family of orientation   The family in which a person was born and raised.

family of procreation   The family one establishes when one marries.

intrinsic marriage   A marriage emphasizing the intensity of feelings of the couple and the importance of the spouse's welfare.

joint conjugal relationship   A marital relationship in which couples share their leisure time and are highly involved emotionally.

joint custody   A legal arrangement in which both divorced parents continue to take equal responsibility for their child's general upbringing.

marriage squeeze   The sociological term that, in the generation from the baby boom following World War II, women reached their most marriageable age range two or three years before men born in the same year. Consequently there was an excess of young women when marriage rates were highest. Because of differences in aging, the marriage squeeze also affects choices in remarriage: Older men have a larger pool of women from which to choose a wife.

mutual child The offspring of a couple who have children from previous marriages.

nuclear family A family group comprising solely the wife, the husband, and their children.

reconstituted family A family consisting of a husband and wife, at least one of whom has been married before, and one or more children from the previous marriage.

simple stepmother/stepfather A person who marries someone with children but who has no children of his or her own.

single-parent family A family consisting of a never-married, divorced, or widowed parent and biological or adopted children.

social parent A person who lives in a romantic relationship with someone who has children.

spousify When a parent, usually a single one, confides in a child and treats him or her more like an adult than a youngster.

10 OUR CHILDREN UNDER STRESS

IMAGINE A WORLD IN WHICH ANYONE OF ANY IMPORTANCE LOOMS SEVERAL feet above you. Imagine a world in which you have little or no say in where you live, what school you go to, what time you go to bed, what you eat, and whom you hang out with. Imagine a world where the person who walks you to and from school may change every few months; where the people who tuck you into bed on weekends may be different from those who tuck you into bed on school nights; where your body shifts and grows with no advance notice. Imagine a world in which much of what you see and experience each day is new.

The life of a young American child in the '90s is exciting and stimulating; it is also full of uncertainty and tension. Consider the following:

- A two-year-old who's been shunted among a series of preschool admission interviews has nightmares and sucks her thumb much more than usual.

- During the first week of kindergarten, a six-year-old boy starts wetting his bed.

- A ten-year-old girl develops chronic headaches, with no apparent organic cause, after she hears that her father is moving out of the house.

Do children feel stress in this country? You bet! These days no child can count on his or her family staying together; child-care arrangements shift quickly, and parents struggle with finances. It's no wonder that doctors now report seeing children as young as three or four with stress-related ailments such as ulcers and colitis. And one study done in the San Francisco Bay area estimated that a whopping 25 to 30 percent of children suffer from chronic stress.

As mothers, we hope we can protect our children from all the bad things that happen in the world. But now more than ever, our offspring will be exposed to events we can't control. How can we help our children get through stressful times, and maybe even become stronger for it? The first step is to recognize that children do experience stress, although they may express it in different ways than we do. The second step is to learn how to spot the symptoms of stress. The hardest step is to help our children deal with it. We can help by offering understanding, support, reassurance, and lots of affection. We can also help by making sure we're not part of the problem, by, for instance, applying unrealistic pressures on our little ones. And finally, we can help by showing children that, in our own lives, stress is surmountable.

THE CHILDREN'S STRESS SYNDROME

Unfortunately, children don't come with instruction manuals. Nor are children, particularly the younger ones, able to articulate fully what's distressing them. And so mothers have to learn to interpret the not-so-obvious signs of stress in their offspring.

Stress makes children act differently. The child who becomes annoyingly whiny all of a sudden may, in fact, be responding to stress. Stress also makes children sick. You should, of course, get any physical symptom checked out by a doctor, but be aware that many ailments can be caused or worsened by distress. These are the stress symptoms to look for in children:

- Tantrums in preschoolers
- A return to behavior that the child has outgrown such as thumb-sucking, bed-wetting, baby talk
- Trouble sleeping
- Frequent nightmares
- Moodiness, irritability, apathy
- Withdrawing from family, friends, and other people
- Picking on younger siblings
- Frequent colds or other minor illnesses
- Headaches
- Stomach aches or other digestive troubles
- Schoolwork slippage
- Deterioration in conditions such as asthma and ulcerative colitis
- Refusing to go to day care or school
- Muscle tension in the neck and head
- Dry mouth
- Sweaty palms
- Excessive or diminished appetite
- Inability to concentrate
- Increased whining and crying
- Frequent daydreaming
- Restlessness

A TALE OF TWO CHILDREN

The night before her "show and tell" presentation at school, eight-year-old Tiffany had trouble sleeping. During the presentation, her voice cracked and her knees got wobbly. Tiffany's best friend, Jennifer, reacted differently. She could also hardly sleep the night before—but because she was so excited. When she gave the presentation, she was glowing. She loved being the center of attention.

The two girls had mothers who were recently divorced; both no longer had a full-time father. But Tiffany reacted by being weepy and irritable, while Jennifer took the whole event more in stride. Although Jennifer missed her father, she was able to see the bright side of things—he had moved to California, and she'd get a chance to see an ocean for the first time.

Why does one child fall apart under stress while another seems to bounce right back? To some extent, the difference is genetic. A long-term study of twins raised apart estimates that about half of the variability in people's stress reactions is inborn. That is, the parents' genes have slightly more to do with how strongly a child reacts to stress than do their child rearing methods. Children on one end of the stress vulnerability scale are nervous, jumpy, easily irritated, and highly sensitive to any kind of stimulation. Children on the other end tend to be resilient and view change as a challenge.

Children may also vary in their ability to deal with stress during different times of their childhood. If a baby has a cold, is cutting teeth, or is colicky, he or she will react more strongly to any other stress, such as a move. Age two is a particularly rough time for children. They can't talk enough to communicate their fears, nor can they walk well enough to feel secure in the world. One study found that children who had tonsil operations at two developed long-lasting fears after the operation, while most five-year-olds bounced back quickly. The five-year-olds are not only in a more secure position than two-year-olds, but are also able to understand (and believe) that they'll feel better the next day.

Another vulnerable time for normally resilient children is pre-puberty, when hormonal shifts make some children depressed or irritable.

Every child reacts to stress differently. Every child may change how he or she reacts depending on what else is going on in his or her life. If you observe your children objectively—see who they are rather than who you'd rather they be—you can quickly pick up how sensitive they are to stress. Then use that information to guide the decisions you make about their lives. For instance, a child who's upset by competition would do better to avoid Little League and sign up for gymnastics instead. A child who's self-conscious shouldn't be pushed into drama classes. But one who loves challenges will probably thrive if you offer a lot of stimulating activities.

STRESSFUL LIFE EVENTS

For most children, every day brings something new—a new word, a new toy, a new smell, a new movement skill to master. But some days bring too many new things. On some days, major life events happen. As with adults, the change can be too much to handle. Here are some of the more stressful life events a child may experience growing up:

- *Death of a parent*. The most disturbing possible event in a child's life.
- *Parents' divorce*. The leading cause of trips to child psychologists and psychiatrists.
- *Financial strains in the family*. There may be a real drop in the child's standard of living, and tensions may rise within the household.
- *Moving*. A child has to adjust to a new home and neighborhood, and make new friends.
- *Changing schools*. Nothing will be familiar to the child.
- *Death of a pet*. For some children, this is almost as traumatic as the death of a friend or relative.
- *Absence of the mother*. The mother may go into the hospital, visit relatives, or go on vacation with her husband. The child may not understand that the mother is coming back, and may experience separation anxiety when she leaves.

- *Parent's physical or mental illness*. A serious physical or emotional problem (such as depression or alcoholism) makes the parent unavailable to the child.

- *Physical abuse*. An estimated eighteen hundred children are abused each day, and they often grow up suspicious and untrusting.

- *Child's illness*. Especially scary to a child when it happens during a time of other stress.

- *Birth of a sibling*. The "king or queen of the hill"—the firstborn—may suddenly find him- or herself dethroned.

- *Parent's dating and remarriage*. A child who's used to the full attention of a parent must get used to sharing that parent.

DEATH OF A PARENT

"I did not want to believe it," says Chelsea, eleven, of her mother's death. "I thought it was a joke. But when my father returned from the hospital crying, I knew it was for real." Chelsea and her brother Paul, eight, say they knew something was wrong that day when their mother didn't pick them up at school. The neighbor who took them home found their mother, thirty one, in the living room, unconscious, after suffering a stroke. She died a few hours later, in a local hospital.

Paul remembers trying to talk to his father about his mother. "Every time I talked about Mommy, Daddy started crying. So I stopped talking about her."

For a child, the death of a parent creates a hole that may never totally heal. The good news, however, is that few children become so distraught that they develop serious psychological problems, according to an ongoing study of bereaved children by two Harvard researchers.

How does sorrow affect children?

- They feel sad, because they miss the lost parent. They may cry, sleep poorly, and have trouble concentrating.

- They will probably have lots of minor physical symptoms, such as headaches and stomachaches.

- They may feel guilty. They may wonder if they hastened the death with an unnecessary quarrel.

- They may feel angry at being abandoned by the deceased parent, over reduced finances, or the need to move from their house or their neighborhood.

- They worry about the health of the surviving parent, becoming excessively concerned about minor illnesses such as colds.

- They may feel anxious or resentful at the prospect of the surviving parent's remarriage and the advent of step-brothers and stepsisters.

- They will maintain a connection to the dead parent by dreaming of the parent, feeling watched by him or her (for both protection and discipline), and talking about heaven. Children weigh more of their behavior on whether it would have pleased or angered the parent they lost. Chelsea works harder at school and tries to keep her room clean "because it would make Mommy happy." Some children keep a personal momento of the parent nearby. Paul sleeps with one of his mother's stuffed animals.

Children who lose a mother (about a quarter of the Harvard sample) have a harder time than those who lose a father. It's not just that the mother is the primary nurturer in the family. It's also that more changes happen after a mother dies. These changes are often small but significant, such as when meals are served, who cooks them, who tucks them into bed, and who takes care of them when they're ill.

Time helps children recover. In the Harvard study, led by psychologist William Worden and social work researcher Phyllis Silverman, most of the children were crying less and concentrating and sleeping better by a year after the death. But they still had more headaches, stomachaches and other physical problems than children with two parents.

If you are the grieving spouse, then it's unfair to yourself to try to cope alone with both your own grief and the grief of your children. Now's the time to call in every source of support you can think of. Your children's grandparents, godparents, and aunts and uncles can offer your children the nurturing they need. Your children will probably also automatically turn to their friends, and possibly their friends' parents, for comfort. And if you're very lucky, you may be able to find a support group for bereaved children, which will allow your kids to talk through their feelings. There are other ways to help your children through this very stressful time:

- Involve them in the funeral arrangements or other mourning customs. All societies have ritualized ways of dealing with death. These rituals help people feel that a community is sharing in their grief. They also mark an ending, a significant passage.

- Allow your children to reminisce about the dead parent. Take seriously any ideas they have about talking to the person. These are their ways of keeping the parent alive. Some grieving children complain that adults want them to talk about their feelings, when what they really want to do is think about the person they lost.

- Change as little of their daily routine as possible. A sense of continuity will help them regain a view of the world as a safe place.

DIVORCE

Each day almost three thousand American children see their parents get divorced.

As with the death of a parent, a family divorce means that a child is losing an important caretaker. But unlike a death, a divorce often makes a child feel wrenched; they often feel they have to pick one parent to feel loyal to. They also frequently feel that they are to blame for the separation.

> When Sarah first learned that her father was moving out, she yelled at her mother, "I'll be better! Daddy doesn't have to leave!" Later, her anger turned on her mother. "You drove him away!" she often screamed. But when she spent weekends with her newly divorced father, she missed her mother. It didn't help that her father asked her, in effect, to "spy" on her mother. He wanted to know if she had dates, if she'd made new friends, if her job hunt was successful. Sarah felt disloyal when she answered these questions, but she was afraid of alienating her dad. She hoped that if he liked her better, he'd come back.

How can you help your child through your divorce? For starters, take the same advice given to widows: Change as little of your child's life as possible in the shortrun; draw on every social resource you can think of; and let your child grieve the way he or she wants. In addition, reassure your child that he or she had nothing to do with the breakup.

Most importantly, stop fighting with your ex-spouse (at least in front of the children)! You can despise, disrespect, and disregard your ex-mate as much as you like, but if you reveal your feelings to your children, they'll feel torn. That louse of an ex may still be the only father your children have ever known.

Divorce has become so common these days that many school systems now offer counseling to the children involved. If you're lucky enough to live in one of those areas, then by all means avail yourself of this opportunity. If you're not that lucky and your children seemed seriously stressed by the separation, then seek out counseling. Your school, pastor, rabbi, and local mental health center can make referrals.

GROWING PAINS

So you think *your* life is complicated! Think of all the worries that are a normal part of growing up. Here's a list of some of the concerns of children found by Lois Barclay Murphy of the

Menninger Foundation, who intensively followed the childhoods of thirty one children originally studied when they were infants:

- Having to do something unfamiliar
- Not enough time to do everything you want
- Not being allowed to do something you want to do badly
- Threat of failure or humiliation
- Competition
- Sibling rivalry (keeping up with older siblings, being displaced by younger ones)
- Body changes, especially when they're out of sync with those of other kids
- Feelings of insecurity regarding the availability of a mother or father
- Unanswered questions about where babies come from and what parents do in bed
- Fears of body damage or loss
- Fears of the consequences of aggressive impulses
- Anxiety regarding accidentally breaking things
- Feelings of being little and perhaps helpless in a world of big people
- Confusion over differences between boys and girls
- Confusion about the fact that big people are both threatening and helpful, and uncertainty about which to expect at a given moment
- Worry about conflicts between adults
- Fearfulness about saying what you want to say when you are angry or scared

In her chapter in the book *The Invulnerable Child*, Murphy reminds us just how powerless children are compared to adults:

Adults have a considerable measure of control over their worlds; they can choose jobs, towns, homes, spouses, friends. By contrast, children may have almost no choice at all; they are stuck with their families, homes, neighborhoods, schools. A child's inability to exercise choice or control over his world can make him feel angry or helpless, or both. It can make him fight or give up; he may feel at a loss as to how to cope with the difficulties he faces.

BUILDING SELF-ESTEEM

Children who like themselves, who feel secure and loved, who feel they are "good," and feel they have some say in their own lives are much more likely to bounce back from stressful events than those who are less self-confident.

For parents, this translates into giving your children lots of physical and verbal affection, as well as providing unconditional love. By unconditional love, I don't mean you fail to set limits; children who know no limits at home have a tough time surviving in the rest of the world, where limits abound. By unconditional love, I mean you accept a child for who he or she is, warts and all. I also don't mean that you should lavish undeserved praise on the child. Children see through that by the time they're in about second grade, and start to distrust you.

Children, like adults, need to have a sense of mastery. To help them attain it, encourage (don't push) them to try a variety of activities. Let them also know that it's okay to fail. I've been told that if you don't fail at least a quarter of the time, then you're not trying very hard to learn something new.

When your child misbehaves, separate the sin from the sinner. That is, for he or she to feel like a good person, make it clear that a bad act doesn't make a bad person. For instance, if your daughter slugs her younger brother, that's a bad act. But she still remains a good person. Tell her that what she did was bad, not that she is bad.

Finally, for children to feel powerful give them choices. Say your daughter wants to paint her bedroom lavender. If it really disturbs you, you can always keep the door shut most of the time. Similarly, it's important to let your children's opinions affect you. They may have a novel viewpoint you'd never come up with on your own. And they'll feel like they have a place in the world if adults really pay attention to them.

The bottom line is that if you respect your children, they'll respect themselves. They may not sail through all of childhood's traumas, but they'll certainly have an easier voyage.

PINT-SIZED PRESSURE COOKERS

Consider the weekly schedule of this overweight child who's having trouble in school.

- Monday, 4:00 to 4:45 P.M., psychotherapy with a specialist in adolescent psychology; 5:00 P.M. to 7:00 P.M., tutoring at a specialized center
- Tuesday, 4:00 to 4:45 P.M., remedial reading with a learning specialist
- Wednesday, 4:00 to 4:45 P.M., drama classes; 6:00 to 6:45 P.M., psychotherapy
- Thursday, 4:00 to 5:00 P.M., nutrition workshop for children
- Friday, 4:00 to 5:00 P.M., prealgebra tutoring
- Saturday, 9:00 A.M. to noon, soccer practice
- Sunday, 9:00 to 10:00 A.M., Sunday school

Are you exhausted yet? I am.

In a misguided attempt to prepare their children for a tough world, some parents push their children too hard. They think their child will excel in school if he or she can read by age three. They think their child will become more "cultured" if he or she starts learning French by age six. Anything done earlier, they think, is done better. And the more learning a child gets, they feel, the more of an edge he or she will have. Between school and various betterment activities, some six-year-olds in this country have sixty-hour workweeks!

It's a mistake. Children who are pushed hard grow up having all the problems of parents who work too hard—and then some. One study found that children enrolled in an academically oriented preschool program had only a short-lived edge when they went to school. What's worse, they suffered emotionally. They had all the signs of the Children's Stress Syndrome—they were irritable, had insomnia, and were unhappy—all at age three or four! And a report, *Right from the Start*, issued by the National Association of State Boards of Education concluded that the wrong kind of education at too early an age stifles the development of children, interfering with their love of learning, pitting child against child, and making kids feel like failures at an early age.

The parents who push have forgotten that children are children, not smaller adults. They haven't allowed their kids to play, to build the fantasy worlds that will allow them to develop into self-confident adults.

How can you prevent a child from feeling pushed?

- Encourage unstructured play. Left to their own devices, most children will find the creativity that will help them enjoy life.

- Let them make some of their own decisions about how to spend their time. If a girl has no interest in ballet, why should she study it? Find another activity to develop her coordination and motor skills—one she likes.

- Try to separate out who your children are from who you'd like them to be. It might be a great ego boost for you if your child gets into Harvard, but if it just isn't in the cards, you're doing no one a favor by pushing your child into advanced classes at age eight.

- Pay attention to how your child is acting. If he or she seems stressed, check out his or her schedule. If it's too much, consult your child and your own common sense and make the necessary adjustments.

What can you replace these structured activities with? How about time with you? The laundry *can* wait.

THE TIME CRUNCH

The most precious gift you can give your child is the gift of yourself. Unfortunately, in the harried '90s, time is one of the first things to go. In fact, the amount of "total contact time" between parents and children has dropped 40 percent over the past twenty-five years, according to an estimate by the Family Research Council.

If you work, you probably don't have a great deal of leeway in how much time you spend on the job. But you do control what you do when you're not at work. If you have small children, now might not be the best time to run for head of the local political party, or to put out the church newsletter.

Even if you can't make any gain in the quantity of time you spend with your children, there *are* ways to improve its quality:

- Offer to do your child's chores alongside him or her. When you're raking leaves or washing dishes together, you have a great chance to gab and to fool around.

- Talk to each child before he or she goes to sleep. Children will love any excuse to stay up a little longer. At bedtime, they won't be distracted by other pursuits—such as running and jumping—and may be more interested in confiding in you. Ask how their day went, what happened that was fun, what happened that wasn't so much fun. Sometimes they'll be more likely to confide in you if you reveal some little fact about your own childhood, such as the time you and your best friend tried to run away but only got as far as the corner.

- Try to eat four or five meals a week together as a family. Again, this is a good time to get children to talk about their lives. And shut off the TV! One family I know gives each child the "floor" for five minutes, to talk about anything he or she is interested in.

- Television can be either a boon to family communication—or a disaster. If you watch shows together and talk

about them, then you're building a feeling of together-
ness. But if each person is off in a separate room, then
you're not connecting. Better than TV are evenings spent
sharing a group activity, such as playing Monopoly or
building a model airplane. One family periodically does
"man on the street" interviews with each other, complete
with fake microphones and cameras, to find out how they
feel about current events.

- Take vacations as a family. When you're all together, getting lost on the freeway, or killing time in an airport, or
fishing in the mountains, you have no choice but to talk
to each other. You'll be surprised at how much you'll
learn during these intense get-togethers.

HANDLING CONFLICT

Kids can be fun! They experience the world with a freshness
we've long lost. They bring out the playfulness in us. They say
the most absurd things. But sometimes children are just a pain
in the neck. And at those times we may forget to listen to them.

When we're under stress, we tend to fall into familiar ways of
doing things. If our parents snapped at us a lot, we'll tend to do
that with our children. If our parents cut us off when we were
talking, we'll also tend to do that. If our parents pointed out our
personality flaws when we did something "bad," then the odds
are good our children will hear the same kind of lecture.

Obviously, if you want your child to trust you enough to tell
you what's going on in his or her life, the child has to feel that
you will listen—even when the news is disquieting.

One of the best pieces of advice I've ever heard is to treat
your children the way you treat your best friend. Do you snap
at your best freind when you've had a bad day? Do you interrupt
her when she's in the middle of a story talking about a mistake
she made? Do you pontificate when she's having trouble making
a decision? Probably not.

To feel confident, a child needs to feel that he or she is treated fairly at home. You certainly should teach your child the logical consequences of his or her behavior, but you should first ensure that your child gets a fair hearing. That means to listen before you talk and to think before you act.

Here are some ways to keep open the lines of communication:

1. Avoid lectures. Long-winded, one-sided "discussions" usually send children off in a daze. Any "conversation" that begins with "I'm so disappointed in you," "In my day," or "Now, look here" is sure to make your children flee to the freedom of fantasy island. As long as you pontificate, you're not making any kind of communication connection. Instead, squelch the urge to lecture, and let your children talk.

   One way to impart useful information without lecturing is to let your children overhear you and your husband, or you and a friend, having a conversation on some important topic, such as staying away from strangers. You can draw the children into the conversation by soliciting their suggestions and ideas.

2. Cool down before you deal with misbehavior. The more serious the misbehavior, the angrier you'll get—and the more likely you are to say something you'll later regret. Remember: Whatever's making you angry is probably already done, and waiting ten minutes to talk isn't going to undo the deed. (Of course, if you have a child who's in the *middle* of doing mischief—like trying out all your lipsticks, or putting the Irish setter into your negligees—you do need to say something fast.)

   You can calm down simply by doing something physical for ten minutes, such as washing the dishes or doing 200 jumping jacks. If you're really furious, suggest to your son or daughter that he or she write a letter explaining what happened and why he or she did the misdeed. Then tell him or her, "We'll talk about the letter later." With a smaller child, simply ask him or her to leave the room for a little while. Say, "I'm too angry to talk right now. We'll talk when I can think straighter."

3. Hear your child out. If you blow up while he or she is in the middle of explaining something, you've severed communication. If you practice, you can learn to listen. By listening, you're telling your child that you trust him or her and that he or she is saying important things. In the book *Back to the Family*, a study of what makes families work well, psychologist Ray Guarendi suggests asking these questions:

- What were you thinking when you did that?

- What else could you have done?

- Did you expect things would turn out the way they did?

- What can you do to make things better?

- What will you do next time that happens?

- Any ideas on how I should handle this?

- What would you do now if you were me?

It's hard to control your anger when a child misbehaves. But children learn how to handle stress by how you handle tough situations. What kind of legacy do *you* want to pass on?

11 SURVIVING TEEN STRESS

THE TEEN YEARS ARE A TIME WHEN YOUR SON OR DAUGHTER WANTS TO stop being a child but is also afraid of growing up. During this time your child might become old enough to drive, vote, and join the military. Yet he or she isn't enough of an adult to understand the consequences of risky behavior. And so the risk of traffic accidents, drug abuse, and illegitimate pregnancy is higher in these years than at any other time in your offspring's life. These are turbulent years, and the rates of depression and suicide are high in this age group. Your teenager's hormones will rage, and a formerly sweet member of the household may turn into a veritable monster. In fact, this may be the first time thoughts of murder pass through your mind.

The key to getting through these years is to remember that your child is struggling to create a new, adult identity that is separate from yours. A lot of teens today, just like their parents before them (remember Woodstock?), use music, hair, and clothes to make statements (sometimes very loud statements). What seems irritating, obnoxious, or even hostile may, from another perspective, just be different. By playing around with new looks and sounds, teens "try on" a variety of identities. The girl who comes home from her friend's house one night with purple hair may well go to school a month later dressed like the model in a Ralph Lauren ad.

One recent survey found that half of teenagers think that their parents' ideas about clothes, hair, and music are wrong. But most also say that "the old folks do have a right to their opinions." In another survey, 63 percent of teens said they would *like* to agree with their parents but can't. And another study found that adolescents want to be able to ask their parents' opinion about how they look, but the kids don't want to have to abide by those judgments. Still, even though they may reject their parents' ideas, teenagers are not necessarily rejecting their parents as people: Almost 90 percent of adolescents say they respect their parents, according to research psychologist Robert C. Sorenson.

So what do teenagers want and need? According to psychology pioneer Abraham Maslow, adolescents need feedback (given tactfully, of course) to help them define themselves and also to learn the rules for getting along with other people. Is your son unusually good-natured? He should know that about himself. Does your daughter annoy the other members of your household by hogging the phone at night? Then you should let her know that she's treating the rest of the family unfairly.

Adolescents also need to put some distance between themselves and their family. To do this, they become part of a clique or group. Whether you like it or not, the opinions of that peer group may count more than yours. They also will rebel by expressing anger at their parents. Teens need to be given the right to feel angry, Maslow says.

Except for a few minor details, teenagers today are basically the same as they were when you were growing up. *You* survived adolescence; odds are, your kids will, too.

THE HORMONAL HURRICANE

"Puberty" is a term that refers to the *physical* development between childhood and adulthood. For some, body changes are gradual as their shape becomes adult; for others, many growth spurts take them by surprise.

"Adolescence" is a term that refers to the *psychological* development between "childhood" and "adulthood." For some, this corresponds to the teen years, while for others it extends into their twenties. The average teen has to cope with the stresses of both adolescence and puberty.

Puberty usually begins at about twelve years and peaks at thirteen to fourteen years, but it can begin as early as ten or as late as sixteen or seventeen. In boys two hormones are produced by the hypothalamus in the brain, and they stimulate the testes to produce sperm and the male hormone testosterone. The production of sperm means that the boy can now become a biological father. The testosterone means that his pubic hair will grow, his penis will grow, and last but not least, his self-consciousness will grow (particularly if he is a late or an early starter).

In girls, a different set of hormones causes breasts to grow, and pubic and armpit hair to appear. Ovulation and menstruation start near the end of puberty. The average age for onset of a girl's period is now earlier than eleven and a half, but anywhere from nine to eighteen years is considered normal. To start menstruating, a girl must generally reach 105 pounds, at which point fat makes up about a quarter of her body weight. To keep menstruating, she needs to weigh slightly more than when she started.

Even if he or she is right on time in developing, the teen's tolerance for change is tested. Never again will your child change so quickly:

1. The preteen is a compact, well-coordinated package. At puberty, however, different parts of the body start to grow at different rates, a process that is called "dysynchrony"—and that feels like disaster.

2. The activity of glands produces strong body odor and acne, for the first time—at just the wrong time!

3. As testosterone increases in a boy, so does the frequency of spontaneous erections, wet dreams, and morning erections. The average teen is embarrassed by the first,

surprised by the second, and misinformed about the third (morning erections have nothing to do with full bladders), and he also tends to be guilt-ridden by his interest in masturbation.

4. If girls become full-breasted early, they receive a lot of attention from boys (and men!) that they don't know how to handle. If they're small-breasted, they worry that they'll remain "flat" forever. Small, medium, or large— most girls will be dissatisfied: plastic-surgery candidates in the making.

5. Many boys have temporary breast swelling when they begin puberty. If they are overweight this will be more pronounced and will compound self-consciousness.

6. Adolescence is the beginning of the dieting years for girls. The thin-hipped figure of preteens is just a fond memory for many teenagers, who can't accept that their genes aren't going to let them look like a model. Adolescence is also when girls begin to shave their legs and armpits and to worry about bikini lines.

7. In boys, voice changes are rarely smooth. As the larynx enlarges, the male's voice deepens—but not without months of squeaks and cracks.

8. Getting her period may mean that your daughter has an excuse not to take gym, but because early periods are irregular and thus unpredictable, your daughter may experience some embarrassing "accidents." What's more, for many girls the first symptoms of PMS start in the teen years (though they tend to get worse during the twenties and thirties).

9. Teen growth seems to be never-ending. In fact, many kids keep growing until their twenties! That's a long time to wait before they see how they are going to turn out.

Adolescence includes puberty but ends with psychological adulthood, not physical maturity. If this strikes you as vague, it is. Adulthood involves emotional, financial, and/or residential independence, and for some the period of adolescence may be very long indeed. As we've seen, the late '80s spawned a whole set of grown-up children who haven't been able to establish an independent foothold in the economy.

Part of a parent's responsibility is to help her child learn to deal with the stresses that accompany maturation so that he or she can move into full adulthood.

THE FOUR DON'TS OF PARENTING A TEEN

The phone rings at ten o'clock on a Friday night. It's your fifteen-year-old daughter Elizabeth, calling from the police station. She was in the car when her friend Betty Sue, also fifteen, was stopped for driving without a license. The police want you to come in. What do you do?

My advice is:

1. Don't panic.
2. Don't personalize.
3. Don't overreact.
4. Don't underestimate.

You could overreact by going into a panic and seeing this one misadventure as the beginning of your daughter's life in crime. You could personalize the behavior by seeing it as a slap in your face. You could also underestimate your teen by taking the episode as a sign of her stupidity.

A better approach is to view the episode as a rite of passage in which your teen can learn the logical consequences of her actions. That is, instead of flying into a rage at your child, or, alternatively, using connections to get her off the hook, help her go through the legal process and whatever punishment it entails. If, for instance, a juvenile court orders the teen to do community service, you could help her pick out the appropriate activity. Adolescents don't yet have the cognitive wherewithal to understand that things that are dangerous can produce unpleasant results. Part of your job as a parent is to help your teens understand that there is such a thing as the future.

The most important ingredient in dealing with teens is a sense of humor. Suppose your son stays up all night to get his term paper finished. The next day he looks funny! He's rumpled, his eyes are half shut, and he's in danger of falling asleep during his most boring classes. If you refuse to write him an excuse to stay home, he'll probably learn that leaving his work to the last minute gives him a rotten next day.

Also remember that what your teen does reflects on him or her, not you. If your daughter has spiked purple hair it means that she has bizarre taste, not you. The best way to ensure that she'll keep that hair is to throw a fit about it. Sooner or later, she'll tire of that look. Or she'll apply for a job and find out she's unemployable as long as she looks strange.

The bottom line is: Don't let your teen's stress become your stress. As we shall see next, your teen has plenty of stress to spare.

THE TURBULENT TEENS

Growing up, most of us wanted to be the pretty cheerleader who had lots of admirers and whose hair never frizzed up or drooped. Not many of us succeeded. Similarly, not many of us will have teenagers who succeed in passing through adolescence unblemished.

Teenagers have an overwhelming need to be accepted by their peers. Much of the anguish of adolescence is over the getting or losing of friends. That anguish is likely to be stronger among girls, who tend to place different demands on friends than boys do. Girls expect their friends to provide not just companionship but also empathy and a forum for sharing feelings. Boys are less demanding; they mostly want companionship. As a result, girls' friendships are filled with many more spats. "High-school and college-age girls tend to be more confrontational than boys. The girls are more likely to break over issues like values or deeds," says Margaret Gibbs, director of the clinical psychology program at Fairleigh Dickinson University. But boys are more swayed by their peer group than girls. And peer pressure isn't necessarily to the benefit of either a boy or a girl. As child development researchers Papalia and Olds put it:

> From time immemorial, parents have worried about the friends their children are seeing, with some justification. . . . It is usually in the company of friends that children engage in petty shoplifting, smoke their first cigarettes, chugalug their first cans of beer, sneak into the movies, and do other antisocial acts.

Unfortunately, it is the teens who are the least secure, the most stressed, and the most dependent who are the most vulnerable to peer pressure and peer displeasure. They are the ones who can least tolerate being shut out, unpopular, or criticized. If they become defensive, they are sure to be picked on. If they become withdrawn, they are sure to be isolated. If they become aggressive, they are sure to be ganged up on. If they become anxious, they are sure to be teased. So they often conform instead—they are angry, perhaps, but they conform.

SELF-IMAGE STRESS

A funny thing happens to girls on their way to adulthood: They start feeling bad about themselves. At age nine, 60 percent of girls are self-confident and assertive. By the time they reach tenth grade, that figure plummets to 29 percent, according to a large-scale study conducted by the American Association of University women. Boys experience a much smaller decline in self-esteem. Some 67 percent feel confident at the younger age, and 46 percent remain that way by high school.

What's more, girls fourteen to eighteen are much more likely to be depressed than boys the same age. But before that age, the two sexes are about equally likely to feel chronically sad.

What makes girls so blue? For many, it's dissatisfaction with the way their bodies are turning out. One study found that the changes of puberty increase boys' satisfaction with the way they look but decrease that of girls. Another study reported that girls' feelings about their worth are much more linked to how pleased they are with their bodies than are boys' feelings. Boys are supposed to be tall, thin, and strong—qualities that a fair amount are blessed with. But girls are supposed to look like Barbie dolls—busty, leggy, and thin-hipped, a combination that doesn't occur often in nature. It's a lot for a girl to live up to!

Across the world, cultures that idealize a preteenlike thin female shape tend to also have higher rates of eating disorders and depression for women than men, says a study cited in *Women and Depression* a report from the American Psychological Association's National Task Force on Women and Depression. "Therefore, female adolescents' dissatisfaction with their bodies may come from an awareness of the conflict between society's obsession with a thin body shape for women and the fact that they are gaining weight as their bodies mature," concludes the report.

Of course, teenage girls are not alone in their preoccupation with their appearances. Boys are acutely aware of themselves, too. Acne, glasses, ears too big, height too short, skinny, heavy, buckteeth, braces, warts, long necks, wide feet . . . just part of the package to adults, but significant sources of stress to teenage boys. Men who participated in the Male Stress Survey I conducted for my book *The Male Stress Syndrome* remember feeling that they were being punished for an unknown failure or inadequacy when they looked in the mirror and saw flaws. Many worked on body building to build up not only their muscles but also their sense of control over their appearances and their bodies. It helped them feel that they could protect themselves, physically and emotionally. No matter how they felt inside, outside they looked strong!

SEXUAL STRESS

Our society has had a double standard for decades: To prove their manhood, boys were supposed to "conquer" as many girls as possible. Meanwhile, to remain feminine, girls were supposed to be the naysayers. Thus one survey found that 71 percent of fathers had sex before they married, but 75 percent—almost the same number!—hoped their daughters would stay virgins before marriage. Both girls and boys are caught in a bind.

The sexual revolution has changed girls' behavior more than boys'. The average American boy loses his virginity between ages fifteen and seventeen—the same age as his grandfather. But, unlike in Granddaddy's time, girls—even "good girls"—are beginning to say yes. These days, 30 percent of girls lose their virginity before they're sixteen; another 47 percent between sixteen and nineteen. By age twenty-five, only 3 percent of American women still haven't experienced intercourse. Still, girls are much more romantic about sex than boys. Two of three girls have their first sexual experience in the context of a serious relationship. With boys, half start their sexual life in a relationship, and half start out with a casual partner. Girls are also much more practical. They are the ones who generally insist on protecting themselves from pregnancy and sexually transmitted diseases (STDs).

Interestingly enough, my male patients tell me that when they were young the torture of anticipating sexual rejection was second only to the torture of anticipating acceptance. If a girl rejected their advances, they felt like fools and usually lied to their friends. If a girl accepted their advances, they felt like fools and often ejaculated prematurely or acted immaturely.

Most young boys believe that their partners are going to judge them on performance rather than pleasure. Unfortunately, this means that they will become very orgasm-focused, and that hugging, petting, and foreplay become moments of anxious anticipation rather than activities enjoyable in themselves.

Pity the girl who has to decide whether to go to bed with a sexually inexperienced boy. If she says no, her boyfriend may go elsewhere. If she says yes, she may end up with a "reputation." Her own feelings about sexual intimacy may have little to do with her ultimate decision.

Sex education classes can help both girls and boys learn how to say yes when they mean it, and no when they mean that. Teens engage in sex for many reasons other than purely physical ones. They want a new experience, they want to prove their maturity, they want affection, they want to be in sync with their peer group, they want intimacy, and they want to lose the anxiety of being a virgin. A good teacher assists students in clarifying their feelings and values.

So does a good parent. Your child will feel much more comfortable with his or her sexual decisions if you open up a line of communication about the subject. You don't need to know *details*—those are for your child's best friend—but you should be able to offer a nonjudgmental forum for discussing issues, including health matters such as protection from AIDS and STDs. Study after study has shown that the more information children have about contraception and STDs—whether they get it in sex education or at home—the more cautiously they act.

During early adolescence, girls carry a special risk. It's at this time that the rates of sexual abuse increase significantly. In a random sample of nine hundred adult women, one researcher found that 12 percent had experienced serious sexual abuse by a family member before age seventeen, and 26 percent had been abused by someone outside the family. Girls are about twice as likely to be abused as boys are.

Some girls who've been sexually abused can react by becoming preoccupied with sex and by becoming more sexually active than their peers, according to research by William Friedrich, a psychiatrist at the Mayo Clinic. Another group reacts by avoiding sex and becoming sexually inhibited. A number of factors combine to push a girl in one or the other direction, including: the age the girl experienced abuse, who the abuser was (mother, father, brother, neighbor, stranger), whether it was violent, whether it involved caresses, and whether intervention happened or not. Either way, these girls go on to become more depressed than their classmates and experience more stress in their lives. They need to talk about their abuse with someone; hidden experience is always more stressful than one said out loud.

DATING STRESS

That first date. He chats listlessly with the parents while waiting for her to make an entrance. She has spent days fretting about the perfect outfit. He doesn't know if he should foot the bill. She doesn't know if she should insist on splitting it. Both are announcing to the world that they're on the path to adult re-lationships. Both now know that they are desirable to at least one member of the opposite sex.

Parents can do a lot to cut the awkwardness of teen dating:

1. Ask your teen in advance what the evening's plans are. If you grill your child in front of his or her date, you'll undo all the adult feelings he or she is experiencing.

2. If your teenager doesn't want to talk about a recent date, don't assume that things went poorly. Your child is entitled to his or her privacy—it's part of separating from you.

3. Remind your son or daughter that she or he has the right to say no to anything that makes him or her un-comfortable. Point out that it's part of your job as a parent to help your children figure out what feels right for them.

4. Don't assume that your child has become sexually active just because he or she has gone on a date. For younger teenagers in particular, the social aspects of dating—rather than the sexual ones—are what count.

SCHOOL STRESS

Some teens are concerned about getting into college, some about vocational choice, some about pleasing their parents with high grades, some about hiding high grades from "the gang," some about bringing up low grades, some about earning a living while they are in high school. All these things and more can contribute to school stress—and almost every teen has it.

After I appeared on the television program *People Are Talking* in Baltimore, Maryland, three teenage boys visited me in the studio. They had heard me talking on the air about stress management, and they raced to catch me before the show ended. A schoolmate had just committed suicide the week before, and they wanted to give me a message to make public to parents in general. Let parents know, they said, that the pressure to please parents with good grades can get to be too much. Sometimes we just can't do it because we're not as smart as they'd like us to be. We think that's why our friend committed suicide, they said.

The pressure to excel has been blamed for the very high rate of cheating that's recently been spotted in some high schools and colleges. In a California survey, for instance, almost three-quarters of high-school students admitted they'd cheated at least once on a test. At Miami University in Ohio, 91 percent of the students admitted to plagiarism.

Girls who feel pressure to achieve—either from themselves or their parents—can experience a double whammy. In some schools, smart girls end up being rejected. In class, a girl might feel conflicted as to whether she wants to raise her hand. She wants to appear smart to the teacher, but not to her classmates. Thus she's ambivalent about the very feeling of mastery that could help her withstand stress throughout her lifetime.

FAMILY STRESS

Suzanne, now twenty-five, recalls spending her teen years "anywhere but at home." She joined every possible club that met after school, spent her weekend nights sleeping at her friends' houses, and took ice-skating classes on Saturdays—all to avoid hearing her parents fight. "My mother blamed everything that had gone wrong in her life on my father, and my father felt the same way about my mother," she says. Yet she remembers the day her father finally moved out as "the worst day in my life."

In the United States, family problems are the number-one reason for admission to day hospitals, for calls placed to telephone hot lines, and for visits to emergency services. An unstable family life is a major factor in 50 to 80 percent of teen suicides, according to a number of studies. At-home discord creates stress for teens struggling to understand their role in the home, school, and outside world. So does a parent's divorce and remarriage.

The teenager is often the center of a family problem if the mother, father, or even live-in grandparents are arguing about rules, regulations, and responsibilities for the child. Some families expect their offspring to participate within the family time and recreation structure; some do not. Some families expect their children to follow the family's traditional career and lifestyle pattern; others do not. There is no single scenario that works for every family, but there is definitely one that never works: parents openly disagreeing with each other about everything, including what is expected of their children. If parents keep changing the rules or sabotaging each other's messages to their children, they're piling emotional flux on top of all the other body, social, and academic changes that a teen is already experiencing. Result? One overwhelmed teenager.

Teens who live with only one parent, or in a blended family, are even more likely to receive conflicting messages from their various parent figures. Ex-spouses can keep fighting decades after a marriage is dissolved, often using the child as a weapon. In other instances, one ex-spouse (usually the father) may completely leave the scene, making the teenager feel abandoned. Even under the best circumstances—where the ex-spouses are friendly to each other and treat the teen consistently—the child is likely to feel that he or she has lost something by the divorce.

It's often said that the mother helps the child learn how to live within the home and that the father helps the child learn how to move out into the world. The mother, then, nurtures emotional bonding, and the father nurtures emotional independence. If a teenager experiences continual conflict between his or her parents, or if one or both of the parent figures are missing (emotionally as well as physically), the teenager is probably not learning either lesson very well.

Although parents may try to hide family problems that do not directly involve their teenagers, teens will soon pick up clues that something is wrong. The mystery of a parent's illness, financial reverses, or potential separation or divorce is usually harder for teens to deal with than the reality. Sharing information, though not necessarily details, with them may help. This is one way of saying that the teen is seen by you as emerging emotionally and that there is nothing too terrible to talk about.

TEEN STRESS SYMPTOMS

Most stress symptoms suffered by teens, such as headaches, depression, and eating disorders, are shared by adults. But teenagers run higher risks of experiencing more life-threatening or serious symptoms: accidents, antisocial behavior, suicide, and substance abuse.

Just as adults become more vulnerable to accidents under stress, so do teenagers. R. Dean Coddington and Jeffrey R. Troxell studied 114 high-school football players and found that those who had experienced more family instability were more likely to sustain significant injuries. The types of instability singled out as especially stressful were parental illness, separation, divorce, and death. Accidents are the leading cause of death among children. And motor vehicle accidents outnumber falls, drowning, and all other accidents put together for teenagers!

In *Coping with Teenage Depression*, Kathleen McCoy reports that many studies link injuries and car accidents to teen depression. Why is the rate of both accidents and car accidents higher for boys? Probably because risk-taking lifts them from their depression in an acceptable or "macho" manner, whereas crying or talking about their feelings would make them feel embarrassed. Their risks lead them toward accidents or even veiled suicide attempts, attention-getting behavior that turns out to be more self-destructive than successful. Girls, on the other hand, are more likely to direct their troubles inwardly, by, for example, developing eating disturbances such as anorexia or bulimia.

Boys are also much more prone to juvenile deliquency, although the rates for girls are climbing dramatically primarily because of drugs. A study by A. Vaux and M. Ruggiero correlates juvenile delinquency with the stresses of life changes. That is, the greater the amount of change a boy must cope with, the greater his chances of antisocial behavior. It makes sense, then, that the more there is overcrowding, family discord, lack of affection, inconsistency, or neglect, the more likely the boy will be delinquent.

TEEN SUICIDE

It's a mother's worst nightmare. This year alone in the United States, five thousand young people will commit suicide and countless more make unsuccessful attempts. In the past thirty years, suicide rates for Americans fifteen to twenty-four years have nearly tripled, according to the report of the Secretary's Task Force on Youth Suicide. More boys than girls kill themselves each year, but more girls try. A single teenage suicide may cause a "cluster" effect in a community, in which other teens attempt to kill themselves. Some of those attempts are successful. To some troubled kids, suicide can appear almost fashionable, or glamorous.

Suicidal teens are depressed teens. Which teens get seriously depressed? Those with low self-esteem and those who aren't connected to their families or their peers or both, say several studies. Their parents provide little support, are often depressed themselves, and fall into one extreme or the other: They are either very lax or very strict.

Any adolescent who's depressed for more than a few days may be a candidate for suicide. A depressed child lacks energy—he or she may have trouble getting out of bed in the morning—and may withdraw from his or her friends. I've already listed some of the other signs of depression. Here are some tip-offs that an unhappy teen may be thinking of suicide:

1. The teen seems to be tying up loose ends, by, for instance, giving away his favorite baseball bat.

2. After being depressed for a while, the teen has a burst of energy and seems resolved. Very depressed people are usually too listless to kill themselves. But when they start feeling a little better, they may get the energy to go through with the act. Sometimes that energy comes from making the decision to die. That decision can lift a big burden off them.

3. The teen starts talking about suicide. It's amazing how many parents ignore such an obvious sign of trouble. Some parents believe that the teenager is just "going through a phase." Others are too embarrassed to seek treatment for the adolescent. And still others believe that nothing as serious as a suicide could happen in their family.

4. Other teens have committed suicide recently. The copycat phenomenon is very real.

DRUG AND ALCOHOL ABUSE

Some teens turn to alcohol and drugs to reduce stress. In the '90s, alcohol and drugs are so widely available that you have to deal with the possibility that your child will be exposed to chemicals. One study, in fact, found that by seventh grade, half of all American kids had already felt pressure to try marijuana.

Fortunately, the use of both alcohol and drugs among young Americans has been declining slowly in the past seven or so years. A national survey conducted by the University of Michigan in 1989 found that 76 percent of college students had had a drink in the past month, compared to 83 percent in 1982. In 1989, a total of 16 percent of the students had smoked marijuana during the previous month, and 3 percent had used cocaine.

Most of us want our children to abstain completely from any

kind of chemicals. But American high-school students tend to be experimental users rather than abstainers. Experimental users try drugs and alcohol infrequently and in small doses, and generally stick to marijuana and alcohol. Experimental users are usually looking for a pleasurable experience rather than a way to escape reality. Still, they risk turning into serious users. They may also experience adverse drug reactions, get in trouble with the law, or become involved in accidents while under the influence. Psychologically, experimental users resemble non-users much more than drug abusers.

For drug/alcohol abusers, the chemical substance has become the focus of their lives. They devote considerable time and energy to getting high. And they need that high; the drugs reduce their pain and alleviate anxiety.

Think of teen drug abuse as an attempt at self-medication. Agitated teens will reach for sedative-hypnotics such as alcohol, barbiturates, tranquilizers, and other "downers." Depressed teens will reach for amphetamines, cocaine, nicotine, and other "uppers." Disenchanted and overwhelmed teens will reach for hallucinogenics such as marijuana, LSD, and hashish, or narcotics such as heroin, to alter their minds or create a state of euphoria.

What are the symptoms of drug and alcohol abuse? According to experts:

1. Weight loss or gain

2. Decreased alertness

3. Atypical moodiness, irritability, depression

4. School problems

5. A switch to drug-related jewelry, clothing, or music

6. Deterioration in relationships or a radical change of friends

7. An increase in spending money

8. Disappearance of money or jewelry around your house

9. A suicide attempt

10. Possession of drug paraphernalia

All these symptoms except the last can come from other kinds of adolescent problems besides chemical abuse. But if your child experiences a bad drug reaction, overdoses, or comes into conflict with his school or the law over dope or booze, you know you have a serious problem on your hands.

Most children, even very stressed ones, don't turn to drugs or alcohol. What separates the non-abusers from the abusers? In *Bringing Up a Moral Child*, Dr. Michael Schulman, a clinical psychologist, and Eva Mekler, a school psychologist, argue that non-abusers possess "personal moral standards" that are incompatible with abusing drugs and alcohol. These values are just the ones that help anyone cope successfully with stress:

1. Caring about your health
2. Enjoying the feeling of mastery
3. A desire for achievement, as well as the ability to plan for it
4. Accepting responsibility for your own actions
5. Wanting to think for yourself
6. An urge to become independent
7. A sense of responsibility to yourself and to society at large
8. A desire to deal with rather than avoid problems

Children pick up behavior not just by listening to you but also by watching you. Homes in which a parent, older sibling, or other family member smokes cigarettes, drinks (even moderately), and/or uses drugs are more likely than other homes to produce drug users and abusers. If you are a well-regulated drinker (or possibly marijuana smoker) and don't want your teen to use drugs, your challenge is to convince your child that controlled use of chemical substances is possible only for an older, more mature person. If you drink (or use drugs) to excess, you are giving off the message that this kind of behavior is normal and acceptable. If you're a smoker, you'll have a hard time persuading your son and daughter that you do—and they *should*—place a high value on health.

TEEN STRESS MANAGEMENT

Adolescence is a time of turbulence for parents as well as for their teenagers. To help both yourself and your teen cope, study the stress management techniques outlined in the final chapter of this book and practice them whenever possible. Unless your child needs professional help because he or she is showing one of the more serious stress symptoms discussed, your own fresh look at the situation—your own sense of perspective—can also help ease a lot of the tension.

Examine your attitude toward your child, especially the issue of control. Are you treating him or her more as a preteenager than an adolescent? Does he or she deserve more autonomy than you're giving? Then change your attitude, if necessary.

Treat your reasonable expectations as being reasonable. It's reasonable to expect a fourteen-year-old to keep his or her room moderately neat most of the time. But don't ask if it's been cleaned up, because this feels like manipulation. It's better to come out plainly with something like, "I see you haven't fixed your room yet, and I'd like you to do it."

As I've noted, adolescence is a time when a boy starts to feel a very strong need to achieve, and it's common for parents to feel that same need. For example, if the son doesn't make a straight-A average, the parents may feel that they, too, have failed. Give yourself and your son permission not to be perfect, not to be Superman or Superboy. If he needs help, see that he gets it, but don't make him live up to your ideals and increase the pressure on you and on him if he seems to be failing. Instead, give him permission to find his own ideals and help him reach them.

The same advice holds true for achievement-oriented girls. But adolescent girls have an additional set of problems. The teen years are when girls start basing a good deal of their feelings of self-worth on their real or imagined desirability to the opposite sex. It's up to you to help her realize that self-esteem springs from within, not from the number of glances she gets from boys.

Let her know if she has a skill for throwing outfits together, a gift for for putting people at ease, or a talent for athletics. Some mothers try to correct or relive their adolescence by pressuring their daughters to be attractive. But instead of squeezing a daughter into a mold, encourage her to learn and become who she wants to be.

Finally, practice. Practice talking to each other, practice resolving problems by discussing them. The results can last a lifetime. Young adults raised in families who settled problems nonviolently are able to handle conflicts much better than young adults from violent families ("violence" being defined as at least two violent incidents in ten years). The main alternative to violence is talking, and that's also the best defense against stress.

Practice setting reasonable limits and sticking to them. Teenagers need limits because they are still learning how to be adults. Teenagers need limits because they want to feel that their parents are still watching over them. Teenagers need limits so they can test them. If you don't set reasonable limits for them, teenagers will push you into doing so with outrageous, self-destructive, or attention-getting behaviors. Don't be afraid to fight the small battles over curfews and grades. They may save you from the larger battles concerning drugs and dropping out. They are likely to inspire your teenager's respect.

Your teen is more likely to accept your rules when you explain the reasoning behind them. A survey of thousands of teenagers in Ohio and North Carolina found that children were much more likely to follow their parents' rules when offered explanations and allowed input rather than when simply given commands. These children were also the most self-confident and independent. And more than other teens studied, they wanted to be like their parents.

Also practice flexibility. Haim Ginott spelled out two criteria for permissiveness in his book *Between Parent and Child*:

1. Allow leeway for learners. A driver with a learner's permit, Dr. Ginott points out, is not given a ticket when he signals right and turns left. The learner is clearly

moving toward future improvement. A teenager can be viewed as an adult-in-training. As long as he is moving in that direction, allow for mistakes.

2. Allow leeway for hard times. Recognize high stress periods and expect disrupted or unusual behavior. A teenager who has just moved, who is coping with his parents' divorce, whose best friend has died, or who has been ill is more likely to be irritable or withdrawn, distracted, or defiant.

Above all, practice keeping your sense of humor. If you can laugh at yourself, your teen will learn to laugh with you and at himself or herself. Things are rarely as hopeless as they can seem to a teenager under stress.

12 THE MALE STRESS SYNDROME

MEN ARE RAISED TO TAKE CHARGE, BUT THEY CANNOT ALL BE THEIR OWN bosses. Men are raised to be primary providers, but they find they are now living during recession. Men are raised to focus on achievement, but success is usually a momentary experience. Men are raised to stand on their own, but they need support systems. Men are raised to express "strong" emotions, but they often feel "weak" ones such as fear and sadness, too.

In the '90s, men must deal every day with mixed messages about the meaning of being male. There are three levels of frustrating confusion. First, society's expectations for men are often in conflict. Second, the individual's expectations for himself are often in conflict with society's expectations. And third, a man's many expectations for himself may be in conflict with each other.

It is no wonder that study after study measures high levels of free-floating hostility among adult men. They claim they are trying to be logical and emotional at the same time; successfully competitive, but appropriately cooperative; stable, but spontaneous; protective, but liberated. The interviews I conducted for the Male Stress Survey revealed hopes of total success but terror of total failure; striving for maturity but mourning over lost youth. Such polarity would make anyone's head spin. Such ambivalence would make anyone upset. Such contradictions would make anyone confused. Add the fear of failure, performance anxiety, and the compulsion to compete, and you have the makings of the Male Stress Syndrome.

The stresses and stress symptoms caused by different psychologies, behavior models, kinds of life change, peer and parent pressures, and cultural reinforcements are quite different for men and women. In this chapter we'll take a look at some of these. Most important, I hope that this chapter will remind us that the question is not "Who has it worse?" but rather, "How can we help each other make it better?"

STRESS AND THE MALE BODY

Are men the stronger sex? In physical size and muscle mass, perhaps, but not when it comes to stress endurance. Although more men than women are conceived and born, by the end of one year the male/female ratio is reversed. From birth to old age, then, men seem to die more easily than women.

Between these milestones, men don't seem to do as well either. They tend to lose the use of their legs and hands earlier, turn gray faster, experience hearing and eyesight loss sooner, and have memory problems at earlier ages. And as far as sex is concerned, the man's capacity to perform (though not his fertility) diminishes with age more sharply than the woman's capacity.

There are still other areas of male vulnerability. Men may be less sensitive to pain, and so they may be less aware of physical problems until symptoms are serious. They are also more apt to minimize or deny their pain, causing them to seek treatment much later in the disease process, according to clinical observations made by Robert Benjamin, chief of the Communicable Disease Bureau of Alameda County, California.

Do men have any stress *advantages* to balance these stress handicaps? Research suggests that they probably have two built-in advantages in dealing with short-term emergencies and temporary stress:

1. According to Karl Pribram, at the University of California at Santa Cruz, young boys show greater right-brain dominance than girls. The right hemisphere of the brain deals with nonverbal, symbolic, spontaneous responses to information, whereas the left hemisphere governs language, logic, and labels. In other words, during their early years, when they are learning to deal with the world, boys may be predisposed to evaluate and react to situations *immediately* and *directly*.

2. The male hormone testosterone is associated with rough-and-tumble play, extroversion, high activity levels, and assertiveness. Equally interesting is the suggestion of John Bancroft, reported in *The Clinics of Obstetrics and Gynecology*, that men with low testosterone levels can more easily be distracted. In short, testosterone may heighten the ability to focus and stay focused on a situation. This would be an important survival capability for early man trying to exist in a physically dangerous world, or for today's man trying to concentrate in a noisy, polluted world.

Adding together both the good and the bad news about male stress management, it is possible to see a *stress responsiveness* that is activated in emergency situations. That is, it may be that since young men seem to react to stress nonverbally, rapidly, and with action; since they can focus and stay focused on high-arousal situations with great intensity; and since they develop more physical strength and can be less aware of low-level pain sensations than women, they are primed and equipped to handle immediate action demands.

What happens to the male body, however, when the stress goes on and on? Disorders, diseases, dysfunctions, and, often, death. For, although both men and women suffer from stress, men find themselves at a higher risk of *fatality* from their stress symptoms.

STRESS SYMPTOMS

Far too often men ignore stress symptoms, denying their potential consequences and avoiding having to address their causes. When women who participated in the Male Stress Survey were asked to check the physical signs of stress they noticed in their men—husbands, fathers, or sons—they most frequently said they saw the following (from a total list of twenty-six items):

insomnia
headaches
allergies (hives, hay fever, and congestion)
teeth grinding, jaw clenching (temperomandibular joint muscle spasms, or TMJ)
nausea, indigestion, and heartburn
backaches and stiff necks

When men themselves were asked about their physical symptoms of stress, one of the few symptoms they consistently reported noticing was that they perspired more under stress! What about all the symptoms reported by the women? Men acknowledge them, but do not usually attribute them to stress; they tend to attribute them simply to age.

In addition to the more general stress symptoms, which are shared by women under stress, men under stress show some symptoms that are uniquely theirs, more frequently theirs, or more dangerous when they are theirs. These symptoms are:

hypertension (high blood pressure)
atherosclerosis (high cholesterol level)
heart attack (myocardial infarction)
heart failure
peptic ulcer (gastric or duodenal)
alcoholism
erectile dysfunction (impotence)
premature ejaculation
retarded ejaculation (failure to ejaculate)

BEHAVIORAL EARLY WARNING SIGNS

In addition to the physical conditions that signal stress or create stress, men must also recognize psychological and behavioral signs of stress. Because behavioral signs are observable, repetitive, and usually consistent for each person, they are potentially the most useful of all early warning signals for the beginnings of the Male Stress Syndrome.

The hundreds of women—wives, mothers, sisters, and friends—who participated in the Male Stress Survey noticed the following early warning signs of stress in their men:

1. Most frequently, women notice that men become *verbally abusive, curt,* or *critical* with their wives or children.

2. The second most frequently reported stress sign for men is *withdrawal*. Men seem to become more sullen, sulky, or silent; perhaps preoccupied.

3. Few men listed *overeating* as their own stress sign, but most women claim that the men in their lives often gain weight during periods of stress.

4. Similarly, women noticed that men *drink more alcohol* during stress periods. Men give other reasons for their drinking but admit that their increased use does coincide with stress periods.

5. *Fatigue* is not among the most frequently noticed symptoms of male stress, but when it is mentioned, it usually heads the list. This would suggest that fatigue is not a universal symptom for all men but that it is a consistent and important early warning sign for some men.

6. For other men, the reverse reaction to stress seems to be characteristic: *agitated activity*. These are men who seem to work off their tension.

7. Among the quick fixes for stress, *smoking* is one of

the most automatic. Smoking rates can easily double before men notice this stress sign

8. The most annoying male stress signals seemed to be *psychomotor habits*: foot-swinging, finger-tapping, and knee-jiggling. Wives add that their husbands often keep them awake grinding their teeth at night.

9. *Somnambulisic withdrawal* sounds like a rare psychological disorder. Actually, it is a common stress reaction. It refers to the tendency to fall asleep when faced with stresses: marital arguments, plane flights, pre-income-tax preparations, or difficult decisions.

10. Other men don't actually slip into sleep; they just become selectively deaf—they *tune out*. They hear but don't listen. In fact, they are dramatically distracted. They see but don't notice; they plan but don't remember.

11. Three times more males than females die in automobile accidents, and many of those accidents are a direct result of stress. *Reckless driving* may reflect anger, anxiety, impatience, impulsiveness, or depression, according to Ming T. Tsuang, professor of psychiatry at Harvard University. Driving after social stress, therefore, is five times more likely to lead to a fatal accident. Many women report that they are terrified of being a passenger when their mate is stressed.

12. There is one sign of male stress that is consistently reported by mothers, daughters, wives, and lovers and that is consistently omitted by males—yet they admit to it when confronted. It's *television tune-in*. Men don't always watch the program they tune in, but it pulls them out of social interaction and into distraction from stress.

Rarely mentioned on the lists but always mentioned in the research literature on stress is the effect of stress on sexual behavior. Sexual intimacy can reduce stress temporarily by providing pleasure; breaking into a work routine; mobilizing and utilizing adrenaline; offering a way to express adult affection, to be giving and to be appreciated; and affording an opportunity to relax. However, when stress relief becomes the motivation for sex rather than the result of sex, another early warning signal is present.

A more common sign of stress, according to clinic reports, is a *loss of sexual interest*. A drop in the incidence of sexual fantasies, the frequency of lovemaking, the occurrence of morning erections or nocturnal erections, or an increase in the frequency of premature ejaculation or erectile problems may each be an early warning signal. Some couples realize this and look for the source of stress. Other couples do not, and focus on the sexual difficulty to the point where a sexual or marital problem is added to the stress mix.

PSYCHOLOGICAL EARLY WARNING SIGNS

The psychological signs of stress that men most frequently exhibit may precede their awareness of stress. Any one of these early warning signs may first appear in mild form or intermittently. As stress continues, so will the psychological signal, and its severity will probably increase.

Some men will show one particular psychological stress sign, others will experience two, three, or all of these early warning signals.

I call the psychological signs of male stress the six *d*'s. There is some overlap with the four *d*'s of female stress, but some very significant differences as well. Check the following checklist for the stress signs you have observed. Any of these psychological signs indicates the beginnings of the Male Stress Syndrome. More than one indicates *moderate to high stress*.

| _____ *Defensiveness* | Defensiveness reflects the unrealistic expectation that a man must "be a man." That is, he should not show weakness; he should not be touched by stress. |

| _____ *Depression* | Underlying the feeling of depression is usually anger or loss. Under stress, men feel angry that they could not control all the aspects of their lives, and they feel a loss of their sense of control. |

| _____ *Disorganization* | Stress preoccupies and diminishes concentration. The resulting disorganization can show up as sloppiness, absentmindedness, or lapses in judgment. |

| _____ *Defiance* | Some men fight back when they feel stressed, even if there is no actual focus for their defiance. They may challenge "authority" figures, become |

argumentative, or deliberately dissent arbitrarily.

_____ *Dependency*

Many men regress under stress. They would love to be saved and to be taken care of, but rarely admit this fantasy to others—perhaps not even to themselves.

_____ *Decision-Making Difficulties*

Feeling stressed usually means feeling a lack of control, choice, or preparation in a situation. Making decisions, even minor decisions, under such conditions becomes very difficult.

What makes men stressed? Like women—but for different reasons—work and love are the two key factors.

THE STRESSES OF STRIVING

It's a boy! The doctor announced the birth of the man in your life, and training for achievement, and all the stress that brings, began. In fact, training for this type of male stress may have begun *before* his birth, with the expectations of his parents.

- In 110 cultures studied by H. Barry, M. Bacon, and I. L. Child, 87 percent of people surveyed expected males to grow up to be more achieving than females, and 85 percent expected males to be more self-reliant as well.

- J. Meyer and B. Sobieszek found, as discussed in Chapter 4, that when men were shown videotapes of a seventeen-month-old child and told that they were looking at a girl, they characterized the baby as passive, cuddly, and delicate. When they were told that they were looking at a boy, however, they more often described the baby as active, alert, and aggressive.

EARLY ASSERTIVENESS TRAINING

Expectations turn into self-fulfilling prophecies, as parents and other adults begin to treat boys in a way that is consistent with their perceptions and expectations. Boys are bounced, pounced, roughed up, and tumbled down. They are taught to "take it." "Put up or shut up." "Talk is cheap." "Fight your own battles." "Get out there and win." "Make us proud of you."

From Little League to the big leagues is a short jump. The message is the same: "Don't let the team down. We're counting on you." The more prominent the player, the more pressure to perform. At first, a boy performs for his parents. Later, for his peers. Finally, for himself. But that does not diminish performance pressure. In fact, living up to his own demands is likely to be the most stressful experience of all!

At work, the striving man has not only internalized early expectations for achievement, assertiveness, and reward, but usually he has added messages of his own. He chooses goals and grades himself continually. Whether it's salary, title, office size or location, number of subordinates, degrees, or awards, they are merely symbols of his quest. The winning is more important than the win itself, and every success means a new, higher goal must be set. As Robert Shultz, chairman of sports medicine at New York Medical College in Westchester County, describes the dilemma, "No man ever wants less than he has become used to, although that is usually more than he needs."

MOVING UP, BURNING OUT

In *The Corporate Steeplechase*, Srully Blotnick outlines four of
the "inner" stresses that those on the management level struggle
with. After interviewing five thousand businesspeople over a
period of twenty-five years, he found that men bring different
worries to their work at different ages.

- In his twenties, the entry-level businessman worries
  about living up to his own image of his father's role model.
  The confident claims and name-dropping that were part
  of his initial interview now haunt him. Can he really do
  the job? Can he fill his own shoes? Will he feel like an
  imposter? Will he look like a fraud?

- In his thirties, he worries about standing out and being
  noticed while functioning as a team player. If he tries to
  go it alone, he is likely to be sabotaged by coworkers or
  even fired for functioning too autonomously. If he melds
  into the crowd, moving up becomes unlikely.

- In his forties, the "dangerous decade," the executive experiences a double stress-threat. The younger generation
  may be pushing their way up from beneath him, and the
  older generation may be blocking his advancement from
  above. "Burnout" may really represent being *burned up*
  about being stuck or unsuccessful!

- In his fifties and beyond, an executive should be enjoying
  his position of elder statesman, his corporate know-how,
  and his political savvy. Many become mentors and receive
  major promotions. But more become stressed by a sense
  of loss of control. Retirement may be mandatory, and
  protégés—or protégées—may become protagonists. In
  fact, 40 percent of protégés get fired by their own mentors, according to Dr. Blotnick.

If the man in your life is an executive, manager, self-employed
professional, or business owner you may suspect that "executive
stress" does not end here. If he deals with clients then he must
worry about their moods as well as his own. Criteria for success

may hinge on their opinions, and his reputation may be only as good as his last success. If contracts or clients go elsewhere, his job may be lost with their revenue.

If his product is a creative concept, as with architects, designers, decorators, and artists, his success or failure may ride on timing, fads, publicity, or endorsement. He must use judgment but avoid being judgmental, or he may "freeze" creatively. He must be original, but avoid being seen as too bizarre to be commercial. He must continue to grow and change, but not lose the style that is identifiably his.

If he is in a highly competitive business, "he must worry not only about moving up, but staying in," according to psychologist Diana Powell. High job insecurity is always a condition for high stress. Behavioral consultant Ron Edelson sampled one thousand accountants, lawyers, and ad-agency professionals and, as expected, found a higher percentage of stress-related cardiovascular, respiratory, digestive, and mental illnesses among the group with the least job security—advertising agency professionals. And Melvin Glasser noted that worrying about their employment termination led to a 700 percent increase in heart attacks and stress illnesses among ground controllers for the Apollo space project toward the end of that project in 1969.

If he is in the sales arena, or selling his personality to the public, as performers and politicians do, he may suffer from the stress that Gail Matthews, a psychologist at Dominican College in San Rafael, California, calls the "imposter phenomenon." She surveyed lawyers, judges, physicians, priests, police, writers, and scientists. The most famous felt the most stress since their work could not be measured by objective standards. "What would happen," they worried, "if I stopped working so hard? Would everyone see that I am not gifted, but only more driven?"

WHEN IT'S ONLY A JOB: THE LOW-CONTROL FACTOR

Some men find it hard to sympathize with success distress. They laugh and say, "I only wish I had *that* problem. I'm too busy taking orders to worry about the stresses of *giving* orders or dealing with success!"

Achievement, self-reliance, and assertiveness are every bit as important to the stress dynamics of the nonexecutive's day as they are to the executive's day. Loss of control, loss of esteem, and loss of position trigger the fight and flight response for both, but the battlegrounds for the fight and the options for the flight are very different. The battleground for nonexecutives is filled with deadening *poor workplace routines*, *workplace conditions*, and *serious workplace risks*, which multiply their stress experiences and undermine their stress-coping patience. What I am saying is that it is potentially *more* stressful to be a nonexecutive achieving personality than it is to be an executive achiever.

What a company as a whole does clearly affects all its employees. As far as the low-level worker is directly concerned, the company can fire him, retire him, move him, change his job, or let him stew in rumors without denying or confirming them. They're all potent sources of stress. Leon Warshaw compiled a group of nineteen job-related "stressors." At the top of the list is loss of job *security*. This is more serious, says Dr. Warshaw, than loss of the job itself (just as unpredictable consequences are often harder to take than known negative consequences). In other words, rumors of layoffs and firings can be as stressful or more stressful than actually being laid off. Consider these other items on Dr. Warshaw's list of workplace stressors:

- loss of job through forced retirement
- job change through relocation
- job change through promotion
- changes within the job through shift-work changes
- work overload without recourse
- work unload, leading to boredom or less income
- unforseen deadlines
- inappropriate work hours
- unhealthy or unpleasant work conditions

- too much job competition
- too little cooperation
- inadequate information supply to workers
- inadequate routes for input into company decisions
- ambiguous or conflicting job duties
- too little recognition of achievement
- too few promotion opportunities
- inadequate financial return
- no incentives or special privileges

These "stressors" have been studied and identified in factories and in fieldwork, in bureaucracies and in department stores. Most men who responded to the Male Stress Survey mentioned at least one. Many mentioned more than one. And in a study conducted by Joseph N. Ruocco, it was found that most of these same stressors plague men throughout the Western world.

"I DO'S" AND "I DON'TS"

Work, of course, is only part of the stress equation for men. There's also the question of warmer relationships.

Although the divorce rate is still high in the 1990s, the marriage and remarriage rates are also high for men. Married men live longer than single, divorced, or widowed men, and report more general life satisfaction, according to most surveys and reports.

In her book *The Hearts of Men,* Barbara Ehrenreich points out that the young man today neither needs nor gets the same type of wife that his father did. Wives most often work full- or part-time now. They no longer reflect their husbands' status by caring for them and their children full-time. In fact, she suggests, the man's "liberation" from being the sole provider for his family has liberated him from the necessity for commitment. Dating becomes entertainment or sexual excitement, rather than a search for the "little woman."

If all this is true, then marriage becomes a decision for men, not a social, economic, or sexual necessity. With an increased sense of choice comes an increased sense of hesitation and stress. "Since I don't really *have* to get married," he thinks, "why do it?"

The answer for most men is that they have an *expectation of* "*primariness.*" A man wants to be the most important person in someone's life. And that person is his wife!

But once married, men often experience stress. Men complain of *role confusion*. Role confusion for men is relatively unique to the last two decades. Traditional husband and father roles had been unchanged for many, many generations. The modern male, however, is faced with mixed messages. He is still supposed to be strong, but he is now expected to be gentle as well. He is still expected to be a hard worker, but he is now expected to be unthreatened by his wife's work. He is still expected to assemble and paint the new crib, but now to change the diapers and feed the baby as well. For many men, it's simply not clear what a husband and father is supposed to be like now. Between the macho male at one extreme and the maternal male at the other is a vast, uncharted territory.

SHARING A WIFE, SHARING A LIFE

The male expectation of primariness, of being his wife's main concern, brings him into parenting with a stress handicap. As much as he loves his child, he must also admit to himself that he is no longer his wife's one-and-only. He is now sharing her time and attention—even her body—with the baby. Compounding this stress is the guilt he feels about any resentment he holds toward his wife or baby. Further compounding it is the reality that his mornings and nights will be different from now on!

Fathers are encouraged to attend Lamaze classes and to participate in the childbirth. They are expected to be caring, sharing, and involved with their children. But men are still also expected to be bread winners and disciplinarians. Where are the role models for these fathers? From whom do they learn the ropes?

Not from women. Women are too busy struggling with the new rules themselves.

DIVORCE DIFFERENCES

Next to the death of a spouse or child, divorce is probably the most stressful event of a man's or woman's life. The type of stress experienced depends on the type of divorce: hostile or friendly, equitable or financially lopsided, with or without a custody battle, coming after a few months or a few decades, mutual or unilateral.

The difference between male and female divorce stress is not actually the type of stress they have, but how stressed other people perceive them to be. Women who are left by their husbands are worried about; men who are left by their wives are treated with less concern:

"Wait until he gets out there—he'll love the single life!"

"He'll be grabbed up in no time."

"No problem. He can start again."

Since men have been raised to appear in control of their emotions and fear the loss of emotional control, they indeed seem to be less affected by their divorces than women. Life and work go on, they seem to be saying. Actually, all the divorced men I surveyed missed daily contact with their children and regretted separation from them even if they were happy with the way their ex-wives mothered.

Listen to me. I've been going through the worst time of my life and nobody believes it. Everybody says, "Hey, free at last." Free at last. Guilty at last, yes. Sick at last, yes. Going crazy, yes. Not knowing what to do with myself, yes. Depressed, definitely. Thinking about my kids with another man, yes. Free? No.

Some fathers say that they dread "visiting days" with their chil dren because they feel their children are, indeed, just visitor "How should I entertain them?" "What should I buy them? "What do they like to eat?" "How do they feel about these visits "Would they rather be with their friends?" How very differe a feeling than that created by the old shout, "Hey, Dad's home!

Discomfort is not for weekends only. Fathers call during th week, ask for their children, and get monosyllabic boys and gir who would rather be watching television. Fathers plan trips ar surprises and get only grunts or tired reminders that they ha done the same thing last year with their Scout troop. Fathe remind themselves that their children are probably better with their mothers and each other than with them, and then t to convince themselves that it's true.

SEXUAL SURVIVAL UNDER STRESS

Men under stress often find that their sexual functioning interest wanes. If you as a couple are experiencing sexual ficulties, examine your attitudes:

- Are you blaming yourself for your man's withdrawal avoidance of sex? Don't. It is probably primarily his pr lem. If it was anger that led to erectile dysfunction, i now his sexual problem, not his original anger, tha stressing him. If he is a victim of inhibited sexual des it is his depression that is probably keeping him the But although it is his problem, it is your problem as w in that his stress interferes with your sexual functioni too. The situation calls for empathy rather than accu tions or defensiveness. See a sex therapist together; the "couple" be the patient, rather than insisting that get help alone.

- Are you linking your self-esteem to his sexual response? Don't. Some women feel that if their husbands or boyfriends don't respond to them sexually, they have failed as women. Again, this is probably much more his problem than yours. To check out the real factors involved, encourage him to check with his internist or urologist, and then see a sex therapist together.

- The next step is to help yourself and your mate relax sexually. Do your best to banish performance anxiety by creating an easy, nondemanding atmosphere. After all, orgasm is not the goal of sex play, it marks the *end* of sex play. Why rush?

- The woman should take the initiative when she is in the mood for intimacy. You may be frightened by your mate's changing sexual capacities, but your mate is probably equally frightened and may be inclined to do nothing. If that is the case, the first move may have to come from you!

- Be prepared to try new styles of making love. Slower responsiveness may mean longer foreplay—which is certainly not bad news. Don't be afraid or ashamed to talk about what is going on. Your talking about your sex life may encourage your mate to do the same. In fact, you may both have been thinking the same things all along.

- Not everyone wants or needs to have an active sex life, but if you are one of those who do, enjoy!

13 FEMALE AFTER FORTY

THIS IS THE GENERATION WHO GREW UP WITH CHOICES. THIS IS the generation who grew up with birth control, kitchen technology, contact lenses, plastic surgery, women's lib, and Weight Watchers. This is the generation of women who rewrote the rules:

- We are not defining ourselves by our age. Some of us are having morning sickness while having hot flashes.

- We are not suffering from empty nest syndrome. When our children leave the nest, we redecorate it—for their return.

This is the generation of women used to being in control of their lives. These are the baby boomers and seven million "babies" became middle-aged this year.

How do you know if you're middle-aged? 1,200 respondents told the American Board of Family Practice their answers:

- 47 percent said you are middle-aged when you think more about the past than the future.

- 46 percent said you no longer recognize the names of the music groups on the radio.

- 44 percent said you begin to take an extra day to recover from skiing and tennis injuries.

- 30 percent said that you get more respect from other people than you used to.

So if everyone is calling you "Ma'am" and the police are looking younger and younger, welcome to those middle years.

Today, the average forty-year-old American woman can expect to live to be at least eighty years old. After the age of forty, then, many naturally start to reexamine their lives. Often they find they are as distressed as these women as they look into their future.

> "I used to think forty was middle-aged. Now that I *am* forty, I wonder if I was right."

> "My mother used to tell me: You live and learn. I have noticed that we live a lot faster than we learn!"

> "Marriage is a state of mind. I don't think I care for the mindless condition my marriage is in."

> "Time seemed to go on and on until now. I thought that I had plenty of time to find a partner or husband, even to have a family. I may have waited too long."

> "I used to think my work was everything. I no longer think *anything* is everything."

> "Now that I am no longer needed by my children, I find that I don't want to be needed by my husband either. I suppose it's part of never having been free to be myself. I went from home, to marriage, to divorce, to marriage . . . without a breathing space. I don't want to divorce my husband, but I wish I had a *wife* for the next half of my life!"

> "I am forty-five and still have not learned to relax. I don't know how to stop worrying about things I can't change."

> "My children have grown up; my husband has regressed. He left me for a younger woman, and I am single, sixty, and sad."

"Just when I finished parenting my children, I had to start parenting my husband's parents. When do I get to take care of myself?"

"Going through menopause was like going through a rebirth for me. I began to think of sex as pure pleasure and looked forward to planning vacations without the kids. My husband, on the other hand, became depressed when he reached middle age, and I feel like I am living with an old man!"

"I'm plagued by this nagging guilt now that my kids are out on their own. I'm so relieved not to have to worry about their food and clothing and schooling anymore. Does that mean I never really wanted to do it?"

"After forty, the crises never end," according to yet another woman. Bigger children have bigger problems, and then empty the nest. Husbands retire, leave, or die. Bodies sag, spirits flag, and backaches nag. Parents die and leave their children and children's children.

Unfortunately, it is during these middle years that many women experience more anxiety and depression than at any other life stage. Think of the many stresses produced by changing self-concepts, marriage dissatisfaction, redefinition of parenting roles, and the double standard of aging.

THE DOUBLE STANDARD OF AGING

In an article written more than twenty years ago, Susan Sontag described the double standard of aging in this society by comparing older women and older men. How much do you think has changed since she made these observations?

• As they grow older, women often keep their age a secret. Most men do not.

- Since women are often judged on their beauty and youth-fulness, their value as partners may decrease as they mature. Since men are often judged on their competence and experience, their value as partners may increase as they mature.

- As she ages, a woman's value in the job marketplace often decreases, as does her pay. As a man ages, he can usually expect to be earning more than when he was younger.

- An older woman is considered less sexually attractive and desirable than a younger woman. An older man, particularly if he is financially or politically successful, does not lose his sexual eligibility. In fact, it often increases as his power increases, and the male/female mortality rates make him a scarce sexual commodity!

- Women experience menopause and, consequently, an anatomical and conceptual change of life; men may change their lives, but not through anatomical destiny.

- Older men can be expected to take younger lovers; older women are not!

- Women are expected to try to maintain facial beauty through cosmetics, moisturizers, and even surgery. Men are expected to have their faces become more rugged, scarred, and marked by the passing years.

Men and women do not approach the aging "starting line" neck and neck. Many of the stresses that affect women as they age have begun to form before they are forty. It is more often the woman than the man who has postponed or interrupted a career for the convenience of marriage or the necessities of parenting. It is more often the woman than the man who has assumed a more flexible position when family decisions had to be made in the midst of pros and cons. It is more often the woman than the man who will end up with no children if parenting is delayed since he can remarry a younger woman, but she can't reset her biological clock. It is more often the wife who is defined by her husband's status than the reverse. It is more often that a wife

takes her husband's name or adds his name than keeps her own—
particularly among women currently over forty. It is not difficult
to see the potential for stress in this sort of situation.

> Shirley flipped through the day's mail. There were eighteen en-
> velopes. Fifteen were addressed to her husband. Two were ad-
> dressed to "Resident." One letter was addressed to her. It was
> a note from her college alumnae association asking for a con-
> tribution to a scholarship fund. She looked again at this last
> envelope. In fact, it was not addressed to her at all. She had
> attended college under the name of Shirley Green, and this letter
> was addressed to Mrs. Richard Ashby. What has happened to
> Shirley Green? she wondered. She felt as though she had be-
> come somebodys' mother, somebody's wife, and nobody at all
> to the outside world. By the time she was forty, she feared, she
> might disappear altogether.

Shirley did not disappear by the time she was forty. Instead, she
wrote to her college alumnae association asking for her name
to be listed as Shirley Green Ashby, took over the fund-raising
division of the association in order to make sure other alumnae
were similarly approached and addressed, and eventually formed
a nonprofit organization that helps postgraduate women establish independent companies and develop self-employed careers.

Other women, unfortunately, see less-happy endings to their
struggles to cope with the double standard of aging. Some lose
their husbands to younger women. Some lose their dating mo-
mentum and settle for partners they would not have chosen a
decade earlier. Some withdraw from the social or occupational
spheres altogether, rather than risk losing out to other women.
Some buy themselves cosmetic surgery and/or younger men.
Whether we are married or single, no matter what our situation,
the double standard of aging affects us and must be considered
one of the special female stresses.

REENTRY AT FORTY

Many women who have spent the first two decades of their adult lives in the home see themselves as "just homemakers," though this is an inaccurate and demeaning view. They complain that they lack job qualifications, social skills, sexual experience, and personal style. By the time they are approaching forty, they would like to reenter the world beyond their homes, but are stressed by what they consider their inadequacies.

Considering that the same activities they have performed are more valued when done by men than by women, low self-concepts among fortyish females are not surprising. Margaret Mead gives many examples of this phenomenon.

- Think of a woman cooking and you probably picture a housewife. Think of a man cooking and you picture a chef.

- Think of a woman working with clay and you probably picture a craftsperson (or Girl-Scout leader, or kindergarten teacher). Think of a man working with clay and you picture an artist.

- Think of a woman assisting a childbirth and you probably picture a nurse or midwife. Think of a man assisting a childbirth and you picture an obstetrician.

- Think of a woman who is assertive. She is probably assumed to be aggressive. Think of a man who is assertive. He is assumed to be successful.

These generalizations help to explain why a woman with twenty years of homemaking experience often feels that she has little of value to offer in her later years. The reverse is true: A homemaker typically has experience in accounting, nutrition, paramedical activities, counseling, decorating, catering, social planning, and sometimes hiring, firing, and even public relations. If she has particularly enjoyed one of these areas, she can begin to focus her job or career ambitions.

In fact, the older woman is more desirable than her male

counterpart both in the job market and as a mate. Research indicates that women have greater resistance to rheumatism, hemorrhages, many cancers, and brain disease. They usually have greater circulation of blood to the brain and suffer less loss of memory than men as they age. Since they retain the use of their hands, legs, and eyesight longer than men, women will remain occupationally and socially active longer.

Despite this positive report on women after forty, the myths often prevail. Husbands advise wives that they could not survive the "dog eat dog" world of business. Men tell women that their rages, hormones, or emotional temperaments make them too illogical to function well in a man's world. Even women often view other women with prejudices, and prefer to vote for male politicians, work for male bosses, hire male employees, use male lawyers, and choose male physicians!

FINALLY FIFTY

At about age fifty, many women have the chance to make a wonderful shift: they can shake off the negative messages society has been sending them about aging and focus on the very large benefits the decade ahead has to offer. Menopause, for example, frees us of the worry that we will become pregnant again, ends PMS, and initiates new possibilities. Now we are free to write the book, open the store, resurrect the career or create the masterpiece of our choice. Husbands may start to be bothered by major health problems about this time and sense the end of their working lives, especially if he is older. We, on the other hand, are often feeling just the opposite: energetic and adventuresome!

Wild horses could not hold us back—but a few others things can slow us down. Like our fiftieth birthday.

There is something unique and symbolic about the number fifty. Fifty percent marks the middle. Fifty is halfway to a hundred, and most of us do not expect to live beyond that (nor do we necessarily want to). Fifty is a turning point: we begin to think more about what has passed than what lies ahead. We ask ourselves whether our lives have been meaningful. It we have not solved the midlife problems of our forties, they come back with renewed intensity in our fifties.

It can help simply to recognize that the turmoil is normal. Midlife crisis is a phase to pass through like adolescence. Talking with other women can be reassuring. However much you may be tempted to avoid the class reunion this time, if you gather up your courage and go, you'll probably see that you are far from alone.

They're baa-a-ack. Another midlife stress can be children—yes, the ones you thought you had raised so many years ago and gently pushed out of the nest. With rents astoundingly high, divorce rates astoundingly high, and the economy heading downward, young adults are returning home in droves, to the chagrin of their parents. The house that was recently so peaceful is now full of activity again. The young person may be unemployed, and you see your savings dwindle as you try to help him get back to speed. After all, he has to eat! He needs a car! Finally, you may be struggling with feelings of failure. After all those years you invested in raising the child, you fear that she has not grown up at all. What is she doing here? Did you forget to teach her something important? When will she go back out into the world again? You may feel some despair that your child's growing-up process could take years more.

What can you do? First, know that your feelings are normal, all normal. To take away some of the tension, talk with your new tenant about your expectations: the amount of the rent, how much housework is expected of you and the child, car use, whether you need to know if he or she will be in for dinner. In time, you can ask, gently, about long-range plans. Encourage the child not to depend on you too much—for example, by setting up a savings account for a co-op, condo or apartment security payment. If you set a deadline for the child to be out, stick with it. That may be hard, since no one knows what the economy will do in the next five or ten years. If you enjoy having them home, remind yourself that they are only on loan.

THE "SANDWICH" GENERATION

Besides the demands of their children, some women in their fifites are overwhelmed with the demands of their aging parents. These women are catering to the young *and* the old—caught in the middle like the filling of a sandwich. (And about to be eaten alive, they sometimes feel!) Parents who are ill, financially unprepared or depressed about aging can drain a middle-years family of even more time, money and emotional energy than the children who have unexpectedly returned home, because older people are sometimes truly helpless. It is hard to say whether it is better to have ailing parents nearby or at a distance. If they are close, the constant pressure of doing little things can be exhausting. If they are far away, the constant worry about who is doing the little things you would be doing if you lived closer is exhausting too!

On the brighter side, since most of the time parents prefer staying in their own home or finding a home-type situation where they have some independence, their daughter can become a manager instead of a servant. It is she who makes sure the nurse is giving good care, the accountant is paying the taxes, and the teenager is keeping up the yard as agreed. If you are tempted to do it all yourself, go ahead and try it—but know that unless you are a professional nurse or unless you have a lot of extra time and energy, it will be a trying experience. By finding other options, you will be able to make more of these years.

SEXY AND SIXTY

The older woman is often more desirable than the older man is still another way—sexually. Although men have traditionally talked more about their sexuality, most women maintain their sexual interest and capacities far longer as they mature.

Excluding individual differences, medical problems, and situational factors, women in general experience fewer sexual problems caused by the aging process than men. Men find that their refractory period (the postejaculation phase of the sexual response when another erection is physiologically unlikely) increases with age and that partial or situational impotence becomes more common. With these problems frequently comes performance anxiety, which can inhibit desire and further interfere with male sexual functioning.

The older woman is in a different position. Menopause frees her from any pregnancy fears she might have had, and coincides with freedom from caring for small children and from her or her husband's career struggles. Menopause can replace premenstrual tension with hot flashes and other body changes, but hot flashes pass, and other changes, such as diminished vaginal lubrication, can be treated medically or compensated for. The majority of women seem to adjust well physically to menopausal changes. Why, then, do we see female stress?

One major source of sexual stress among older women is older men.

Irene had been a bookkeeper for over twenty years, always looking forward to the time she and her husband would retire and move permanently to their country house in Maine. Her fantasy was that their time would be spent as their vacations there had been spent: gardening in the summer, reading, playing cards, and repairing in the winter, entertaining their children's children during holidays, and being close to each other. For Irene this meant romance. She and her husband had always been physically affectionate, cuddled, hugged, kissed, and found themselves making love with leisure and pleasure. Although she expected that the frequency of their lovemaking might diminish as they aged, she found her interest and enjoyment still held steady.

To her dismay, Irene found that as the retirement date drew near, her husband drew away. He seemed less interested in both Irene and his own sexual pleasure. By the end of their first year in Maine, Irene and her husband were no longer making love. Disappointed and depressed, Irene tried to convince her husband to talk to a therapist. Her husband refused. She eventually came to understand that her husband's loss of interest reflected both his loss of self-esteem when he retired from a responsible job and began to live on his wife's pension as well as his own income, and his expectation that to continue to be sexually active might stress his health. Perhaps, she speculated, intermittent intimacy was all her husband could handle emotionally. Being sexual as well as being together constantly would be too much for him.

Although their closeness and cuddling were restored, Irene and her husband did not share an active sex life in their later years. For Irene, this was a source of stress and frustration.

One point of this case history is that marriage itself does not ensure that a sexually interested woman will have sex available in her later years.

Husbands may, for example, withdraw sexually after they have suffered a heart attack or other serious illness, even though their physicians have given them a go-ahead. The statistics on heart attacks, in fact, show a surprisingly low incidence rate of attacks during intercourse with a spouse. (It is slightly higher among men with new partners!)

Out of misguided concern, a man may also withdraw after his wife has suffered an illness. My mother, psychologist Mildred Witkin of the Payne-Whitney Clinic, has found that often a woman needs confirmation that she is still desirable after surgery, and waits for her partner to make the first move out of her own insecurity. Not surprisingly, Witkin found that the sooner women who have had breast surgery resumed their love lives, the more rapid and complete was their recovery from the psychological and physical effects of the operation. Indeed, this was a major factor in the recovery.

Husbands may withdraw sexually after high blood pressure medication, diabetes, or aging interferes with their erections. Most men do not know that they can have an orgasm with no erection at all. Furthermore, since women can enjoy all types

FEMALE AFTER FORTY   **273**

of pleasuring and can have an orgasm from clitoral stimulation without intercourse, even total impotence does not have to mean an end to a couple's sexuality.

Husbands, finally, are often older than their wives. This is financially advantageous when a couple is young but sexually disadvantageous when a couple matures. Add to that years of familiarity, routine, and daily problems. Add anxiety about appearance and performance. Add social taboos against "dirty old men." The result? Wives experiencing the Female Stress Syndrome!

Older women who are not married, or who never married, run the risk of additional problems in this area. Sexuality may be an inner quality, but sexiness, like beauty, is in the eye of the beholder. Without appreciative eyes around to behold you, it is all too easy to become lax about your exercise, diet, or appearance. Women over forty who are finding sexual partners less available should know that this is not so much a reaction against them personally, but rather the result of the double standard of aging as well as the unfortunate imbalance in the male/female populations in this age group.

The life expectancy for women in our society is still greater than that for men—six to eight years greater, on the average. By the time a woman is fifty, there will be approximately eighty men for every hundred women of the same age. By the time she is sixty, the number drops to seventy-two men per one hundred women; and after seventy-five, there are only about sixty-three men per one hundred women. Now consider that two-thirds of these men over sixty-five are still married; that leaves approximately one single man for every four single women over sixty!

Furthermore, as Susan Sontag noted, it is expected that men will date women their own age and younger. It is not expected that older women will do the same, even if they could. When an older woman is seen with a young lover, even today, most people assume that she is rich. These and other societal factors result in far fewer dating opportunities for older women than for older men.

STRESS AND THE
NOT-SO-MERRY WIDOW

Another source of stress in the older woman is the experience of widowhood. There are now more than ten million widows living in the United States, and, although women can of course be widowed at any age, they are on average sixty-four years old.

When it comes to remarrying after the death of a spouse, the odds are not in a woman's favor. Only one-quarter of all widows remarry within five years, compared to half of all widowers and three-quarters of divorced women.

Sheer loneliness is one of the biggest burdens of widowhood, whether it happens at a young or older age. H. Z. Lopata identified ten kinds of loneliness in widowhood that illustrate the stress experienced by many of these women:

> missing the particular person
> missing feeling loved
> missing being able to love the other
> missing an in-depth relationship
> missing having someone else around the house
> missing sharing work
> missing the married life-style
> missing the status of being escorted
> increased strains on other relationships
> difficulties meeting new friends

Compounding loneliness are ten additional sources of stress that have emerged from stress workshops I have run with widows.

1. Approximately 44 percent of widows must cope with a drop in their incomes when their spouses die. In addition, immediate funeral and other death costs average $4,000!

2. The majority of men die without leaving a will. This precipitates lengthy and confusing court procedures for their widows to handle.

3. Many widows can't escape the need to find an object of blame for their loss. They begin a litany of "if onlys" that prolongs their mourning.

4. The woman who occupied a traditional role as a house-wife usually suffers a sense of confusion and helpless-ness when the head of the household dies and she must take over.

5. Women whose husbands were financially and socially successful find both their status and feelings of security are diminished.

6. Depression in reaction to the death is often associated with early awakening and other sleep disturbances. These, in turn, reduce the widow's coping capacity and raise the risk of female stress symptoms.

7. If the widow's spoken communication is reduced with the loss of her husband, she may gradually withdraw from social contact. Such withdrawal may become chronic, but it may not be obvious initially.

8. Many widows feel guilty if they find that they still have sexual needs. They feel disloyal to the deceased and inhibited about masturbation. Moreover, they are un-likely to find a suitable male partner. At present, two of three women over sixty-five years in the United States are unmarried.

9. Widowhood is so common that it may not rally the social-support reaction it warrants. Since women tend to marry older men and then live longer than they do, for the most part, widowhood is epidemic! According to Metropolitan Life Insurance Company statistics, a woman's chance of widowhood is approximately 54 percent if her spouse is five years younger, 64 percent if her spouse is five years older, and 80 percent if her spouse is ten years older.

10. If a widow is forced by practical or financial circum-stances to move after her husband's death, she must

deal with the stresses of a significant change in routine, control, familiarity, and neighborhood support system. If, in addition, the change is to a child's home or to an old-age home, the loss of dignity and/or power and autonomy can be devastating!

AGING IN THE '90S

Although some of the stresses that beset women as they age are both universal and inevitable, others are unique to this time and place in history.

Women in the '90s are caught in the divorce deluge. Some women over forty are leaving their husbands; some are being left. They have no models for their new life-style and no idea of what is to come. They are on the forefront of a new social world, caught in the stresses of changing expectations.

Women in the '90s are affected by the unique economic situation in which inflation is coupled with a recession/depression. The golden years have become tarnished as pensions and incomes fall short of today's financial needs. Women worry about their own wage-earning capacities; about their retirement plans; about their security should they remain unmarried, or should their husbands die or leave; about medical costs; about their independence in their later years; and about their children's economic survival.

Women in the '90s are concerned about their daughters. Just as the lives of women over forty are radically different from the lives their mothers led, so are their own grown daughters' lives different. Their daughters are marrying later, working more, having fewer children, and divorcing more quickly. In *A Room of One's Own*, Virginia Woolf imagines the fate of an equally talented sister of William Shakespeare. As the story evolves, she is continually blocked from developing her talent by ridicule and prejudice. Today her fate might have been very different, but so might her stresses! With opportunity has come responsibility, choices, and risks. Today's women over forty do not escape the Female Stress Syndrome.

MANAGING AFTER-FORTY STRESS

MENOPAUSE

Perhaps more than at any other time in your life, your mind can make the difference in your experience of the Female Stress Syndrome after forty. Menopause, of course, is biologically programmed (unless surgery precipitates it), and the physical changes it brings are not totally under your control. But you can reduce the stress of feeling helpless and victimized by Mother Nature by maximizing your sense of *predictability*.

Women going through menopause should learn all they can about the changes they are experiencing. Learn that they are normal; learn that some have a limited duration; learn that they are not all mysteries; learn what changes will come next.

Although the menopause symptoms themselves may not be under your control, other areas of functioning are.

- Maintain control of your weight, following a nutritionally sound diet, and you will continue to enjoy your body.

- Set up and follow an exercise program. This will maintain your muscle strength and stimulate your energy supply.

- Schedule your time. Decide on your own priorities and handle time as if it were a very valuable commodity. Your time will truly be yours.

- Be good to yourself. This can help to reduce that feeling of being controlled by physical changes rather than your own decisions. Treat yourself well: Take bubble baths, read good books, eat delicious, nutritional food. Be as considerate of your own feelings as you are of others'.

- Take notice of your needs and be ready to *ask* for what may be needed from others: sympathy, support, closeness, distance, respect, or attention.

- Take care of your health. Have regular check-ups and mammograms, and deal with problems such as high blood pressure and cholesterol which can damage your health in the future.

- Discuss estrogen replacement with your physician. Estrogen therapy after menopause helps prevent osteoporosis and there is some evidence that it may reduce the risk of heart disease, according to Dr. Marjorie Luckey, Director of the Osteoporosis and Metabolic Bone Disease Program at Mt. Sinai School of Medicine.

Calcium and exercise both help to prevent osteoporosis, although the body doesn't absorb calcium well without estrogen. So Dr. Luckey advises women who decide not to take estrogen to take 1500 mg of calcium daily. Women who do take estrogen, she says, still need at least 1000 mg of calcium daily, either from food or calcium supplements. Since it is not yet clear, however, if estrogen slightly increases the risk of breast cancer, every woman needs to weigh carefully the benefits and potential risks of hormone replacement before making this important decision. If the physical symptoms seem excessive, consult a gynecologist or endocrinologist.

If stress symptoms seem excessive, consult a psychologist or psychiatrist.

If you have a hard time deciding whether the symptoms are excessive, ask a professional that question.

As previously mentioned toward the beginning of this book, there is a very positive side to menopause. Many women experience it as a relief, even as a rebirth. They find freedom from fear of pregnancy that is liberating both sexually and practically. With menopause comes a rite of passage into a period of personal choices and self-defined life-styles, free from premenstrual tensions and postpartum blues. With menopause often comes a reexamination of goals and roles, free from preparental anticipation and filled with postparental relaxation! Here at last is the opportunity to make resolves and choose courses of action that had been postponed, or not even considered. "It is time to get paid for my work," a mother of two college girls declared. "A job with pay will give me dignity and give my daughters a new way of thinking about me and themselves." And there are many women like Lena, who never considered that the years after mothering would be any less full or important, and planned for them.

> Lena, now sixty-two years old, began planning for her eventual retirement from mothering when she was only thirty-eight. She started by enrolling in a counseling program that had evening classes, and by the time she reached menopause she had received her master's degree in social work. She had also completed her full-time mothering responsibilities. Lena feels that the fun has just begun since she started her private practice five years ago. She is pleased with the way she pursued her interests sequentially, rather than trying to juggle them simultaneously.

MANAGING THE STRESS OF GRIEF

Although, of course, there are individual differences, widows may find comfort in the fact that grief and mourning often have distinct, predictable stages. Each is a necessary step in the natural healing process. Be aware of your own bereavement process and its stages. This awareness will not change your mourning, but will reassure you that your feelings are normal, and that mourning is a period that should gradually evolve into reengagement with the life around you. Milton Matz, a clinical psychologist and a former rabbi, has outlined the phases of bereavement.

Phase I: "If I deny it, it's not true"

The widow will try to avoid any thought or mention of the loss in an attempt to escape pain. This can be done in many ways. Some will act as if nothing had happened, for a while. They will attend to business and continue their work. Others will withdraw from friends and family to avoid mention or association with memories of the deceased. Still others seem to be numb and unfeeling. Their lives and actions seem to be on automatic pilot.

Phase II: "I have the power to undo it"

During this stage, Matz suggests that many widows may try to escape the sadness of acceptance by utilizing magical thinking. Attempts to keep the spouse alive by "seeing" and "hearing" him are not uncommon, nor are beliefs that he is still right here on earth in spirit, to be communicated with. Women who have been raised to believe that women need men to survive daily life may try to undo the death of a spouse by immediately substituting someone—a son, a new spouse. Since the initial loss is not confronted, however, the mourning will continue and often interfere with new relationships.

Phase III: "I can't do anything about it"

The loss is faced and felt during this difficult period. The reality of the death of the spouse can lead to despair and even suicidal notions. The turning point will be not the acceptance of helplessness with regard to her husband's death, but power and control with regard to the widow's own *life*. As she makes choices and reshapes her life, reengagement will begin.

Phase IV: "I am rebuilding, and every now and then I remember"

According to Matz, there are as many reconstruction patterns as there are lives. In my clinical experience, I have noticed one common characteristic: the widow's healthy sense of surprise that she has been able to manage her loss and grief, and often to feel stronger for it. Widows realize that they were not merely half of a pair, but are, in fact, a whole person in their own right. Many choose to remain on their own and enjoy the control they have over their lives.

If you have a friend who has lost her husband, try helping her in the following ways:

- Allow her to formulate her own alternatives without overwhelming her with advice or threatening her sense of self-confidence.

- Do not deny her sorrow and loss. Reminding her that her spouse had "a good life" or died without pain will not address her personal separation anxiety, but, rather, may make her feel guilty for thinking of herself!

- Don't stay away. Although she may be withdrawn, upset, or proud, even silent company offers security.

- Offer social and work activities without pressure. Don't try to guess what is appropriate for her; everyone handles reengagement differently. Let her know that she is welcome to join life rather than being left to mimic death. It does not imply disrespect for her loss for her to function as fully as she can.

LIVING ALONE AND LIKING IT

If your marriage or long-term relationship ends, or you have difficulty adjusting to the fact of being forty-plus and on your own, there are a number of steps you can take to make the experience more positive.

First of all, don't *judge* your needs. Don't stand back from yourself with your imaginary eyebrow raised and foot tapping while you assess whether you *should* need company. Instead, put yourself squarely on your own team and help yourself go after what you need to feel good without harsh self-judgments.

Turn to your family and friends. This is not a sign of weakness, not a lack of self-sufficiency. You're not the only one who needs to be needed. Think how good and useful it will make others feel to be able to give you pleasure or assistance.

Don't try to run away from intermittent sadness or loneliness. If you repress these feelings, the same repressive system will likely put the lid on *all* strong feelings—including joy and humor as well.

If a long-term relationship has just ended for whatever reason, accept the fact that you have gone through a transition and that any change, particularly one over which you have little or no control, will aggravate the symptoms of the Female Stress Syndrome. You may be more prone to depression or illness, depending on your "weak links." You may feel social stresses more, be more sensitive to insults and injuries from others. Remember that the Female Stress Syndrome is real—it's not all in your mind. Help yourself and be good to yourself.

If you have recently been widowed, be aware that guilt is a common side effect: guilt that you are still alive while your spouse is not, guilt that from time to time you felt anger toward him when he was alive, guilt that you may even be enjoying some aspects of your widowhood, guilt that feelings for another man may be developing.

Also, especially at first, take as much time as you can to make big decisions (such as whether or not to sell the house, where you should live if you do). If possible, don't let yourself be pressured into something before you're ready; in the midst of grief and coming to terms with a major life change, it is difficult to think clearly, and you may make decisions you will later regret.

Develop a network of people who share the same problems and feelings; you'll feel less alone. Fight some of the injustices of age prejudice, if that is your style. It will make you feel more potent. Keep in mind that as your sense of control increases, your stress decreases, so anything you can do to put yourself more in control of your life will go a long way toward easing the Female Stress Syndrome.

14 MANAGING THE FEMALE STRESS SYNDROME

UP UNTIL NOW WE HAVE BEEN EXAMINING THE STRESSES THAT MAKE UP the Female Stress Syndrome, and the symptoms associated with those stresses. We have seen how the stresses that stem from a woman's biology and conditioning can trigger a wealth of physical and psychological ailments that, to one degree or another, are a fact of life for most of us. Now it is time to focus on *living with* the Female Stress Syndrome.

The aim of Female Stress Syndrome management is threefold. The first aim, which we have been discussing throughout this book, is to increase a sense of control. The higher one's sense of control, the lower one's stress. To take just one example, it has been shown that institutionalized, elderly people who are given certain choices—about which movie to see, which houseplant to own, which foods to eat—seem to cope much better, both physically and psychologically, than those who do not have such choices.

The second aim of Female Stress Syndrome management is to encourage realistic assessment of the stressful situation. Some stressful situations are short-term and require minor management efforts. Others are long-term and chronic—more likely to put women at high risk for stress symptoms, and requiring major stress-management efforts. Realistic assessment will not only help to distinguish between the two types of stressful situations but also will help determine which are best handled through *action* and which are best handled through *acceptance*. The women of the '80s learned to take control of their lives. Now, in the '90s, we must learn when to stop trying to take control of some aspects of our lives. We must learn to recognize where our efforts are futile, unwanted, or unnecessary. We must teach ourselves to know when enough is enough.

The third aim of Female Stress Syndrome management is to improve problem-solving skills and coping strategies. Successful stress management should produce more than situational relief. Ideally, the process of managing stress should generate information on one's particular vulnerabilities and strengths, one's susceptibilities and capabilities. Every encounter with the Female Stress Syndrome should leave a woman better equipped to deal with stress when it next appears.

HELP FROM OTHERS

Years ago, my mother's mother taught her about the dangers of female friendship. She warned her daughter that her so-called girlfriends would talk behind her back, be jealous of her accomplishments, and probably even lust after her man. In some instances, my grandmother was right—but not always.

Through the years, my mother learned that many of her female friends could be trusted, were loyal, and truly cared about her happiness. So she reexamined her mother's teachings. Unfortunately, by that point my mother had passed on my grandmother's words of warning to me—so I had to learn the truth about female friendships the hard way, on my own.

During the past 20 years, I've studied the dynamics of women and friendship—the envy, the anger, the bonding. And I've learned that not only is friendship *natural* among women, it also fills a number of basic needs in our lives. Your female friends can add warmth, fun, and meaning to your life in a way no one else does.

For example, have you ever told your best friend something you thought you'd never be able to tell *anyone*? Or called her in the middle of the night because you just *had* to talk? Have you altered your career, moving or vacation plans because you wanted to avoid the separation anxiety you'd feel being away from her? Broken up with a boyfriend just after she had broken up with hers? Or gotten divorced within a year of her divorce? Or even decided to have a baby after she had one? Maybe you've kept her company at the dentist's office. Or simply felt like she's the only person in the world who *really* understands you.

If you've answered yes to even one of these questions, you've experienced the powerful effects that friendships between women can have.

Female friendships can tell us a lot about our nature and our needs. In fact, by midchildhood most young girls have already developed at least one best friend to whom they can reveal their innermost secrets. Boys, on the other hand, are less self-disclosing with each other and more private with their personal feelings.

This pattern of female bonding seems to be true across time and cultures, and researchers are trying to figure out why. Is the need for female friendship learned or instinctive? When does it start? Studies conducted by Eleanor Maccoby, Ph.D., director of human development in psychology at Stanford University in Palo Alto, suggest that female infants react to touch more readily than male infants. And Karl Pribram, Ph.D., says that girls begin to talk earlier and express emotions more verbally than boys. Does this push females toward conversation and contact? Does this mean that mothers, fathers, other girls and even boys will more easily communicate with us than with males? Probably so.

Moreover, developmental psychologists have demonstrated in clinical studies that by eighteen months of age, girls have better-controlled, less aggressive tempers than boys. This means that even as toddlers, most girls can already think first and act later—a wonderful quality for the development and nurturing of friendship.

How do successful female friendships form? The formula

seems to require one part shared values and one part attraction—mixed with a tremendous amount of commitment. If you're surprised to hear that attraction is an important part of women's platonic friendships, think about your favorite friends. It's likely that each of them possesses a special quality that you have always been attracted to: vivacity, intelligence, beauty, grace, gentleness, assertiveness.

By the way, shared values need not refer to politics. Instead, sharing values about honesty, achievement, family, and fun can mean that you and your friend inhabit the same psychological world. And as for commitment, many women tell me that their friendships with other women have outlasted their marriages and more than one career. But keep in mind that this kind of staying power requires a commitment from both of you. After all, you must give time and effort for any relationship to be rewarding.

There really aren't any rules, guidelines or scripts that can guarantee a successful friendship. But there *are* vital considerations that seem to enhance it:

1. *Accept your friend as a package deal.* Don't expect her to be perfect. Accepting her as she is will also help you learn to accept yourself as *you* are. You don't have to be perfect to deserve devotion, and neither does she.

2. *Don't be a closet competitor.* Sometimes we use our friends as models for comparison. We may feel better about who we are when we compare ourselves to our friends, but sometimes we may feel worse. Either way, we are misusing our friendships when we compete, because the products of competitions are winners and losers, not equals. Instead, use each other for inspiration, feedback, sympathy, humor, empathy and as sounding boards.

3. *Don't treat female friends as in-betweeners.* In between men, that is. Too many women cancel appointments with their female friends whenever a man calls, and yet expect their friends to be there for them through thick

and thin. No matter how loyal, friends won't last if we keep disappearing when a new man comes into our lives.

4. *Don't abuse the power of friendship.* A friend cares what you think of her and cares how you show it. She has given you emotional power. Don't abuse it by using her to vent your own bad moods. (Even if you call it "constructive criticism," she *will* be hurt). And don't endanger it by invading her privacy. Friendships, like all living things, need room to grow!

Remember, the key to making and keeping lasting, loving friendships is, ultimately, learning how to be a good friend yourself.

HELPING OTHERS

Everybody knows someone who is suffering from female stress and having difficulties managing it. It may be your mother, your sister, your daughter, your neighbor, your good friend. Fortunately, there is a great deal you can do to help her manage her Female Stress Syndrome. The plan I recommend embodies many crisis-intervention techniques and family counseling approaches developed by psychologists throughout the past decade.

1. Remember the four *d*'s. They will let you know when a woman feels that she is in a crisis.
   Dependency needs are increased (though often denied!).
   Decision-making is difficult.
   Depression dominates the emotions.
   Disorganization and even panic sets in.

2. Show her that you *care*. Even if you share her alarm, do not show it—express concern instead. Try to understand the stress from her point of view, not your own. In this case the reality is not as important as the experience. Here are some things you might say: "I want to understand what you're going through."

"I'm glad to have a chance to spend some time with you."

"Have you ever gone through this kind of thing before?"

3. Encourage her to *talk* about her problem. Talking gives one a sense of "doing" something. Talking gives her an opportunity to "hear" herself, "listen" to herself as she would to another. Try saying:

"Tell me a little more about this."

"How do you explain that?"

"I'm not clear about . . ."

"What've you done that made you feel better (worse)?"

4. Be what psychologist Carl Rogers calls an *active listener*. Rogerian psychologists would recommend that you repeat what your friend or relative has said as a check for accuracy; repeat what you have heard to reassure her that you have really been listening. Repeat with warmth and sympathy to indicate that you accept the feelings being shared with you.

"What I hear you saying is . . ."

"I think I understand. You feel as if . . ."

"You certainly seem to think . . ."

"Do you mean . . ."

5. Help her to *help herself*. Taking over for her will only increase her sense of being overwhelmed, helpless, and out of control. Taking over will interfere with any learning that might otherwise result from managing a stress experience. To increase her self-help capabilities, follow the rest of the steps outlined.

6. Ask for a *plan of action*. Assess the risk-reward ratio. Discuss alternatives.

"How do you plan to . . ."

"What do *you* plan to do?"

"Did you ever think that you might also try . . ."

7. Work on her *fine-tuning*. That is, help her to focus on the problem without blurring the picture with exaggeration, anxiety, or anticipation. Sort the facts from the fictions.

   "From what you're telling me, it seems . . ."
   "Let me see if I can say that another way . . ."
   "What's the most practical way to go about this?"
   "If you decide to do that, then you'll probably also have to . . ."

8. Develop a *contract* for a specific course of action. This accomplishes two stress-management goals. It makes her responsibility for self-help clear, and it gives her a chance to increase her self-esteem by carrying through a plan during a stressful time.

   "So by Wednesday, you're going to . . ."
   "Now, I'm counting on you to . . ."

9. *Recapitulate* as often as necessary, since your friend or relative is likely to be easily distracted.

   "Now, you told me that you'd . . ."
   "Let's make sure we know what we're doing . . ."
   "Tell me again what you're going to do next."

10. Provide a *safety net*. Discourage withdrawal from friends and family or support systems. Encourage her to develop a network of resource people—informal "hot lines."

    "Remember, I'll be around tonight at six and tomorrow at . . ."
    "Let's get together again tomorrow (Tuesday, etc.) . . ."
    "Who're you planning to spend the evening (weekend, holiday, etc.) with?"

11. Set up *structure*. We all do better when we are not at loose ends with time on our hands! Mourning rites

(wakes, shivas, etc.), baptisms, confirmations, bar and bat mitzvahs, and even weddings can provide structure during periods of transition or stress. Make use of such social institutions.

12. There are cases in which we are dealing with a problem that cannot be truly "solved" (one-sided love, fatal or chronic illness, etc.). In these cases, promote appropriate *acceptance*. This will help reduce useless persistance and directionless activity; and it will help reduce the effects of the Female Stress Syndrome.

HELPING YOURSELF: SHORT-TERM STRESS MANAGEMENT

Always remember, as I said at the outset of this book, that *you are entitled to try to reduce the stress in your life*. Give yourself permission to take control over your life, to stop feeling guilty, to worry less about the "shoulds" that inevitably crop up.

Once stress has started and your adrenaline level is climbing, start short-term stress management immediately. Don't wait until you have time—it will be too late. Burn up that adrenaline before it burns you out by squeezing in some physical exercise right now, or shut off the adrenaline flood with relaxation techniques.

BECOME YOUR OWN CATHARSIS EXPERT

For short-term or emergency stress, catharsis techniques can help you cope. Catharsis is the emotional equivalent of a pressure cooker blowing off some of its steam through the lid valve. If the valve becomes stuck and the pressure builds to the point of eruption—pot roast on the ceiling! Catharsis techniques aim at discharging the tension that accumulates during stressful situations. They increase our sense of control by giving us the means to moderate our pressure levels, vital during times of stress. They exercise and relax our bodies, make good use of the extra adrenaline produced during stress, and direct "nervous" energy. They provide a healthy distraction from our immediate stress.

Some cathartic activities are self-regulated and self-contained. They don't require a partner or equipment. They include

- Walking—The most common exercise for both men and women of all ages.

- Calisthenics—About 17 percent of men and women twenty to forty-four years of age work out at home or in health clubs.

- Swimming—15 percent of women surveyed report that they find swimming very relaxing.

- Jogging—Fast becoming the most popular stress antidote!

Other cathartic activities are competitive. They include

- Tennis
- Racquetball, paddleball
- Team sports
- Marathons
- Games (backgammon, cards)

And there are many others: aerobics, biking, bellydancing, tap dancing, scrubbing, buffing, waxing, hoeing, or mowing. Or just put on the radio to music faster than your heartbeat (seventy-two beats per minute) and dance around your bedroom for twenty minutes. Remember, any sustained, rhythmic, self-regulated physical exercise not only uses up the extra adrenaline that stress stimulates, but it also increases your sense of control, distracts you from your stressors, gives you a sense of accomplishment, and leaves your muscles relaxed.

FAST FIXES

If your physician or your life-style says "no" to physical exerc
try games as your short-term intervention: competitive ga
like cards, backgammon, or word games; team games and ac
ities; or individual games like jigsaw and crossword puzzle
you enjoy it, and it is engrossing, it will counteract bad str
And if you compete openly, if you give yourself the victory
if you win and a pat on the back if you lose, if you stop pretenc
that nice girls don't try, you'll give yourself the added satisfac
of counteracting any non-assertiveness training you may h
picked up in the past.

And did you know that reorganizing part of your world
also be short-term, fast stress therapy? Clean our your wa
arrange your closet, rearrange your kitchen drawer and th
out the junk in it—part of the brain will register the result
an increase in control. And when your sense of control goes
stress goes down. The women I surveyed also recommend bc
store browsing, listening to music slower than our heartb
plant pruning, carpentry, and needlepoint for minivacations fr
stress.

MIRROR, MIRROR

A survey I did revealed that we women look at our reflecti
on an average of seventeen times a day: when we get ready
the day, when we wash our hands, when we pass a reflec
picture window, when we adjust the car mirror or try on clot
retouch our makeup before or after dinner. Try using your
flection as a feedback tool. Everytime you check your hair
makeup, check your brow for furrows, your jaw for clench
and your shoulders for hunching. If you see that your post
position is like someone about to be jumped from behind,
then and there, and begin one of the following relaxation te
niques.

BECOME YOUR OWN RELAXATION EXPERT

As important as using up the "fight" and "flight" adrenaline is shutting off your stress adrenaline before it wears and tears you into the Female Stress Syndrome. Soothing environments work like tranquilizers. Both relax your body enough so that your mind says "there's no stress here—no need for adrenaline, muscle tension, worrying, watching, or waiting." Try a hot bath with fragrance, bubbles, candles, and flowers, a book and soft music, or a long, long shower. Give yourself a massage—start with your face, and work your way down to your feet. Be creative. You may have heard all this before; the trick is to do it.

Stanley Fisher, in his book *Discovering the Power of Self-Hypnosis*, recommends that you use autohypnosis to let your body know that this is its time to relax. The simple steps for entering and exiting from autohypnosis are as follows:

1. Sit comfortably in a chair facing a wall about eight feet away. Pick a spot or an object on the wall that is about one foot above your sitting eye level. This is your focal point.

2. Look at your focal point, and begin counting backward from 100, one number for each breath you exhale.

3. As you count and continue to concentrate on your focal point, imagine yourself floating, floating down, down through the chair, very relaxed.

4. As you stare at your focal point you will find that your eyelids feel heavier and begin to blink. When this happens, just let your eyes slowly close.

5. While your eyes are closed continue to count backward, one number for each time you exhale. As you count, imagine how it would feel to be as limp as a rag doll, totally relaxed and floating in a safe, comfortable space. This is your space.

6. As that safe, comfortable feeling flows over you, you can stop counting and just float.

7. If any disturbing thought enters your space, just let it flow out again; continue to feel safe and relaxed.

8. When you're ready to come out of autohypnosis, either let yourself drift off to sleep, or count from one to three and exit using the following steps. At *one*, let yourself get ready; at *two*, take a deep breath and hold it for a few seconds; and at *three* exhale and open your eyes slowly. As you open your eyes, continue to hold on to that relaxed, comfortable feeling.

You can also counteract tension with progressive relaxation. Some of my patients make a tape of their own voice issuing the following instructions:

1. Starting with your toes, relax them.
2. Then the feet and ankles: relax.
3. Then the calves: relax.
4. The knees: relax.
5. The thighs: relax.
6. The buttocks: relax.
7. The abdomen and stomach: relax.
8. The back and shoulders: relax.
9. The hands: relax.
10. The forearms: relax.
11. The upper arms: relax.
12. The neck: relax.
13. The face: relax.
14. Drift off.

Finally, try counteracting tension with the following technique. You will first slowly contract and relax each part of your body for ten seconds each; and then contract and relax each part of your body more quickly to become aware of the tension-relaxation contrast.

1. Frown as hard as you can for ten seconds; then relax those forehead muscles for ten seconds. Now repeat

this more quickly, frowning and relaxing for one second each and becoming aware of the different feelings of each movement.

2. Squeeze your eyes shut for ten seconds, then relax for ten seconds. Repeat quickly.

3. Wrinkle your nose hard for ten seconds; then relax for ten seconds. Repeat quickly.

4. Slowly press your lips together; then relax. Repeat quickly.

5. Press your head back against the wall, floor, or bed (real or imaginary)—then relax. Repeat quickly.

6. Bring your left shoulder up in a tight shrugging motion; relax. Repeat quickly.

7. Do the same with your right shoulder; repeat quickly.

8. Press your straightened arms back against the wall, or floor, or bed; relax. Repeat quickly.

9. Clench your fists tightly for ten seconds. Relax your hands and let the tension flow out through your fingers. Repeat quickly.

10. Contract your chest cavity for ten seconds and release. Repeat quickly.

11. Press your back against the wall or floor; relax. Repeat quickly.

12. Tighten your buttock muscles for ten seconds; relax. Repeat quickly.

13. Press your straightened legs against the wall or floor or bed; relax. Repeat quickly.

14. Slowly flex your feet, stretching your toes as far back toward you as possible; relax and let tension flow out through your toes. Repeat quickly.

15. Check for tense spots and repeat the exercise where you find any.

Soon you will begin to recognize muscle contractions caused by tension before these contractions can cause spasms and chronic pain.

BIBLIOTHERAPY

Don't neglect the wealth of self-help books written by credentialed professionals which can teach you new techniques for getting along with others, negotiating at work, getting married, staying married, ending a marriage, and worrying less and enjoying life more. Bibliotherapy is self-paced, not expensive, unambiguous, educational, and often the first step toward therapy. In fact, 60 percent of psychotherapists who belong to the American Psychological Association say they tell their patients to read self-help books for guidance in parenting, personal growth, relationships, assertiveness, sexuality, and of course, stress reduction.

But, buyer beware: if the answers seem too easy or the claims are excessive, close the book. If you are approaching problems too intellectually, or reading too passively without taking notes or practicing what you read, close the book. And if your problem is a depression that interferes with eating and sleeping, an anxiety that interferes with your daily life, or an addiction that is hurting you or others, choose a two-way interaction with a therapist instead of a one-way do-it-yourself book.

HELPING YOURSELF: LONG-TERM STRESS MANAGEMENT

Now that you're managing the symptoms of the Female Stress Syndrome with short-term techniques, it's time to do something about the *causes* of the Female Stress Syndrome. Long-term management is built on prevention, planning, perspective, and practice.

- *Prevention* means knowing the difference between stimulation and stress.
- *Planning* means knowing your weak links and vulnerabilities and protecting them.
- *Perspective* means knowing when you can make choices and take control and it means knowing when it's time to give up control.
- *Practice* means that reading this book is not enough. Make management part of your daily life.

PARENT YOURSELF

We parent our children, we parent our spouses. We parent our friends and we parent our parents. Now parent yourself, too. Monitor your own nutrition and sleep. Schedule your own playtime.

GIVE YOURSELF SELF-ESTEEM

Some women get self-esteem as a gift from their parents. Some of us must give it to ourselves. How? Give yourself pats on the back, compliments, encouragements, and even hugs and kisses. Parent yourself just the way you would have wanted to be parented. You can't "do-over" your childhood, but you can do it right in your adulthood.

THINK "INCONVENIENT"

Have you noticed how often we women blame ourselves for life's snags or dwell on what we could have done and should have done? It's time to think of those snags as "inconveniences," not failures. Some are very big inconveniences—like bankruptcy or divorce. Some are smaller—like parking tickets or broken dates. But most things that befall us are not punishments. They are the result of bad luck, or human nature. Make room for both.

PRIORITIZE

You've heard this before. Now think about it again. You can't expect to carry on at all costs—the cost is too steep. You can't expect to add new roles to old roles without becoming overwhelmed. You can't make all your commitments priorities, so make fewer commitments. A recent study at Northwest Kaiser Permanente Hospital in Portland, Oregon found that the incidence of angina chest pains has increased by 69 percent for women over the past fifteen years, compared to an increase of 31 percent for men. So make your own physical and mental health a priority starting today. Underwhelm yourself.

TAKE CHOICES

In the '80s, we learned to *make* choices—we had to. We became single parents, divorcées, single-never-marrieds, and widows, all at an explosive rate. Now, in the '90s, it's time to *take* choices. Don't avoid them because you fear criticism or the responsibility. Don't say "I don't care" or "It's up to you." The next time someone asks you to choose a movie or pick a restaurant, do it. If everyone is disappointed with the food or film, don't think that they are disappointed in you. Remember, disappointments are not failures, merely inconveniences. Try saying, and thinking, "better luck next time."

SEPARATE YOUR PAST FROM YOUR PRESENT

Don't re-create old scenarios again and again with the new people in your life. They will not change in the reliving. They will not give you mastery over the past. Instead, address the present: It is the present over which you can really take control.

Don't assume the future will be the same as the past. Our view of the past is never objective anyway. Our earliest introduction to the world leaves a lasting impression, it is true; however, this first impression can be sorted out from the more complex reality of the present. The child's view in each of us can be recognized by us, tolerated with self-affection, and then redirected and guided by the adult in us.

ACCEPT YOURSELF AS A PACKAGE DEAL

You cannot be perfect. Don't even try. Instead, as I recommended before, aim at being able to describe yourself accurately. As you allow yourself to be a less-than-perfect package, you will allow others to be so also. As you begin to describe rather than evaluate yourself and others, your stress level will go down. Replace "This is who I should be" with "This is who I seem to be." Work with your reality, not your ideal. This is vital to managing the Female Stress Syndrome.

BREAK THE HABIT OF LIVING LIFE LACED WITH GUILT

When we are young, most of our guilt follows behavior that we learned was *bad*. When we are adults, however, we have little time or impulse to be "bad." More often, our guilt follows behavior that falls short of what we learned was *good*. Women say to themselves "I should have . . ." all day long.

"I should have said yes . . ."
"I should have said no . . ."
"I should have called . . ."
"I should have offered . . ."

This type of guilt serves no purpose except to increase stress. It is after the fact and therefore cannot be helpful. Replace self-recrimination with self-observation.

"It seems I did not want to say yes . . ."
"I wonder why I did that . . ."
"Would I prefer, next time, to . . ."

LEARN TO SAY NO

Learn to say no without feeling guilt (as to a child).
Learn to say no without justifying yourself (as to your spouse).

Learn to say no without defending yourself (as to a parent).
Learn to say no graciously, not tentatively (as to your lover).
Learn to give explanations, not excuses (as to the boss).

GIVE YOURSELF THE FREEDOM TO CHANGE YOUR MIND

Don't persecute yourself every time you change your mind about something or someone. Reassessing is a mark of flexibility, not instability. Although a "whim of iron" may represent too much mind-changing, a happy medium is better than rigid, inappropriate consistency.

BECOME YOUR OWN PERMISSION-GIVER

You don't need permission from others to take care of yourself, to reduce your own stress level. Don't wait until the whole world can see that you are under stress before you allow yourself a rest. Don't wait until you feel you can't cope with one more problem before you start to take care of yourself. If you wait for others to take care of you, you might wait forever. Even if no one else in your life recognizes the reality of the Female Stress Syndrome, by now you do.

Give yourself permission to

- Rest: take a nap, a bath, or whatever—you're entitled!

- Relax: read a book, watch television, write a poem, listen to music, nap—and don't *contaminate* this relaxation time with chores.

- Set realistic limits: underwhelm yourself, underschedule yourself, and underdemand—don't worry, I'm sure you'll find that you still have too much to do!

BECOME YOUR OWN BEST FRIEND

Be on the lookout for stressors that trigger your stress symptoms. Protect yourself as you would your other loved ones.

BECOME YOUR OWN RESOURCE PERSON

Learn how to manage *emergencies* that are inevitable or highly probable: funeral arrangements, medical crises, auto disasters. Compile lists of hot lines, professionals, and references.

Learn how to manage your reactions to those *situational stresses* that particularly affect you: holidays, in-law problems, or financial worries. Don't be caught upset; anticipate and alleviate your reactions.

Learn to manage *chronic stress* in order to protect yourself from serious Female Stress Syndrome symptoms. Pay attention to the factors that make such situations better or easier for you—and the factors that make them worse.

CREATE SELF-FULFILLING PROPHECIES

Expect the best. Even if things do not work out the way you might have wanted them to, at least you have not stressed yourself *before* the problem or disappointment. In other words, reduce *anticipatory anxiety*, which does not change outcomes but only increases the risk of the Female Stress Syndrome.

Use the "as if" technique. That is, behave *as if* everyone would be delighted to treat you just the way you want to be treated.

Rosalie was meeting her friend David for dinner. She very much wanted to attend a party for city singles later on in the evening, but worried that David might be insulted if she tried to socialize with other men, or angry if she added another activity to their plans. She decided, however, to put the "as if" technique to work before abandoning the singles' party idea. After all, she reminded herself, she and David were "just friends," not lovers.

Rosalie presented the party plan to David as if she expected him to be delighted and appreciative. "Guess what," she began. "After dinner, I've arranged it so that I can take you with me to the best singles' party in town. We can compare notes when it's over. Aren't you lucky to have me as a friend?" Indeed, David responded by agreeing.

Similarly,

> Ellen was trying to attend a college in the evening and run a three-child household at the same time. She needed her husband's moral support, financial aid, and household help. She was feeling that she wasn't entitled to them, however. "Going to college is so self-indulgent," she thought. "I really should be working part time, rather than studying part time," she chided herself. Although her husband had not said a word against her studies, she was always prepared for his criticism. She read things into his remarks, became defensive if he was tired, and felt angry if he wanted her time. She put herself under so much pressure with this anticipatory anxiety that she was ready to quit college.
>
> As a last resort, Ellen decided to try the "as if" technique. She gave herself permission to be a part-time student and began to behave as if she believed it was fine with her husband, too. Now she was able to react to his helpfulness with appreciation rather than guilt, and she never let an opportunity go by to praise his support in front of friends.

In Ellen's case, the "as if" assumption was closer to reality than her own pessimistic assumptions. Her husband increased his efforts to be helpful and understanding, and she felt less stressed.

The "as if" technique, as I have suggested before,

- Facilitates asking for favors without a trace of defensiveness.

- Facilitates asking for favors without the flavor of anticipatory anger.

- "Teaches" others that we see ourselves as worth positive treatment and entitled to consideration.

- Flatters others by making *requests* of them—not demands.

- Reinforces reactions in others that will reduce, rather than increase, stress.

Remember, don't sabotage your own communications by broadcasting expectations of disappointment or by broadcasting criticism.

ENJOY YOUR OWN SEXUALITY

If you have a sexual partner, don't neglect the sexual side of yourself when you are under stress. For many women, sexual activity is an important outlet for tension. It helps women remember that they are desirable, attractive, needed, or wanted. And by being intimate, they close out the rest of the world temporarily, providing a vital respite from stress.

If you are orgasmic, your sexual experience will leave you relaxed due to the role of the parasympathetic nerves in orgasm. The capacity to masturbate, therefore, is also very important as a stress reliever.

STAY SELF-CENTERED

By self-centered I do not mean selfish; I mean self-aware. Remind yourself continually to look at yourself and at the world through your *own* eyes, not through others' eyes. Looking at yourself through others' eyes is called "spectatoring," and it can raise performance anxiety, which is a component of the Female Stress Syndrome. If you suffer from shyness, self-consciousness, and lack of spontaneity, spectatoring is probably your problem.

Do not constantly view yourself through others' eyes and change your opinion of yourself and of your decisions, even when important people in your life disagree. Don't reevaluate yourself every time your partner, children, or friends disapprove. Don't give others the power to knock you off balance. Stay centered.

ASSESS YOUR STRESS

You cannot manage stressors or symptoms until you can identify them. With pencil in hand, review the list of stress symptoms provided here. Add others in the blanks provided. During the course of a day, note the time when you experienced any symptom on the list. Next to the time, jot down the activity you were engaged in or about to begin. Do you find a pattern?

TIME	ACTIVITY	SYMPTOM
		Headache
		Heartburn
		Nausea
		Cold sweat
		Dizziness
		Memory block
		Asthma
		Hyperventilation
		Allergic reaction
		Backache
		Swallowing difficulty
		Rapid heartbeat
		Increased blood pressure
		Urinary frequency

If you find that certain activities seem to trigger stress symptoms for you, deal with them in the following ways:

1. Assess the timing of the activity. Could you do the task earlier or later in the day? Would this make a difference in terms of stress?

2. Assess your performance level. Are you overinvested in this activity? Are you spending too much time and energy in this area?

3. Assess your motivation. Are you letting a sense of "should" dictate your behavior? Too often an activity we might enjoy is resented because we feel compelled rather than motivated to complete it.

ANTICIPATE THE STRESS OF HOLIDAYS

Don't feel guilty or surprised if holidays are stressful. Everyone finds them so. Holidays involve a change in schedule, a gathering of family, and high expectations—usually too high! For many, they evoke upsetting memories of good times lost or bad times past. For some, they emphasize feelings of being alone and isolated. Holidays can also encourage regression to childlike feelings without childhood's satisfactions. And most people find that holidays require extraordinary preparation, work, and cleanup. Don't be fooled by the fantasy that everyone else's Christmas is warm and wonderful. Some are, of course; most aren't.

Take holidays one moment at a time. Some moments will be memorable; some will be disappointing. Enjoy what each *does* bring: food, a break from work, visual beauty, religious feelings. Try not to compare a holiday experience with those past, or with those to come.

AIM FOR SELF-MANAGEMENT, NOT QUICK CHANGE

As we noted before, your personality structure was years and years in the making. Your earliest years constituted your introduction to "reality." Because those years preceded speech, they are not even accessible through your memory. Think back to your earliest memory. Chances are you are thinking about something that happened when you were two or three years old. Your sense of safety, security, and self had long since begun to form. Think back to your twelve years in grade school. Can you remember every teacher you had? No? And yet you spent a *year* with each!

Restructuring a personality would obviously take as long as the five most formative years and then some. Although psychoanalysis attempts this, most stress reduction can be more quickly and realistically achieved by *knowing* your personality structure than by changing it. Work *with* your defenses, strengths, and weaknesses, not against them. Self-deprecation increases stress; self-management does not. Unrealistic attempts at personality change are frustrating and increase stress. Self-acceptance does not.

MOVE INTO THE HERE AND NOW

Many women increase their stress by being so pulled into reliving past problems and so pushed into "preliving" future fears that they are rarely living in what gestalt psychologist Fritz Perls called the "here and now." Life is literally passing them by, and so are opportunities for quiet moments, little pleasures, and deep breaths. If this is one of your problems, continually bring yourself back from upsetting hypothetical scenarios into the present, and try to live life as an ongoing process, not a series of upcoming crises.

PRACTICE, PRACTICE, PRACTICE

Therapists have learned that insight is usually not enough to change behavior. What is needed after insight is practice, practice, practice. Practicing new behaviors leads to new types of reactions from others, new information about alternatives, and new views of realities. Start practicing now.

When you are under stress, practice *acting*, not reacting.

1. Help yourself do this by taking the time to collect information about a situation or person before you draw

conclusions. If someone's behavior is upsetting, don't take it personally. Process what you are seeing and feeling as information, not insult. Decide how *you* feel about what they are saying or doing, and what their behavior says about them.

2. Help yourself do this by determining the logical consequences of the situation or of someone's behavior, not by dwelling on illogical "what ifs," or "This must mean that . . ." Check out all assumptions you are making before acting on them.

3. Help yourself by *not* giving others the power to make you react before you are ready. Take your time.

4. Help yourself conquer spectatoring by practicing placing your focus on others as you interact, not on yourself. If someone's reaction threatens to throw you off balance, practice staying centered. Mary Beth does this when she is confronted by saying, "I understand your point and I will think about it." Laurie tells her friends: "I find what you say very interesting." Paula just says: "Hmmmmmmmmm!" when she feels stressed and ready to react defensively.

5. Help yourself by recognizing when you are backing off from a goal because of fear of failure, rather than moving forward toward it. Remember the ring-toss study? Practice focusing on the stake. Walk right up to your goals; don't back off. Since you will try to achieve your goals anyway, why make your job harder by handicapping yourself?

LAUGH, LAUGH, LAUGH

Laughter is the signal for the Female Stress Syndrome centers to turn off the emergency adaptation system. As Norman Cousins suggests in his book *Anatomy of an Illness*, laughter may even promote healing. What a delightful tool for stress management! It defuses tension when an embarrassing topic has come up in a joke, when an unacceptable thought or impulse has been spoken out loud, or when a perspective has been changed or regained. It lights up our faces, relaxes our muscles, lowers our sense of vigilance, restores our objectivity, and enhances hope.

PURSUE BOTH SHORT-TERM AND LONG-TERM REMEDIES

As you begin to develop your own stress-management program, keep in mind that you will continually need to pursue both short-term *and* long-term remedies. Exercise, autohypnosis, relaxation techniques, sex, and even laughter are short-term remedies that will help you feel more comfortable with your body and more positive about yourself. They provide immediate gratification and release. Long-term solutions, including the various aspects of behavior modification discussed in this chapter—learning to live in the present rather than in the past, learning to feel less guilt, accepting what you cannot change about your life, giving yourself permission to take time off and reduce stress—will increase your sense of control and help reduce chronic stress. Both kinds of techniques are vital to counteracting the stress in your life.

The stresses that plague women are a part of our lives; so, too, are their symptoms. We cannot ignore them, feel guilty about them, or let them overwhelm us. Recognizing the effect they have on us means that we will no longer need to turn to others for an incomplete explanation of what is going on. Learning how to manage them means we will no longer need to settle for the recommendation that we simply get a good night's sleep—or take two Valiums. Female stress must be taken seriously—by women, their families, and their friends. It must be countered with understanding, self-help, and, where appropriate, with professional help.

Turn your hand palm-up and look at what is called your lifeline—the line that starts between the thumb and first finger and curves around the base of the thumb almost to the wrist. Your lifeline has a beginning, a middle, and an end. It does not go on forever. Life, too, has a beginning, a middle, and an end; it, too, does not go on forever. From now on, whenever you look at your hand, be reminded that the time to reduce stress is *now*! Don't wait until stress symptoms overwhelm your capacity for work or play. Don't wait until your doctor, family, or friends beg you to start taking care of yourself.

I began this book with a quotation from Hans Selye, "Complete freedom from stress is death." Contrary to public opinion, he points out, we cannot avoid stress. We are in fact *surrounded* by stress, especially where money, work, family, children, and sex are concerned. We experience stresses connected with our physiology, stresses hidden in our daily routines, and stresses that crop up at holidays and even on vacations. Short-term stress can help us achieve what we want to achieve. Long-term stress can help us mature—but only if we gain control over it where possible and, where it is beyond our control, try to manage the effects it has on us. More than ever, it is vitally important that we learn how to live with stress, so that we can really enjoy the full, healthy lives we were meant to have.

SELECTED BIBLIOGRAPHY

ABERLE, D., and NAGELE, K. "Middle Class Fathers' Occupational Role and Attitudes toward Children." *American Journal of Orthopsychiatry* 22 (2) (1952): 366–378.

ABRAMSON, M., and TORGHELE, J. R. "Weight, Temperature Change, and Psychosomatic Symptomology." *American Journal of Obstetrics and Gynecology* 81 (1961): 223–232.

AMERICAN PSYCHOLOGICAL ASSOCIATION'S NATIONAL TASK FORCE ON WOMEN AND DEPRESSION. *Women and Depression: Risk Factors and Treatment Issues.* Washington, D.C.: The American Psychological Association, 1990.

BARRY, H.; BACON, M.; and CHILD, I. L. "A Cross-Cultural Survey of Some Sex Differences in Socialization." *Journal of Abnormal and Social Psychology* 55 (1957): 327–332.

BARUCH, GRACE K., and BARNETT, ROSALIND C. "Implications and Applications of Recent Research on Feminine Development." *Psychiatry* 38 (1975): 318–327.

BLOCH, J. H. "Conceptions of Sex Role: Some Cross-Cultural and Longitudinal Perspectives." *American Psychologist* 28 (1973): 512–526.

BREIT, ETTA BENDER, and FERRANDINO, MARILYN MYERSON. "Social Dimensions of the Menstrual Taboo." In *Psychology of Women*, edited by J. Williams. New York: W. W. Norton, 1979.

BRODER, MICHAEL. *The Art of Living Single.* New York: Avon Books, 1988.

BRYSON, R. B., et al. "The Professional Pair: Husband and Wife." *American Psychologist* 31 (1976): 10–16.

BUDOFF, PENNY WISE. *No More Hot Flashes and Other Good News.* New York: G. P. Putnam's Sons, 1983.

CAINE, LYNN. *Widow.* New York: Bantam Books, 1975.

COLEMAN, J. C. *Psychology and Effective Behavior.* Glenview, Ill.: Scott, Foresman & Co., 1969.

COSTRICH, N.; FEINSTEIN, J.; and KIDDER, L. "When Stereotypes Hurt." *Journal of Experimental and Social Psychology* 11 (1975): 520–530.

COUSINS, NORMAN. *Anatomy of an Illness as Perceived by the Patient.* New York: W. W. Norton, 1979.

DALTON, KATHARINA. *The Premenstrual Syndrome.* Springfield, Ill.: Charles C. Thomas, 1964.

DOHRENWEND, B., and DOHRENWEND, B. "Sex Differences and Psychiatric Disorders." *American Journal of Sociology* 81 (1976): 1447–1454.

DOUVAN, ELIZABETH. "The Role of Models in Women's Professional Development." *Psychology of Women Quarterly* 1 (1976): 5–20.

EDELMAN, BARBARA. "Binge Eating in Normal Weight and Overweight Individuals." *Psychological Reports* 49 (1981): 739–746.

FREEDMAN, ALFRED; KAPLAN, HAROLD; and SADOCH, BENJAMIN. *Modern Synopsis of Comprehensive Textbook of Psychiatry/II.* Baltimore: Williams & Wilkins, 1978.

FRIEDAN, BETTY. *The Second Stage.* New York: Summit, 1981.

FRIEDMAN, MEYER. "Type A Behavior: A Progress Report." *The Sciences* 20 (2) (1980).

FRIEDMAN, MEYER, and ROSENMAN, RAY. *Type A Behavior and Your Heart.* New York: Alfred A. Knopf, 1974.

FRIEDMAN, MEYER, and ULMER, DIANE. *Treating Type A Behavior and Your Heart.* New York: Alfred A. Knopf, 1984.

GINOTT, HAIM. *Between Parent and Child.* New York: Avon, 1969.

GOODE, WILLIAM J. *Women in Divorce.* New York: The Free Press, 1956.

GUARENDI, RAY. *Back to the Family: How to Encourage Traditional Values in Complicated Times.* New York: Villard Books, 1990.

HOLMES, D. S., and JORGENSEN, B. W. "Do Personality and Social Psychologists Study Men More than Women?" *Representative Research in Social Psychology* 2 (1971): 71–76.

HOLMES, T. H., and MASUDA, M. "Psychosomatic Syndrome." *Psychology Today*, April 1972, 71–72.

HOLMES, T. H., and RAHE, R. H. "The Social Readjustment Rating Scale." *Journal of Psychosomatic Research* 11 (1967): 213–218.

HORNEY, KAREN. *Feminine Psychology.* New York: W. W. Norton, 1973.

KAPLAN, HELEN SINGER. *The New Sex Therapy.* New York: Brunner/Mazel, 1974.

LAMANNA, MARY ANN, and RIEDMAN, AGNES. *Marriages and Families.* Belmont, Ca.: Wadsworth, 1981.

LEVI, LENNART. "Environmental Factors in Stress and Coping." *Stress and Coping*, Report No. 3. Philadelphia: Smith, Kline & French, 1981.

LEWIS, MICHAEL. "Early Sex Differences in the Human: Studies of Socio-Economic Development." *Archives of Sexual Behavior* 4 (1975): 329–335.

LOPATA, H. Z. "Loneliness: Forms and Components." *Social Problems* 17 (1969): 248–261.

LOPICCOLO, J., and LOPICCOLO, L., eds. *Handbook of Sex Therapy*. New York: Plenum Publishing Corp., 1978.

LUETGERT, M. J., et al. "Today's Feminist: Her Place is in the Home!" Paper presented at meeting of American Psychological Association, Chicago, Ill., 1975.

McCLINTOCK, M. K. "Menstrual Synchrony and Suppression." *Nature* 229 (1971): 244–245.

MACCOBY, ELEANOR E. "Sex Differences in Intellectual Functioning." In *The Development of Sex Differences*. Stanford, Calif.: Stanford University Press, 1966.

MACCOBY, ELEANOR E., and JACKLIN, C. *The Psychology of Sex Differences*. Stanford, Calif.: Stanford University Press, 1974.

McGUINESS, DIANE. Quoted in "Just How the Sexes Differ," by D. Gleman et. al. *Newsweek*, May 18, 1981, 72–74.

McKINLAY, S., and JEFFREYS, M. "The Menstrual Syndrome." *British Journal of Preventive and Social Medicine* 28 (2) (1974): 108.

MASTERS, WILLIAM H., and JOHNSON, VIRGINIA E. *Human Sexual Inadequacy*. Boston: Little, Brown & Co., 1970.

MEAD, MARGARET. "On Freud's View of Female Psychology." In *Women and Analysis*, edited by Jean Strouse. New York: Grossman, 1974.

MEYER, J., and SOBIESZEK, B. "Effect of a Child's Sex on Adult Interpretations of Its Behavior." *Developmental Psychology* 6 (1972): 42–48.

MONEY, JOHN, and EHRHARDT, ANKE A. *Man and Woman: Boy and Girl*. Baltimore: Johns Hopkins University Press, 1972.

MURPHY, LOIS BARCLAY. "Further Reflections on Resilience." In *The Invulnerable Child*. New York: Guilford Press, 1990.

1990 Virginia Slims Opinion Poll. Storrs, Conn.: The Roper Center, 1990.

PAIGE, KAREN. "Effects of Oral Contraception on Affective Fluctuations Associated with the Menstrual Cycle." *Psychosomatic Medicine* 33 (1971): 515–537.

PARLEE, MARY BROWN. "The Premenstrual Syndrome." *Psychological Bulletin* 80 (1975): 454–465.

PERLS, F., HEFFERLINE, R., and GOODMAN, P. *Gestalt Therapy*. New York: Delta, 1965.

PRIBRAM, KARL. Quoted in "Just How the Sexes Differ," by D. Gleman et. al. *Newsweek*, May 18, 1981, 72–74.

PUNER, M. "Will You Still Love Me?" *Human Behavior* 3 (1974): 42–48.

REBELSKY, F., and HANKS, C. "Fathers' Verbal Interaction with Infants in the First Three Months of Life." *Child Development* 42 (1971): 63–68.

REES, L. "Premenstrual Tension Syndrome and Its Treatment." *British Medical Journal* 1 (1953): 1014–1016.

ROGERS, CARL. *Client-Centered Therapy*. Boston: Houghton Mifflin, 1951.

RUBIN, J.; PROVENZANO, F.; and LURIA, Z. "The Eye of the Beholder: Parents' Views on Sex of Newborns." *American Journal of Orthopsychiatry* 44 (1974): 4.

SCHMALE, A. H. and IKER, H. P. "The Effect of Hopelessness and the Development of Cancer." *Psychosomatic Medicine* 28 (1966): 714–721.

SEARS, R.; MACCOBY, E.; and LEVIN, H. *Patterns of Child Rearing*. Evanston, Ill.: Row, Peterson, 1957.

SELYE, HANS. *The Stress of Life*, rev. ed. New York: McGraw-Hill, 1976.

———. *Stress Without Distress*. New York: Signet, 1974.

SERBIN, LISA A., and O'LEARY, K. DANIEL. "How Nursery Schools Teach Girls to Shut Up." *Psychology Today*, December 1975, 56–58.

SHERMAN, J. A. *On The Psychology of Sex Differences: A Survey of Empirical Studies*. Springfield, Ill.: Charles C. Thomas, 1971.

———."Social Values, Femininity, and the Development of Female Competence." *Journal of Social Issues* 32 (1976): 181–195.

SONTAG, SUSAN. "The Double Standard of Aging." *Saturday Review*, September 23, 1972, 29–38.

SPEROFF, L.; GLASS, R. H.; and KASE, N. G. *Clinical Gynecologic Endocrinology and Infertility*. Baltimore: Williams & Wilkins, 1973.

STAFFORD, R.; BACKMAN, E.; and DIBONA, P. "The Division of Labor Among Cohabiting and Married Couples." *Journal of Marriage and the Family* 39 (January, 1977): 43–57.

STEDMAN, NANCY. *How to Keep Your Family Drug Free*. New York: GCR Publishing, 1986.

TASCH, R. "The Role of the Father in the Family." *Journal of Experimental Education* 20 (1952): 19–61.

TELLER, SANDY. *This Was Sex*. Secaucus, N.J.: Citadel Press, 1978.

U.S. BUREAU OF THE CENSUS, Statistical Abstract of the United States: Washington, D.C., 1981.

WILLIAMS, JUANITA H. *Psychology of Women*. New York: W. W. Norton, 1977.

WILLIAMS, JUANITA H., ed. *Psychology of Women, Selected Readings*. New York: W. W. Norton, 1979.

WOLFBERG, L. R. "Hypnotic Experiments in Psychosomatic Medicine." *Psychosomatic Medicine* 9 (1947): 332–342.

WOLMAN, BENJAMIN B. *Handbook of General Psychology*. Englewood Cliffs, N.J.: Prentice-Hall, 1973.

WOLPE, J., and LAZARUS, A. A. *Behavior Therapy Techniques: A Guide to the Treatment of Neuroses*. New York: Pergamon Press, 1968.

WOOLF, VIRGINIA. *A Room of One's Own*. New York: Harcourt, Brace & World, 1929.

INDEX